Tales from the Dead-House

For Well-Beloved
Mimi II,
Pomchi, of the highest intelligence,
understands everything.

Tales from the Dead-House

Richard Whittington-Egan

AMBERLEY

First Published 2016

Amberley Publishing
The Hill, Stroud
Gloucestershire, GL5 4EP

www.amberley-books.com

ISBN 978 1 4456 5404 1 (paperback)
ISBN 978 1 4456 5407 2 (ebook)

British Library Cataloguing in Publication Data.
A catalogue record for this book is available from the British Library.

Typesetting and Origination by Amberley Publishing
Printed in the UK.

CONTENTS

1

THE CAUTIONARY TALE OF THE GOOD DR SHIPMAN

His was far and away the most popular practice in town. Patients vied to get on to his packed list. His reputation for patient-care and kindness was legendary. He would even make home visits without being asked, just turning up. He always seemed interested in his patients' lives. He would chat with old ladies about their pet cats and wax sympathetic about their arthritic aches and pains and 'bronichal' spasms. He was always at hand with his ever-ready hypodermic syringe to ease away the pains ... of life itself. What nobody nurtured the faintest suspicion of was that he was Britain's greatest-ever serial killer. His total of an estimated 284 murders smashed the record of Britain's previous champion murderer, Mary Ann Cotton (1832–73), of West Auckland, who poisoned fourteen or fifteen – perhaps even twenty – and made him one of the most prolific serial killers in modern criminal history.

He was the Dr Jekyll of Hyde, Greater Manchester.

He was Dr Shipman.

The rogue doctor, the Hippocratic saviour turned hypocritic slayer, is a mercifully rare medical phenomenon in Britain. Of doctors who commit murder within the context and confines of their private lives, and for personal reasons, there has never been any shortage – uxoricides mostly, from Dr Pritchard (Glasgow, 1865), through Dr Crippen (London, 1910), to Dr Ruxton (Lancaster, 1936), and Dr Clements (Southport, 1947).

The case of Dr Harold Frederick Shipman bears remarkable similarities at one latter-day level to that of the acquisitive, late, unlamented, and avaricious Northern Ireland medico, Dr John Bodkin Adams, who was in practice in Eastbourne in the 1950s. I attended his trial at the Old Bailey in 1957. Although he was there found not guilty of murder, I was far from impressed as to his entire blamelessness in the matter of the convenient demises of various doting old ladies who bequeathed to him their Rolls Royces, family silver, coveted valuable antiques, and so forth. Shipman, of course, did not thus benefit, until, that is, he tried to clumsily in the case of Mrs Kathleen Grundy; it was his undoing.

To bring the matter closer in time, there was in the mid-1980s the case of the consultant surgeon whose invalid wife stood in the way of his preferential alliance with a distinctly more glamorous partner, and who conceived a plan to eliminate his wife with the help of a drug difficult, if not impossible, of detection. Doubtless he would have succeeded, had not chance intervened to expose his fell design. And in the late 1990s, a consultant obstetrician at a London teaching hospital bludgeoned his wife, who, although it was by no means certain that he knew it, was also involved in an extramarital dalliance. Relations had otherwise, it seems, become somewhat strained because of the husband's unreasonable constitutional parsimony.

But the practitioner who practises the killing skill within the practice of his healing art is a rare patient risk. The series of exhumed patients who proved to have been murdered by their apparently caring general practitioner, Dr Shipman, raised the worrying question as to how we are able to safeguard ourselves from Dr Cain; for what distinguishes the Shipman case is that his victims were individuals emotionally remote, albeit in the doctor–patient relationship, and scarcely, at least within the parameters of normalcy, presenting any powerful motivation to such excessive action or reaction.

*

Harold Frederick Shipman was born on Monday 14 January 1946. He was the second of the three children of Harold and Vera Shipman. The family, unashamedly working-class, lived in a 1930s red-brick council house at 163 Longmead Drive, on the Edwards Lane Estate, in the Sherwood district of Nottingham. His father was by vocation a lorry driver. Harold the younger was always known by his second name, Fred, to differentiate them. His mother, Vera, was the fruit of the illegitimate union of a bricklayer's labourer and a lace clipper. She had been eighteen and working as a printer's assistant when, in December 1937, she had belatedly married twenty-three-year-old Harold. Their first child, a daughter, Pauline, arrived in March 1938, and, in 1948, two years after the advent of Harold Frederick, a second son, Clive, was born.

Futurity's aspects for their first son were scarcely of the best. Superficially, heredity yielded scant promise. The genealogical roots were depressingly mundane. His father's father had risen no higher than a hosiery warehouseman. His mother's father had been a bricklayer's assistant. But, by beneficence of Mendelian law, the young Shipman had been endowed with sound cerebral potential, and it was this that pointed his way from Burford Infants' School, where he struggled initially with besetting problems of sinistrality, via Whitemoor Primary School, at age six, to success in a scholarship examination which took him, when he was eleven, to Nottingham's prestigious High Pavement Grammar School.

Raimented in the distinction of a brown blazer, edges smartly braided with intertwined brown and yellow, brown college cap, new school tie striped with brown, yellow and blue, neat school socks, and flannel trousers, short and sober grey – all blazoned resplendent, in spirit if not in physical actuality, with the Paviorian Latinate motto, *Virtus Sola Nobilita* (Virtue is the only nobility), he walked tall. Physically maturing early, he began to shave at fourteen and was soon sporting luxuriantly hispidulous sideburns which were the cynosure and envy of all school-fellow eyes. He walked even taller.

Never distinguished for sociability, transparently a bred-in-the-bone loner, Fred minor's athleticism characteristically manifested itself primarily as that of the lonely long-distance runner – celebrated by that other Nottingham native, Alan Sillitoe – but he nonetheless achieved a moderate degree of popularity because of his sporting prowess on the rugby field, where, however, admiration was blended with a not so moderate degree of fearful wariness, because of the renowned crippling savagery of his tackles. He was an aggressive player. Forgiven on this score, he ended up vice-captain of the school athletics team.

His classroom performance was adequate. He worked hard and passed in seven GCE subjects, including, at A level, and after two attempts, those needed to make him an acceptable candidate to read medicine – chemistry, physics, and biology.

In September 1965, just over four months short of his twentieth birthday, he entered Leeds University Medical School. His father being a low earner, Shipman qualified for a full student grant. He and another medical student, Peter Congdon, lodged with a Mr and Mrs Copley at Harewood House, the veritable 'apotheosis of suburbia' at 164 Wetherby Road, in the Wellington Hill area on the outskirts of Leeds. Studying medicine proved a full-time job; lectures every weekday from 8.30 a.m. to 4 p.m., with just a short lunch break. By long and sacred tradition, Wednesday afternoons were left free for various healthy sports' indulgences, a laxity redeemed by compensatory nose-to-grindstone lectures on Saturday mornings.

Thin, small, and dapper, Shipman was viewed by his medicinal cohort as a quiet lad, generally kindly, albeit somewhat withdrawn, a hard worker, but too inward-turning and self-preoccupied to present any great impression to the world at large. The one thing that was noted and unfailingly remembered was how fascinated he appeared to be by the corpses in the dissecting room. He was in no way squeamish and showed a creepy tendency to linger on alone with the cadavers after the other students had melted away. Was this, perhaps, when the flame of serial killing was lit in his skull?

It was in that same September of 1965 that an out-of-the-blue bolt descended upon him. He got a girl 'into trouble', as the old euphemistic phrase had it. She was 16 years old. Her name was Primrose Mary Oxtoby.

*

The daughter of George Oxtoby, a Yorkshire farm foreman, and his wife, Edna (*née* Constable) – whom George had met when she was a general servant at the same farm at Upper Poppleton, where he was at that time (1924) a labourer – Primrose Mary had been born on 19 April 1949. By then her father had attained to the ranking of foreman, at a farm at Huttons Ambo, near Malton.

From there, the family moved on to East Rigton, a hamlet situated between Leeds and Wetherby, where George Oxtoby was again employed as a farm foreman, and it was from here, in 1954, aged five, that Primrose started her education at Bardsey Primary School.

The family moved again, this time to the market town of Wetherby, where Primrose's father obtained a new urban job as road labourer with the council, and where, thanks to a modest family legacy, the Oxtobys were able to buy a house – Prospect

Villa, No. 4, Prospect Terrace, a substantial, stone semi-detached built in 1876, on a hillside overlooking the centre of the town.

It was an austere home in which Primrose was brought up; God-fearing to the exclusion of virtually all merriment. Both parents were strict Methodists of pious turn, devotees of Bank Street Church. Mother was the boss. Sunday was drenched in Victorian churchgoing. Morning service; afternoon, Sunday School; evening, another service. Tuesday evenings, Methodist Fellowship meetings. Weekdays were only a little less restricted. Visits to youth clubs or Wetherby's Rodney Cinema were forbidden. She was not allowed to go out to afternoon tea with, or in the evenings to meet, her friends, or to go with them to local dances. She was the prisoner of other peoples' consciences in the dark, dank interior of Prospect Villa, with its prospect of heavy mahogany furniture and sole frivolous alleviation of a piano, at which she would, in desperation, and without any real musical aptitude, tinkle out tunes. Her one permitted avenue of escape was her attendance at meetings of the Girl Guides.

In 1960, having failed the eleven-plus exam, which, had she passed it, would have made her eligible to go to grammar school, she was channelled to Wetherby County Secondary Modern; but, following her parents move to Prospect Villas, she was transferred instead to a school in Crossley Street, a mere five minutes' walk from her new home. The pupils' skills were there honed towards practicalities rather than academic achievement.

Early in 1964, after four years – from her eleventh to her fifteenth – of education which led to no particular qualification, she was wondering what on earth she was going to do when she left school. And that was when chance played a hand. She heard that, with a remarkable painting that she had done of some hats, and which was considered to show a distinct flair for art, she had earned herself a place on an art and design course Unsurprisingly, her mother was disappointed. She would have preferred Primrose to have taken up a career in nursing, as her older sister, Mary, had. Art was such a flimsy-whimsy subject – not much of a living to be made out of it. Never mind. Hope for the best. Art went hand-in-hand with catering. Prim would learn to decorate cakes artistically, to a professional standard; perhaps even wedding cakes. In fact, Primrose did well on her course, and, armed with her college certificates, went job-hunting and found herself a place as a trainee window-dresser. Around 7.30 every morning, she and a number of other girls would catch a Number 38 red double-decker bus, or 'West Yorkshire Road Car', to bear them on the 41-minute journey along the A58 to Leeds.

That bus ride was to prove a fateful one for Primrose.

*

Another bus-riding regular was Harold Frederick Shipman. He and Peter Congdon caught the selfsame 7.30 a.m. Number 38 bus every morning to convey them into town, to the medical school in Great George Street, and they could not, of course, possibly fail to notice the parrot-bright and noisy flock of chattering young women who shared their daily transport with them.

What did Shipman perceive? Surrounded by a gaggle of giggling girls was a sturdily built lass, plump rather than fat, some 5 feet 4 inches tall, well-scrubbed looking, unflattering pudding-basin hair-cut, perhaps a shade butch. But, overall, jolly, perky, bright. Indeed, described by one of the gaggle of gigglers as 'a bundle of laughs, good fun, down to earth, bubbly, vivacious, very good company'. But her parents' edicts had not allowed her to make the best of herself. Any hint of make-up was taboo. Her clothes designed to deliver a frumpish and spectacularly non-sexually stimulatory effect, she was caparisoned in camouflage of twin-sets and pleated skirts.

Shipman and Primrose were both essentially shy people. He was a loner by choice; she was a lonely child isolated from her family by differences of temperament. Both were sexually frustrated. In all innocence, they began to exchange diffident chatter, then bolder banter. The burgeoning had begun, but it took the passage of many days, weeks, before they plucked up the courage for unselfconscious conversational interchange. It is not recorded who spoke first, but they began to talk. Things gathered momentum. Acquaintance burgeoned into friendship, friendship into love. Shipman had a girlfriend: his first. And he was her first boyfriend. They made a date. They went for a drink. They went to the cinema. They held hands. They kissed. Finally, Prim took Fred home to meet her parents. Disaster. From the start, Mother took an instant dislike to him – found him 'smarmy and superior'. Father wasn't too keen either. After that, Primrose never took him home again. They met instead at nearby cafés and went occasionally to the pictures.

Quite speedily, the burgeoning ripened into fruit-bearing. Fred had not attempted to use a condom when they inevitably made love. He subsequently clean-breastedly confessed that he had been too embarrassed to go into a chemist's and buy a packet. So far as Prim was concerned, it was a case of *ignorantia excusat*; parentally uninstructed, the territory of sex had been total *terra incognita* to her. The subject had never come up, nor been discussed, around the Oxtobys' rabidly religiose hearth side; their whole concern being that Prim should be proper. When the tidings of great joy – that of the impending nativity – were conveyed to them, both sets of parents were somewhat less than overjoyed. They were horrified.

What, impolitely but accurately, may be termed a shotgun wedding was arranged for fireworks day, Wednesday 5 November 1966, a rapid splicing to be carried out, at Edna Oxtoby's insistence, at Barkston Ash Register Office – a good ten miles away from the home territory of Wetherby, as Prim's bump of sin might show! The bride wore a long blue dress. The groom was apparelled in clean white shirt, dark tie, and black suit, funereal and ill-fitting. The respective unenthusiastic fathers supplied the legally demanded brace of witnesses.

On St Valentine's Day, 14 February 1967, at Harrogate General Hospital, seventeen-year-old Primrose was delivered of a daughter, Sarah Rosemary. Shortly after baby Sarah's arrival, the Shipmans found themselves a tiny flat near Blackman Lane, in the Woodhouse district of Leeds, the heart of the city's rather run down bedsit-land student territory. For all its shortfalls in luxury, Primrose, well instructed in matters of domesticity by her mother, succeeded in making it cosy and homely, and Shipman and his new bride were very happy together there.

And here it was, to the all-pervasive scent of damp napkins drying before the fire, and the intermittent music of baby cries, that Fred came home each evening to wear the night away poring over his textbooks.

Three long-seeming years later, in 1970, Shipman sat a month of finals. He passed, winning the entitlement to write MB, ChB. after his name, and on 23 July 1970 was granted his provisional registration – Number 1470473 – with the General Medical Council. The whole course, studying anatomy, histology, embryology, physiology, biochemistry, and materia medica had taken five years (1970–75), three of those years (1967–70) devoted to gaining clinical knowledge and experience, walking the wards of Leeds General Infirmary.

The next mandatory step which every pre-registered medic had to take prior to registration was that of one year's service, working in a hospital as a junior doctor. This obligatory year was usually divided into two periods of six months, dedicated to medicine and surgery respectively. Shipman elected to apply to, and was accepted by, Pontefract General Infirmary. His choice was dictated by the fact that the infirmary offered resident doctors the great advantage of staff houses provided in the hospital grounds.

The newly laureated Fred Shipman, along with his wife and

three-year-old daughter, moved into a good, solid, red-brick house, one of a 1930s complex of a dozen council-style houses, sitting astride Friarwood Lane, just below the market, and settled down to twelve months' hard graft.

From 1 August 1970 to 31 January 1971, he was junior house officer with the surgical firms of consultants Mr L. C. Bell, general surgery, and Mr K. Mayall, aural surgery. From 1 February 1971 to 31 July 1971, he was junior house officer, medicine, under consultant physician, Dr John O'Turner. It was during this spell that, on 21 April 1971, his second child, a son, christened Christopher Frederick, was born to Primrose in Wakefield Maternity Hospital.

Traditionally, the life of a junior houseman in a British hospital was very hard labour: slave-like servitude to the hierarchy. And, many years later, when in Strangeways Prison awaiting his trial, Shipman drily observed that if one could cope with the regime of a junior houseman, then prison life was certainly no worse.

At last, on 5 August 1971, a day of great significance and triumph, it was all over. The year's compulsory drudgery under his belt, Shipman was fully registered with the GMC; he was a *real*, full-blown doctor. He decided to spend a bit longer at Pontefract, Actually, he stayed on there for another two and a half years, during which time he was promoted from senior houseman to registrar, took his Diploma in Child Health in September 1972, and, the following September, gained his Diploma of the Royal College of Obstetricians and Gynaecologists. He also most sagaciously contrived to get his membership of the College of General Practitioners.

Now it was time to venture out into the world of competitive medicine.

In March 1974, Dr John Michael Grieve, the senior partner of the group practice, at the Abraham Ormerod Medical Centre, in Todmorden, West Yorkshire, gave him his first job as assistant GP. Shipman blew in like a breath of fresh air and covered himself in glory. He figuratively took of his jacket, rolled up his sleeves and seized the opportunity by the throat. He worked all the hours God sent. Nothing was too much trouble; nothing was too insignificant for his full endeavours. Night and day his enthusiasm bubbled and boiled over. He took sheaves of the practice's patients' records home with him at night to burn the midnight oil summarising the notes and preparing them for the as yet unrealised advent of the computer. Having so recently emerged from medical school, he was bang up to date as prime source of the latest information and could even help his colleagues with the technique of fitting those (then) new-fangled intrauterine devices. He was brimful of ideas for modernising the practice. He was described, somewhat sinisterly as things turned out, as 'brilliant with a needle'.

This paragon was adored also by the patients. His strong Nottingham accent conveniently exonerated him from any condemnation of being posh. He was, moreover, no mincer of words. Spades were spades with him. They liked his medical manner and manners, too; vaguely avuncular. They liked even more the fact that he was a generous prescriber and could be relied upon to supply amphetamine tablets for slimmers. He was lent a certain winning air of paternality by his altogether beguiling air of prevenient ageing. 'He had a lot of fans,' said Dr Grieve.

After a month's trial, his hard work and patent enthusiasm was rewarded: he was upgraded from assistant to principal GP. Made permanent, 'He was almost too good to be true', was Dr Grieve's ungrieving, but alas premature, verdict.

Aglow with optimism, Fred and Primrose and Sarah and Christopher took out a mortgage on, and moved into, a solid, stone, semi-detached house, appropriately named Sunny Bank; (confusingly, the name of the house is also given as Penrhyn. *vide*: *The Good Doctor.* Wensley Clarkson. John Blake, London, 2001. p. 76) on equally appropriately named Sunnyside, a terrace of mixed Victorian and 1930s houses clinging to the tree-clad steep valley side to the west of the town.

The workload at the practice proved heavy. Even so, Shipman found time outside surgery hours to labour mightily as a member of the Rochdale Canal Society, a group dedicated to the digging-out and ultimate reopening of the disused and sludged-up canal. Although considerably less skilled at DIY, he also contrived to build a garage and, after a fashion, some walls at Sunny Bank. He shaped up much better horticulturally, laying out a beautiful symmetry of pink and red roses in his front garden.

Things looked set fair. Then the dark wind of pethidine blew up ... and blew everything away.

Pethidine is an opioid analgesic. Injected subcutaneously, intramuscularly, or intravenously, its properties are similar to those of morphine, Since, however, it requires the use of much larger quantities than morphine, it is therefore easier to fine-tune doses, and so avoid the dangers of addiction. It is used peri-operatively, and for longer term to combat the pain of gallstones and renal colic, but, its most widespread usage is in obstetrics. It is a drug which midwives are permitted to prescribe and dispense – and, because of its smooth functioning as an anadynic and a spasm relaxant, they were often tempted to 'take a bit of pethidine' themselves to help with a painful period. It has also the reputation of being a drug that can keep one going through long hours of work; it is said, moreover, to produce the pleasant side-effect of euphoria.

*

The first sign that things were not as they should be with the doctor was when he started blacking out.

The year 1975 was his *annus horribilis.*

There had been several disconcerting blackouts at the surgery, dismissed as the likely legacy of overwork, since it was nothing unusual for his days to stretch punishingly from 8 a.m. to 9 or 10 p.m. The crisis came one day in May, when he and Primrose were decorating the family bathroom at Sunny Bank. Suddenly, the doctor crashed down into the bath, and lay there unconscious. Terrified that he had had a heart attack, Primrose summoned an ambulance, and he was taken to the casualty department at the Halifax Royal Infirmary. There, having recovered consciousness and gathered his wits about him, he managed to hoodwink a consultant into a diagnosis of idiopathic epilepsy.

Back in the practice, it was business as usual, with just one difference: Primrose now chauffeured him on his rounds. Actually, there was another difference. It was noticed that Shipman seemed to have undergone something of a sea change. From presenting a previous modesty of demeanour, an ever ready willingness to oblige, a patent desire to please, a manner verging on the positively ingratiatory, he had erupted into an attitude of overbearing superiority, truculent self-importance, and a tendency to display open contempt for Dr Grieve and his older colleagues.

In July, a Home Office drugs inspector, Donald McIntosh, interviewed all the doctors at the surgery and interrogated Shipman about apparent discrepancies in prescriptions. He fielded the questions and succeeded in convincing the inspector that it was an unfortunate misunderstanding.

All seemed to be going along swimmingly until the day that Mrs Marjorie Walker, one of the practice receptionists, decided to cross the road to Boots the chemists to pick up some bandages and wound-dressings for the surgery. She telephoned Harold Lever, a pharmacy dispenser there with whom she usually dealt, and told him that she would be coming over. He then made certain secret preparations for her visit. Fate decreed that she was to be the innocent instrument of the revelation of the true cause of Dr Shipman's blackouts.

Due to pure chance, it seemed, or perhaps sheer carelessness, the book in which was kept the written details of the prescriptions dispensed was lying open in the dispensary. It was not by accident but design that that book's contents were thus displayed, for Mr

Lever had deliberately so arranged matters. Mrs Walker could not help noticing – as indeed it was intended that she should, the hackles of Lever's suspicions having risen high regarding the prescriptive habits of Dr Shipman – that the doctor had been prescribing gargantuan quantities of pethidine in the names of a large number of patients, as well as ordering very substantial additional amounts of that drug on the practice account.

Predictably, Mrs Walker went, as Mr Lever had hoped that she would, straight back to the Medical Centre and told the first doctor that she met – Shipman's colleague, Dr John Dacre – about what she had seen in the chemist's dispensary. He, understandably, told her to say nothing to anyone else about it for the time being. He then made it his business to check with Lever, and, that weekend, visited various patients of Shipman's whose names had appeared in the chemist's book. One and all they assured him that they had never been given pethidine.

The first that Shipman and the other practice doctors knew about Dacre's investigation was at the normal Monday morning practice meeting. 'What's all this then, young Fred?' was Dacre's jovial way of kicking off the sticky proceedings. And he went on to lay the distasteful facts before the taken aback and utterly surprised assemblage. From Shipman, there was no denial, no embarrassment, no mouthings of remorse. Maintaining an inscrutable, outward, cucumber calm, he there and then made full and frank confession that he had become hooked on pethidine at medical school, where, he said, he had been required to try it experimentally as part of his training. He seemed to think that if he cured himself of what was obviously an addiction, he would be able to carry on working.

'Can't we just ride over this?' he asked.

This delusion was rapidly dispelled. No, they could not. Quite rightly, his brother doctors insisted that he had to go into hospital for treatment. If the partners thought they were going to get rid of him as easily as that, they had another thing coming. After a fine public display of fierce ill-temper, in the course of which he kicked his medical bag across the room, he shouted, 'Bugger this, I'm off!' and vanished like a pantomime demon.

Next, up through the trapdoor burst a furious, scarlet Primrose, vengeance bent. Breathless, she harangued the meeting. 'My husband will not be resigning. You'll have to force him out.'

They did. But it took six weeks of full pay and a solicitor's no frills letter to accomplish it. The official date of his dissolution from the partnership was 10 October 1975. That month Sunny Bank, standing dark and gloomily empty, was put up for sale. Incidentally, its next owners were horrified by the filthy, neglected state in which they found the house. Clearly, Primrose's latter-day household pride, efficiency, and hygiene had drastically deteriorated. Primrose, with six-year-old Sarah and three-year-old Christopher, had had to move back to stay for the time being with her parents – home to Mother, and the old dark house at Wetherby, where 'I Told You So' was writ invisible, but nonetheless detectable, on the Not-So-Welcome mat.

Meanwhile, accepting his whilom partners' earnestly proffered advice, Shipman had, without further ado, admitted himself to the Halifax Royal Infirmary where the consultant psychiatrist arranged for his voluntary admission to The Retreat, the celebrated private clinic, just outside York. He was to remain there, an in-patient treated with anti-depressants, until his discharge on 30 December 1975.

In the November of 1975, Shipman faced the same drugs inspector, Donald McIntosh, whom he had seen before, but accompanied this time by Detective Sergeant George McKeating of West Yorkshire Police Drugs Squad. They turned up at The Retreat. At first he refused to see them. Then ... sudden collapse ... all pretence abandoned, he made a clean breast of his medical malfeasances, admitting that he had been injecting himself with pethidine over a period of more than six months. He was arrested, given police bail, pending trial.

By the time his case came up at Halifax Magistrates' Court on 13 February 1976 – six weeks after his discharge and the day before his daughter's ninth birthday – Shipman had restarted his chequered career. Immediately after his emergence from six months in The Retreat, putting his best foot forward, he had found and taken short-term positions with the National Coal Board at Doncaster, and, on 12 September 1977, with the South-West Durham Health Authority, which latter involved responsibility for children's health in the Bishop Auckland, Crook, and Willington areas of the county. Ironically, this was within the ambit of West Auckland, the killing ground where Dr Shipman's homicidal numerical rival, Mary Ann Cotton, had lived and practised the secret poisoner's art nigh on a hundred years before.

Pleading guilty in answer to charges of eight offences – three charges of obtaining ten ampoules of 100 milligrams of pethidine by deception; three corresponding charges of unlawful possession of pethidine; two charges of forgery of NHS prescriptions – he now unhesitatingly confessed to having been ingesting 600–700 milligrams per diem of pethidine, which would amount to as many as fourteen injections, and agreed to have seventy-four other charges taken into consideration. It had all started, he claimed, because he had been depressed, the result, he had his solicitor not very fairly suggest, of his being frustrated by the indifference of his partners to his ideas for improvements to the practice. The presiding magistrate, Dr Maurice Golding, treated him with sympathy and comparative leniency. The sentence of the court was a fine of £600 plus the payment of £58.78 compensation for illegally obtained drugs.

Remarking, 'This is indeed a sad case,' Dr Golding told Shipman: 'It is something which, it seems, has been going on for a long time, and no one could be more aware of the dangers involved than yourself.'

After his conviction the General Medical Council, turning a blind eye, merely sent him a letter of warning, and Dr Shipman, virtually absolved, returned to reunion with the family in their brand-new rented semi in Rylestone Close, on the Burn Hill Estate, at Newton Aycliffe, just 8 miles north of Darlington. He kept himself to himself there, and no one even knew that he was a doctor.

The next crooked milestone in the somewhat dubious career of Harold Frederick Shipman was when, in October, 1977, despite his assurance to the Halifax Magistrates' Court that, 'I have no future intention to return to general practice or work in a situation where I could obtain supplies of pethidine', his yearning to return to general practice was such that he answered an advertisement in the *British Medical Journal*, was offered, and accepted, a position in the Donneybrook House Medical Centre group practice, at Hyde, in Greater Manchester. Hyde, where nightmare memories of the infamous Moors Murderers, child killers of the early 1960s, Ian Brady and Myra Hindley, still blotted the town's conscience more than a decade on.

He was to remain there for fifteen years. After one year and 294 days in the wilderness, the Shipman ship – of luck – seemed at last to have come home.

*

At first, all shining fresh and handsome in Donneybrook House, the devil a saint would be, but, as custom staled, the devil a saint was he. To be fair, new broom Dr Shipman did manage to maintain affability and courtesy towards his medical confrères, but to the non-medical staff – receptionists and cleaners – he became progressively more and more rude, unpleasant and intolerant.

At interview he had made a good impression. Freely admitting his passage at arms with drugs and conviction for his pethidine habit, he insisted, 'but I'm off it. I don't use it. You'll have to trust me'. They liked what they saw and heard. Oh, he was plausible. They felt it was only fair to give him a second chance.

Taken into the practice on a trial basis for six months, Shipman agreed on a year's leasehold renting of a neat, modern-style, semi-detached house in Lord Derby Road, Gee Cross. Picture-windowed, light and airy, with a fine lawned garden and conveniently situated for several schools, it stood on the summit of one of Hyde's many hills.

Now began the battle in earnest to establish himself. That autumn and winter Shipman snapped back into his top gear medical mode. He arrived earliest, left latest. He made himself universally useful. He shouldered vast quantities of work. He sought to relieve and oblige. He was willing to help anyone. Nothing was too much trouble. It worked. He received the grand news that he had been accepted as the seventh doctor in the group practice.

He found the family a permanent home, purchased on mortgage No. 15 Roe Cross Green, a leafy, cul-de-sac enclave of Mottram, an attractive village in Longdendale, some fifteen minutes' drive from the centre of Hyde, and where, incidentally, at The Elms, Stalybridge Road, the artist L. S. Lowry lived from 1948 to his death in 1976. The Shipman house was an unpretentious four-bedroom semi, with a long rear garden backing on to the busy, rather noisy, A6018 trunk route. It was to be the family home for twenty-two years.

Here he set about rebuilding his life. It was, he recognised, Shipman's last stand. He plunged into the work with his usual vigour.

As his backside became more comfortably ensconced in the leather of his consulting room chair, the carefully painted, mild-mannered expression on his face vanished beneath the suffusion of upsurging inner fury that bubbled continuously away at the core of the man. Ever shimmering, just below the surface, were brusquerie, arrogance and aloofness, waiting to break through. Only let an overstretched receptionist forget to lay before him, with suitable servility, his morning cup of coffee, and he would turn white with tremulous rage.

He seemed to view all of the non-medical staff with hatred, but a particular hate was reserved for Miss Vivien Langfield, Val as she was known to her colleagues, practice manager and in private life a lay preacher. Her loyal service with the doctors extended over twenty-five years. But Shipman took against her. The trouble was that she stood up to him. She made a great thing of looking after the practice receptionists; 'my girls', she called them, and she was thoroughly upset by Shipman's continual snapping and bullying attitude to them. She spoke up defending them, Shipman's wrath was deflected on to her, and he conscientiously strived to make her life a misery.

Having been ordained in 1991, she took early retirement in 1992 in order to become minister at the Abbey United Reform Church in Mosley, near Oldham. The Reverend Vivien Langfield remembered, 'Dr Shipman was known for his bad temper. It was a joke among the reception staff. We would tell each other: "If you do that again you'll have Fred blowing his top". We would say "Good morning" to the doctors as they arrived, but Fred would never reply. He would just go to his room, the last one at the end of the corridor without saying a word. He never responded to our greetings. We all felt that he was ignorant.'

One of the speak-as-you-find receptionists dubbed him 'a divisive, despicable man'.

The surgery threw a party for Miss Langfield upon her departure. Fred Shipman did not go to it. He made a point, however, of hanging around, and once the presentation and speeches were over he went up to her and asked her when she was retiring. Somewhat taken aback by the question, she told him, 'today'. 'Oh, you won't be here on Monday, then', he said, turned his back on her, and, without another word, walked away.

For the last year or eighteen months that he had worked at Donneybrook, he had refused to speak to Miss Langfield, telling her, 'Don't speak to me, write everything down and put it on my desk'. Prior to that, he had refused to exchange words with any of the receptionists, insisting that they had to go through the practice manager if they wanted to speak to him.

Neither was it only in-house discourtesies in which he indulged himself. Exceedingly ugly was the display he put on, patently to demonstrate his intellectual superiority and clinical supremacy, when a young woman in her twenties paid a visit to the practice as a drugs representative, trying to persuade the doctors to prescribe the drugs which her company manufactured. It was her first day on the road. At the end of morning surgery she was conducted upstairs to say her rehearsed piece to the three or four doctors who were waiting there to receive her. She was clearly very nervous, but did her best. With one exception, the doctors were charming to her. The one exception was Shipman. From the start he was hostile. He badgered and browbeat her, and treated her to a cross-examination so fierce and trenchant that, within minutes, her careful patter disrupted, she was reduced to a trembling bundle of tears. Glancing round with an aren't-I-clever expression buttering his admiration-questing look, Shipman found nothing but contempt and disdain on the faces of his disgusted audience. He rose from his seat and, still enmantled in the irrefragable belief that he had shown the breadth, width, and depth of his superior clinical knowledge to his intellectually inferior co-partners, walked smartly out of the room.

Such bully boy tactics did not make him popular. Acerbic Fred of the caustic tongue was earning himself a wide berth. Cracks were beginning to increase and multiply in the temporarily smoothed surface. It required no great diagnostic ability to discern the new doctor's tendency to patronise and overbear in some quarters and circumspectly to fawn and ingratiate where discretion's dictates lay.

But his patients ... his patients positively adored him. He was hailed as a good, old-fashioned family doctor of the type that was virtually dodo dead. And it was true. Nothing was too much trouble for him. He developed a theatrically perfect bedside manner of positively hypnotic impact. He listened attentively and became his flattered patients' adviser and confidant in all manner of matters other than medical. The sole clue to a hidden, inner impatience was the way that he drummed with his fingers when dealing with certain patients.

His idolaters might not have been so flattered or so lavish with their praise had they known of the descriptive acronyms he employed. Scribed on their medical records – WOW: Whining Old Woman. WDSS – What Drivel She Speaks. FTPBI – Failed To Put Brain In.

Externally, what manner of man had he developed into now? Smallish, thinnish, with his grey beard and thinning dark grey hair, thick-lensed spectacles, narrow face, 'scratchy' voice, and already unmissable paunch, his general aspect was older than that of a young man in his thirties. Pedantic, and tending to the tetchy, he dressed in an inconspicuous sort of middle-aged way – sober grey or brown or grey-brown suits, conservatively dark-hued ties. He has been compared to an old-fashioned schoolmaster or a middle-ranking civil servant; hardly a Lothario, but respectable and dependable.

He was concerned about his public image. He was desirous of gravitas. To that end he joined the local St John Ambulance Brigade, and held the posts of Divisional Surgeon, Area Surgeon, and Area Commissioner, became treasurer of the Small Practitioner's Association, was on the Tameside Local Medical Committee, and on the School Board of Governors. At a lower level of public good works, he would at weekends, armed with a suitably capacious bag, go round knocking at the neighbours' doors collecting old newspapers for the local scout group.

His fulfilment of the role of paterfamilias is more equivocal. As a father, he was erratic and intermittently bad-tempered. Sarah was the only one of the children who managed to handle her father's mood swings. She simply laughed at his ill-humour, whether mere grumpiness or more violent, a technique which never seemed to fail to change his mood instantly.

Sarah and Christopher, the two older children, were joined by David, born on 20 March 1979, and Samuel, born on 5 April 1982. Fred's tolerance level where the two young boys were concerned was not high. When he was at home during the day he invariably insisted that they should be confined to the bedroom – Sarah and Christopher shared a rather cramped bedroom, as did David and Samuel – and only let out after his departure. He offered little or no help with the children's homework, supervising it only to the extent that he always insisted on inspecting it and approving of what he saw before permitting them to sit down in front of the television set.

Albeit, Shipman was a strong disciplinarian and distinctly autocratic – despotic in some ways. It is told how, when Primrose would telephone him at the surgery with the tidings that dinner was on the table and everyone sitting there awaiting his arrival, he would bark, 'Nobody eats until I get there'. But Primrose was dominant in her own household roles as good wife and caring mother. Sadly, in her role as cook she was no longer what she once was. Over the years, her culinary skills seem to have slipped several notches.

Fred considered himself an expert on wine and haute cuisine. He delighted in confounding Primrose by flaunting his vinous expertise, making a grand show of it when choosing a wine for them on one of their not wildly frequent visits to Ferrero's or Maestro's – their two neighbourhood Italian restaurants. More modestly a great real ale man, he set up vast plastic bottles of home-brew beer behind the living-room settee.

He and Primrose did not go out a great deal, but they would

occasionally turn up at their local, The Dog and Partridge, to enjoy a night out. They were notoriously partial to stodgy pub grub, especially roast beef and Yorkshire. They were to be glimpsed, too, at church fetes, games of tombola, community quiz nights, and parents' sports days at the local junior schools. At these latter events, Fred could often be run to ground in the beer tent. 'There's no doubt', commented his fellow doctor, David Walker, 'he liked a pint of ale.' Family summer holidays were spent in Brittany and Spain. In the summer of 1984, Fred and Prim accompanied daughter Sarah on a school exchange visit to the Haute-Marne department of north-eastern France.

The following year – on 5 January 1985 – Fred's father died, aged seventy, of a heart attack. He collapsed in the kitchen of the old family house in Longmead Drive, Nottingham. When practice manager Vivien Langfield said, 'I'm sorry about your father', Shipman replied, 'Are you? I'm not,' and walked off. He appeared to be totally unmoved, and did not take time off work to go to the funeral. One suspects that his father's attitude all those years ago to his marriage to Primrose still rankled, and he was undoubtedly angry, too, that the family home had been left entirely to his sister, Pauline, who had sold it and used the proceeds to buy herself a granny flat attached to the large modern house at Long Eaton, where her brother, Clive, his wife and their two children lived. Things would, he felt, have been very different if only his dearly loved mother had been alive.

Fred loved to ramble about the long garden of his home, which was his pride and joy. He liked to sit there, too, at the table, writing letters with the beautiful tortoiseshell fountain pen which he cherished. It was the one place where he felt able truly to relax; in that garden, where as well as planting a rainbow myriad of flowers and neat borderings of green bushes, he had built a rockery and garden wall with his own hands. Bare-torsoed, wearing only shorts, leather sandals, and a floppy white sunhat, he would sit out there with Primrose for hours. Back from doing his rounds, he would be there contentedly sipping wine, seeing the warm summer's evening slipping down the sky.

Although it had been known for the Shipmans to host a couple of barbecues in their garden, the house itself was, in the words of Dr Walker, 'like a cocoon and few adults ever got in there'.

That most likely had something to do with Prim's fall from grace as a housekeeper. The place was described as a tip. It was dirty and its air was tainted by a most unpleasant smell. The family's black and white cat contributed to the odour of the place, the poor creature being often forced to urinate in the corners of rooms because it could not get out into the yard through the frequently jammed catflap in the back-door. Fred was enormously attached to the cat. He was not a dog man: 'Dogs are too needy. I like the fact that cats always retain their sense of independence.'

Interior walls, once pristine white, had faded to a bilious yellow. The living room was covered with a scattered, chaotic confetti of children's colouring books, great drifts of papers of various kinds, newspapers, magazines, and discarded shoes; in the kitchen, where the oven grill was thickly coated in fat, were three-foot standing stacks of unwashed clothes. Nothing was ever tidied away. Days' accumulations of dirty saucepans and soiled plates lay around in shameless profusion. Simple cleanliness and elementary hygiene seemed to be disregarded. Said one visitor, Dr Wally Ashworth, 'Your feet stuck to the carpet, it was so filthy'.

The internal disorder extended to the outside. The place had been allowed to deteriorate. It was frankly shabby. Some of the paintwork was peeling. There were toys littering the lawn. Standing forlorn in waiting were Prim's battered Fiat Mini and Fred's rusting Ford, in the glove compartment of which he kept a phial of antidote against the danger of bee stings, to which he was, or so he informed all and sundry, allergic. In actual fact it was an ampoule of pethidine.

In any event, whatever the reason for it, the Shipmans did not go in for entertaining in their own home. They did not do dinner parties nor even informal suppers there, although they did hold their daughter, Sarah's, eighteenth birthday party in February, 1985. On the other hand, Fred's fortieth birthday, on 14 January 1986, was celebrated at the York House Hotel, Ashton-under-Lyne, where he astutely invited a strategically selected company of his fellow medics to join him and his family as his guests at a sit-down meal.

More and more after his departure into solo practise did the doctor slip into rigidities of routine. Each evening at 6 p.m. precisely he would leave the surgery and drive home to Roe Green Close, where Primrose would invariably be just about finishing cooking the evening meal. His greeting to her would be equally invariable: 'Good evening! What time is dinner?' Never a kiss or warmer salutation. Just off with his jacket, a scrupulous washing of his hands, and into his favourite armchair to await the serving of the meal. The family seated about him round the table, he would proceed to bark out orders to his two youngest sons: 'Samuel, serve the potatoes. David, the carrots.' Then ... silence. Conversation at the dinner table was neither permitted nor tolerated. The food was not all that good, either. Sausages frequently undercooked pink, potatoes hard, not properly baked, only the tinned sweetcorn was palatable. Dinner over, the doctor would most evenings slink off into the sitting room, there to bury his nose in the financial pages of the newspaper, checking up on the movements of his thin portfolio of stocks and shares.

A stern father, Shipman brooked no insubordination in his house, and there was, indeed, internal evidence that, a strict disciplinarian, severe physical punishments were meted out to those who chose to disobey his edicts. It has been tellingly observed that the boys seemed afraid to speak to him, unless he spoke to them first.

Always inclined to be prickly, Shipman refused to attend the joint twenty-first birthday party of the Donneybrook and

Clarendon group practices of Hyde, held at the Dukinfield Golf Club at the end of 1989, for the staffs past and present of both practices – a total of more than 150 people. The Mayor of Hyde, who happened to be a Labour councillor, had been invited, and this prompted Fred to accuse the organisers of being politically motivated. He would, consequently, have nothing to do with the festivities.

He was growing restless, anyway. To start with, he did not at all care for the government insistence that, as part of the Patients' Charter proposals, all practices should be computerised. Neither did he like the practice talk that was going on about becoming fundholders; taking charge, like limited company directors, of their own finances. By 1991, the proactive Donneybrook partners were actively gathering practical information, clearly bent on entering the scheme. If they were to do so, that would, Shipman realised, be bad for him; it would mean increasing use of computerisation, and that would mean that other doctors would be able to look at the medical notes he made on patients' records. Such potentially constant scrutiny would seriously interfere with his secret practice.

Carefully, cautiously, deviously, Shipman allowed, drip by drip, the rumour to slip out that he was planning to move back to Yorkshire, but had so far failed to find a suitable practice there. Eventually, he was to make no secret of what he claimed was the reason that he did not want to stay at Donneybrook. It was that he was opposed to GP fundholding.

But the manner of his leaving was to betray the trust of his six fellow doctors in the Donneybrook professional brotherhood. He – or perhaps his solicitor – found, and crawled meanly out through, a legal loophole in the partnership contractual agreement. Shipman had faithfully promised that, in the event of his departure, he would not poach any of the staff, but, devious to the end, he carried off with him not only three receptionists and a district nurse, but also 3,000 patients. This last was contrary to established custom and practice, and, in the view of his former colleagues, unethical and immoral, it being an unwritten law that any doctor who left the group practice would pass his list of patients on to the incoming doctor who was to succeed him. That was what Dr Bennett had done when Dr Shipman had replaced him.

This final stroke of Shipman's hit the six remaining doctors to the tune of some £73,000. They lost his annual contribution to the running costs of the building and the payment of the associated non-medical staff (£23,000), and they were obliged by agreement to pay his tax bill on the previous year's earnings (£30,000). Shipman found new premises at 21 Market Street. It had been a shop, and was bang in the centre of a row – on one side a chemist's, two Italian restaurants on the other. He arranged for the erection, above its frontage, and below a smart green-painted architrave, of a mammoth sign, 'The Surgery'. Another equally prominent sign read 'Dr Shipman's Surgery Entrance 21 Market Street'. Although hardly the smartest of buildings, it occupied a prime location, 300 yards from, and virtually opposite, Donneybrook House, and about a hundred yards from the Market Square and the Town Hall in the centre of Hyde. The rent was roughly £300 per week. He took up a twenty-year lease. He puffed out his chest. Monarch of all he surveyed. *Ecce gubernator.*

External appearances were deceptive. There was very much more to No. 21 than a first street glance might suggest. It provided an amplitude of space. The doctor's demesne covered three floors. At ground level was the reception area, a consulting room, and an examination-cum-treatment room. Shipman cherished an inordinate penchant for pigs, and had seeded his home with decorative pig ornaments. This positive porcine mania was further demonstrated by his plastering of the walls of the waiting area of the Market Street Surgery with pig posters, and the presence on the reception desk of a big pink piggy bank – for the collection of loose change for the Patients' Fund. Corridor walls were hung with prints of steam trains. A large caricature, drawn by one of his patients, of the doctor himself, without his beard but with a large moustache and an even larger grin on his face, was accorded pride of place, and on his desk was displayed the, in the circumstances sinisterly cautioning, maxim: 'Every Day's a Bonus'.

Up on the first floor, there were a couple of offices, one of which was reserved for the use of nurses and a psychotherapist, Colton Reid. A large room on the second, top, floor was the administrative centre.

Officially starting up in sole practice on 1 January 1992, he continued for the time being, while Market Street was being got ready, to work from his old room in Donneybrook House. Being a raging psychopath, he was able to do this without embarrassment or an atom of emotional unease. He moved into his new surgery on Monday 24 August 1992. Just six years of dignified professional life were all that remained in the draining upturned glass of his existence.

Throughout that half-dozen years he was the Great Dissembler. Brian Whittle (*Prescription Murder*, Warner Books, London, 2000. pp.319-320), sums him up most acutely: 'Fred Shipman managed, superficially at least, to have a "normal" life, with a wife and children, with colleagues who, while perhaps not liking him much, did not find his behaviour bizarre or alarming. He made social contacts, although perhaps in a contrived and unsatisfactory way, always on his terms ... He maintained a job, and did it well by most accounts.'

For all his much-vaunted disapproval of fundholding, it was not long after his severance from the Donneybrook practice before he was pointing a toe in the direction of the establishment of a fundholding arrangement with certain other single-handed practitioners. When a nearby branch of the Halifax Building Society closed down, he seriously considered the possibility of extending into its premises. With that end in mind, he initiated partnership negotiations with a young woman doctor, Lisa Gutteridge; but the plan went awry, and there was no second meeting with Dr Gutteridge.

A mercurial, charismatic character, he has been felicitously limned by Wensley Clarkson (*The Good Doctor*, John Blake, London, 2001. p. 88) as having 'become like a magician with his mysterious bag of tools and potions, his secret vocabulary, his impenetrable handwriting, his hidden knowledge. He could cure and listen'. Indeed. But, all unguessed, he could kill and turn a deaf ear. The Good Doctor had become something else ... the Master Eliminator ... the Medical Bagman ... the hypodermic wielder *par excellence*, the Syringe Slayer. And he was the best of British in his killing field – an estimated 264 murders; the closest runner-up, Mary Ann Cotton, with a measly twenty, then, quite a drop, Dennis Nilsen, sixteen. Peter Sutcliffe, the Yorkshire Ripper, thirteen. The Wests, twelve. John Reginald Halliday Christie, six. Ian Brady and Myra Hindley, five. Jack the Ripper, five.

*

The plain truth is that no one knows for sure how many murders Dr Harold Frederick Shipman perpetrated in the course of his twenty-three years as a self-asserted life-saving, healing disciple of Hippocrates. The figures with which to juggle range from the fifteen murders for which he was safely convicted, through the 284 ultimately hazarded by the careful calculations of Dame Janet Smith, DBE, the High Court judge who presided over the Shipman Inquiry – ordered by the then Secretary of State for Health, Alan Milburn, and held in Manchester Town Hall – to the not necessarily extreme tally of one thousand, a possibility aired by the coroner for South Manchester, John Pollard.

The likelihood that the good doctor picked up the syringe of serial slaying practically as soon as he emerged from Leeds Medical School and secured his first job at Pontefract General

Infirmary, seems now to have escalated persuasively from distinct possibility to virtual certainty. The trigger of the transition was the contacting of the police, in January, 2004, by Mrs Sandra Whitehead. Between October, 1971 and October, 1974, Miss Goddard, as she then was, had been a student nurse at Pontefract General Infirmary, and she had now recognised Dr Shipman, from his photograph in the newspapers, as a doctor with whom she had been working from February to July, 1972, and had, at the time, become concerned, thinking that he might have been killing patients. She had, she said, ever since retained bad memories of her time on Ward 1 – the female medical ward – and a long-lingering unease, because of the high number of deaths that had occurred there. She also recalled how on many occasions when a patient had died she would find an empty injection packet next to the bed. For decades it had remained for her the stuff of nightmares.

Between July 2002, and December 2004, Dame Janet Smith produced five Shipman Inquiry Reports. In them she had tended to the belief that Shipman's first killings had not taken place until after he had moved from Pontefract to Todmorden. Alerted by Mrs Whitehead's disturbing recollections, she made a further close scrutiny of Shipman's years at the Infirmary, and in her sixth Shipman Inquiry Report, of January 2005, she finds that those whose demise at Pontefract are certified by Shipman, and present, as to a degree, suspicions, include ninety-one-year-old Albert Sidebottom, obit. 18/11/70 of alleged coronary thrombosis; William Turner, aged fifty-two, obit. 06/03/72 of alleged myocardial infarction; Thomas Cullumbine, aged fifty-four, obit. 12/04/72 of alleged ventilatory (*sic*) failure; John Brewster, aged eighty-four, obit. 28/04/72 of alleged left ventricular failure; James Rhodes, aged seventy-one, obit. 22/05/72 of alleged coronary thrombosis due to ischaemic heart disease, pernicious anaemia, and coronary thrombosis.

Three deaths, all occurring on the same day, 14 April 1972, gave

Dame Smith particular pause. They were those of Agnes Davidson, aged seventy-three, at 10.15 p.m. of alleged left ventricular failure; Elizabeth Thwaites, aged seventy-four, at 10.30 p.m. of alleged congestive heart failure; and Alice Smith, aged eighty, at 11 p.m. of alleged congestive heart failure. She observed that Shipman 'liked to inject with fatal doses of opiates, usually on late shifts between 6 p.m. and midnight, when the wards were quiet, when there would be no other doctors about, and when there would be a reduced level of nursing'.

In a revised conclusion, she estimated that while at Pontefract he had probably caused the deaths of between ten and fifteen patients. She thought it quite likely that he had killed one or two patients while working on the medical wards in 1971, and very likely while working as a Senior House Officer on the medical wards in 1972. 'I do not think that he killed anyone while working on the surgical or gynaecological wards and I have concerns about only one death that occurred while he was working on the paediatric wards.'

The only one, she said, 'in which I think he might have killed a child (Susie Garfitt), he was convinced that she was very ill and that she would never have any reasonable quality of life'.

It transpired that during his time at Pontefract Shipman had done occasional locum work for the practice of a Dr Michael Hessel and his wife, Dr Gwendolen Hessel. Upon investigation, however, they reported no concern about his work, or suspicious sudden death alarums.

Of the doctor's homicidal performance at Todmorden there can be small dubiety. Within a few weeks of moving there, Shipman had begun obtaining quite large quantities of pethidine from Boots the chemist's.

21 January 1975 was a good day for Shipman, and a bad day for three of his patients – Elizabeth Pearce, aged eighty-four, who died at 4.10 p.m. (cerebrovascular accident), sixty-two-year-old Robert Lingard, who died around 7.30 p.m. (Bronchiectasis and

emphysema), and Lily Crossley, aged seventy-eight, who died later that evening (Terminal carcinoma).

All three died in their own homes. All conformed to the Shipman modus operandi. Typically, he would pay a domiciliary visit to an elderly patient who lived alone, either by request or, quite often, out of the seeming goodness of his heart, unsolicited. With elderly ladies he was wont to adopt a pseudo semi-flirtatious stance, impersonating an avuncular Romeo, chatting away like an amiably babbling brook, pouring forth soothing sympathy, empathetically sharing their manifold personal distresses, and bemoaning with them the human lot. With a kindly smile of reassurance, he would draw forth his alleviating syringe from his bag, where it always nestled, ever lethally ready-charged with 100 milligrams of diamorphine. Then, with some well-practised and plausible excuse for intravenous injection slipped smoothly out, a sleeve would be trustingly rolled up ... a faint pinprick ... and, thanking the Beloved Physician, his grateful patient would float gently far, far away, to that 'undiscover'd country from whose bourn no traveller returns', and where 'the pain' could no longer beset her.

Shipman was not, like most serial killers, of sadistic turn, loving to hurt. He did not, as they generally do, exult in the infliction of pain. He had no taste for torture. There is evidence that he gave some patients overdoses of such phenothiazine drugs as largactil, to induce a deep sleep.

Secure in the knowledge that the victim had been safely despatched, Shipman would tend to vary the subsequent proceedings. Sometimes he would remain on the premises, telephoning the victim's relatives, friends, or neighbours, explaining that he had happened to be there, that the death had taken place in his presence, and assuming the role of master of funereal ceremonies Other times he would profess to have discovered the patient dead upon his arrival – he would actually, the deed done, have sneaked quietly away, only to return to 'find', preferably with a neighbour as witness, his patient dead.

Throughout his fifteen-month tenure of office at the Abraham Ormerod practice, in Donneybrook House, Hyde, Shipman killed sporadically. He was personally present at a suspiciously high number of his patients' deaths, and would be constantly urging relatives of the deceased that there would be no need for a post-mortem. 'I know all about it. I was her doctor. I was there when she died. You don't want her body messed about with. It isn't necessary.' And he was careful to advise speedy cremation. Back in his consulting room, he would be busy in front of his computer, falsifying the patient's medical record, cramming it with notes of bogus symptoms, busily justifying to echo his death certificate diagnostic verdict.

But the real, the crowning epoch of his toxicological triumph, were the seven years between 1992 and 1998, when he was a sole practitioner, unobserved, unchecked, master of all he surveyed. Between 1994 and 1997 five women actually died on visits to The Surgery. Joan Harding was the first of them. Shipman said that she had had a fatal heart attack while he was examining her. That was on 5 January 1994. She was eighty-four. On 30 June 1995, sixty-eight-year-old Bertha Moss succumbed to a Shipman-alleged massive heart attack while attending The Surgery. Also in 1995, on 26 September, Dora Ashton, who had reached the respectable age of eighty-seven, made her way to Dr Shipman's surgery to undergo her regular three-monthly check up. She was sitting in the waiting area, Shipman called her name, she stood up and collapsed. He took her into his consulting room, and, according to him, she promptly keeled over again. He certified a second and final stroke. Edith Brady, seventy-two, also a regular, attending The Surgery for her three-monthly B12 injection for her pernicious anaemia, met her end on Monday, 13 May 1996, on the table in Shipman's examination room. Fifthly and finally, Ivy Lomas, a generally healthy sixty-eight-year-old, walked into The Surgery on 29 May

1997, to keep a 4 p.m. appointment for a routine check on a pain in her arm, and never walked out again. Shipman took her into the treatment room. He emerged twenty-five minutes later to inform the receptionist that the ECG machine was giving problems. He then saw three more patients before calling the receptionist to tell her that Mrs Lomas had died in the treatment room. He duly inscribed her death certificate with heart attack and obstructed airways, caused by smoking, as the reasons for her demise.

Shipman struck with the speed of a rattlesnake, but without the warning rattle. Mrs Alice Kitchen and her grown-up son, Mick, lived in a council house in Kirkstone Road, Hyde. She was aged seventy. At 1.30 p.m. on 6 June 1994, Mick left his mother at home in her usual health and the best of spirits. At 6.30 p.m. he returned to find her stone-cold dead on the settee, and a note from Dr Shipman saying that he had called at about 4 o'clock and found Mrs Kitchen slurring her words and dragging her foot. It was clear to him that she had had a slight stroke. She had, he added, refused to go into hospital, and would not let him ring any of the family, because someone would be home at teatime. And so he had left her.

In the kernel of every tragedy there seems always to be the heartening story of the one who got away. In 1966, Jim King arrived back in Hyde from Texas, where he had been working as a high-flying engineer. Just a week after marrying his fiancée, Debra, he started to get backache and noticed blood in his urine. Shipman, his doctor, immediately referred him to hospital, where a consultant diagnosed bladder, urethral, and prostate cancer. Shipman prescribed morphine, and told King that he had only eighteen months to live. What, wickedly, Shipman failed to tell him was that he had received a letter from the hospital consultant informing him that a misdiagnosis had been made. Instead, he allowed King to go on believing that he was terminally ill. Why? Because King was being prescribed and fed massive doses of morphine, and Shipman was snaffling considerable quantities of the drug from those prescriptions for his own purposes. The normal dosage for pain-killing is 30 milligrams. King was getting as much as 360 milligrams per diem. Shipman was prescribing up to 24,000 milligrams at a time.

Just before Christmas, 1996, King's health took a serious turn for the worse, and his wife telephoned Dr Shipman and asked him to come round to see her husband. Said Jim King, 'He tested my chest and said I'd had a bad dose of pneumonia and I'd got liquid on the lungs.'

'I need to give you an injection to help all this,' the doctor told him.

'No,' interjected Mrs King. 'Can't you just write out a prescription for him?'

But Shipman was adamant.

'I kept telling him, "No",' said Mrs King afterwards. She hadn't liked the doctor's insistence, 'the way he was being so arrogant about it. He had a real snotty attitude towards me.'

In the end, Debbie King's will prevailed. Her determined demeanour set alarm-bells chiming in his head, and he decided that it would be unsafe to forge ahead with his lethal plan. Jim King was convinced that at that moment his life had been saved by the tenacity of his wife, who felt certain – and correctly so – that what Jim needed was antibiotics rather than morphine. King summed it up: 'I honestly believe that if I had had that injection it would have killed me. He would have said it was cancer. Debbie would have gone back to the States, and no one would have known any different.'

It was shortly after this that King learned that he did not have cancer – and never had had.

*

As the massed clouds of years passed over his thinning hair and thickening waist, Shipman's status as a doctor and adroitness as a serial killer advanced exponentially. But, a quinquennium on from his establishment as solo practitioner at The Surgery, there were faint stirrings in the conurbationary undergrowth. Some of the people of Hyde were beginning to seek, and what they sought was a fuller, more in the round, view of the man they thought to glimpse behind the smiling image.

Flashes of him had shown up when an anxious relative of seventy-seven-year-old Harold Eddleston, dying of terminal cancer, had asked Shipman how long he had to live. The droll reply was, 'I wouldn't buy him any Easter eggs.' Mr Eddleston's death took place on 4 March 1998. Easter came thirty-nine days later, on 12 April. Shipman almost certainly killed him.

Not everyone in Hyde fell for the doctor. Seventy-three-year-old Kenneth Smith, affronted by his arrogant and overbearing manner, was not at all partial to Shipman. 'Don't let him come here,' he told a relative. 'He's the Angel of Death.' But come he did, on 17 December 1996, and finished poor Mr Smith off.

From 1994, the killing rate had increased. By 1998, Shipman was beginning to display a Dr-Bodkin-Adams-like interest in the acquisition of consumer goods. Mabel Shawcross had died, aged seventy-nine, at her house in Stockport Road, Hyde, on 22 January 1998. She had died alone. Her body had been found by a neighbour. Shipman had diagnosed the cause of her decease as 'probably a stroke'. Among her furniture was a very handsome polished dark-wood settle, a fine piece of old oak, the sort of thing that would make antique dealers' mouths water. Shipman had cast a beady eye on it.

When, the day after her maiden aunt's funeral, Joan Sellars and her husband went to Shipman's surgery to collect the death certificate, they were shocked to be greeted by the doctor with the intimation that Miss Shawcross had promised him the settle. Mrs Sellars promptly and peremptorily dismissed his claim, telling him that the matter of the settle had long ago been settled: it was going to her son, Miss Shawcross' grandnephew. The police later informed Joan Sellars that her aunt, who had been cremated without benefit of post-mortem, had most likely been murdered by Shipman.

Bianka Pomfret, who was only forty-nine when she died on 10 December 1997, was one of Shipman's younger victims. Mrs Pomfret, born in post-war Germany in 1948, had been diagnosed in the 1970s as manic depressive (bipolar). At 5 p.m. a psychiatric social worker had called at her house in Fountain Street, Hyde. Getting no response to her persistent ringing of the doorbell, the social worker had looked in through the window and seen Mrs Pomfret stretched upon the settee, as though asleep. Knowing that her son, William, had a key, the social worker telephoned him, and together they went round to the house. Mrs Pomfret, fully dressed, was still lying motionless on the sofa. The television was on, a half-drunk cup of coffee was beside her, and in an adjacent ashtray lay a cigarette, burnt halfway down. It emerged that Dr Shipman had called earlier – at half-past twelve that Wednesday. He certified coronary thrombosis and ischaemic heart disease as the causes of her demise, and created a false computerised medical record – angina for ten months. No post-mortem needed.

Joan Dean was seventy-five when she died on 27 February 1998. Her death was a totally unexpected tragedy. That very day she had gone to see Dr Shipman at The Surgery, complaining of dizziness. In the afternoon she failed to turn up at her usual weekly hairdressing appointment. The salon rang her home at 4 o'clock. There was no reply. Dr Shipman told her son that it was probably a stroke that had killed her. Asked if there ought not to have been a post-mortem in the circumstances, Shipman was brusque. 'She doesn't need one of those. I'll speak to the coroner. Leave it to me.' He certified death due to coronary thrombosis, heart disease, and high blood pressure. She was buried in the mink coat bought for her by her father many, many years before. Going through her possessions, her son found that a watch worth more than £1,000, an engagement ring valued at £5,000, and £300 in cash, which she had drawn from her bank account earlier on the afternoon of her death, were all missing. There is no evidence for it, but good reason for wondering, had the good doctor come a'calling?

*

The year 1998 was to prove to be Fred Shipman's *annus fatalis*. Nemesis half-struck in the month of March. That was when – on 24 March– Dr Linda Reynolds, a fellow GP who worked in a surgery diagonally opposite to his in Market Street, became seriously exercised about the number of times that Shipman was asking her to countersign cremation certificates for his patients; by the end of 1997, one every ten days. She was anxious, too, about the unusually high mortality rate of those on the Shipman list. So worried did she become, that she felt obliged to alert the coroner, John Pollard, to her suspicions, frankly stating her belief that Shipman was murdering his patients with some sort of drug, adding that the bodies of two of his elderly patients – Lily Higgins and Ada Warburton – were at the undertaker's and would be available for post-mortems. This, taken in conjunction with information from Deborah Bambroffe, who worked in her father's undertaking business, as to how the bodies of Dr Shipman's patients presented disturbingly frequently as elderly, always fully dressed, and with no sign of any long-term illness, plus the fact that, over the course of the previous year or so, Dr Shipman had required practically three times as many cremation forms as the Donneybrook practice's total deaths, surely merited official attention. Moreover, although the Donneybrook was three times the size of Shipman's practice, his had ten times more deaths, causing the coroner considerable unease.

Deborah Bambroffe's father, Alan Massey, trepidatious to a degree, felt it his duty to pay Shipman a frank-speaking visit; they had, after all, had a long-lasting acquaintance which must surely by now skirt friendship. The anticipated burst of the furies did not eventuate. Instead, a studiedly nonchalant Shipman, open and genial, protectively cloaked by doctors' jargon, simply pushed his medical records and death certificates towards Massey; 'Here, have a look at them'. And, after what Massey described as 'quite a pleasant two or three minute chat', the undertaker floated home on a cloud of unknowing, knowing that there was 'nothing to worry about'.

On the other hand, the coroner, also unknowing, had the distinct feeling that there might well be something to worry about, and, without further ado, spoke to the police. Unfortunately, Detective Superintendent Bernard Postles was away, and it was Detective Inspector David Smith who undertook an investigation. He was not up to it, and on 17 April 1998 it was reported to the coroner that nothing untoward had been found as regards Dr Shipman. Subsequently, at the Shipman Inquiry, Detective Inspector Smith said that he had not been told that the Mrs Higgins' and Mrs Warburton's cadavers were available for autopsy; but Dame Smith concluded that he *had* been told. There are straws in the wind that indicate that the police may have taken the view that suspicion against Dr Shipman was the exclusive province of Dr Reynolds, and consequently did not put themselves to the trouble of interviewing the other doctors concerned. In any event, Smith failed, falling dismally short of his remit. He made no notes of interviews with Dr Reynolds or Mr Massey and his daughter; he neglected to check Shipman's criminal record, thereby missing his conviction for drug abuse and falsifying documents; he neglected to check the number of death certificates signed by Shipman, as compared with the numbers signed by other local doctors; he failed to arrange for post-mortems to be carried out on Higgins and Warburton. (Five weeks after Shipman's ultimate conviction Dr Reynold died, aged forty-nine, of liver cancer.)

Smith was moved to a desk job.

But another pair of eyes was watching. They belonged to John Shaw, taxi driver of a blue Volvo, proprietor of K Cabs. Since the founding of his company in Hyde in 1988, he had built up rather a specialised clientele. It consisted for the most part of elderly ladies, often widows, who required ferrying on short journeys. A jovial, companionable man, he tended to look upon all his customers as friends, and as well as driving them around made a point of always being available to do little jobs for them, like the changing of light bulbs or the carrying of heavy weights. However, in spite of his excellent customer relations, he could not help noticing that within a few years of starting his business he was beginning to lose clients. Looking at the situation more closely, he came to realise that what was happening was not that they were transferring their allegiance to other firms, but that various ladies were suddenly dying – ladies whom he had seen weeks, or possibly even days, before their deaths, when they had given every appearance of being in perfectly satisfactory health. The first of these so rapidly declining ladies had been Mrs Monica Rene Sparkes, who died on 7 October 1992. By the time he had lost four more of his ladies he was beginning to harbour suspicion.

'I seemed to be seeing a pattern that caused me a lot of concern. They all died in similar circumstances. They were fully clothed, sitting in a chair. I didn't hear of one of these ladies going into hospital and dying. They all appeared to be dying at home and, in the course of conversation with others, it always seemed to be Dr Shipman who was their doctor.'

Shaw began to wonder if the doctor was practising euthanasia; but took himself to task for 'being paranoid'. However, when, in January 1994, Miss Joan Harding died in Dr Shipman's consulting room, all his worst suspicions seemed to be confirmed.

For the next four years Shaw struggled to come to terms with his conviction that a GP could really be killing his patients, but it was the death of Mrs Kathleen Grundy that finally convinced him that a GP named Fred Shipman really could. He added her name to the list of twenty, going back to 1992, that he had already compiled.

Shipman would, in fact, do away with Winifred Mellor (11 May), Joan Melia (12 June) and Kathleen Grundy (24 June) before his crude attempt at forging a will would snap the trap on him. Kathleen Grundy was healthy, wealthy and eighty-one years wise. She was also a lady of station, a former Mayoress of Hyde. She lived in a beautiful, £200,000, seventeenth-century house – Loughrigg Cottage – at 79 Joel Lane, Gee Cross, owned a £90,000 terraced cottage nearby, and a £60,000 flat in the Lake District, as well as a portfolio of nicely prospering investments. She was possessed of estate totting up to some £386,402. Her health was excellent, apart from one potentially lethal defect, from which her sixteen lustra had failed to deliver her: she was a patient of Dr Shipman's.

On Wednesday, 24 June 1998, Mrs Grundy was expected at Werneth House, a social centre for pensioners, where she was due to help with the lunches. There was no sign of her. Telephone calls went unanswered. Anxious colleagues calling at her home just before noon, and getting no reply to their knocking, let themselves in through a door that they found unlocked. And there, in the living-room, they found the dead – the body of Mrs Grundy, curled up, fully dressed, on the sofa. They sent for her doctor. Dr Shipman arrived within ten minutes. He told them that he had seen Mrs Grundy earlier that morning – 'only for a talk' – and, after carrying out a cursory examination of the corpse, said that she had suffered a cardiac arrest. He also advised them to contact a firm of solicitors, Hamilton Ward & Co., of Century House, 107–109 Market Street, Hyde, who, he said, would handle everything.

Duly contacted, the solicitors denied that they were acting for Kathleen Grundy, but added that that very morning they had received in the post a will ostensibly from her. It was accompanied by a typewritten letter:

Dear Sir,

I enclose a copy of my will. I think it is clear in intent. I wish Dr Shipman to benefit by having my estate but if he dies or cannot accept it, then the estate goes to my daughter. I would like you to be the executors of the will. I intend to make an appointment to discuss this and my will in the near future.

The will, dated 9 June 1998, also typewritten, read:

I give all my estate, money and house, to my doctor. My family are not in need and I want to reward him for all the care he has given to me and the people of Hyde. He is sensible enough to handle any problems this may give him. My doctor is Dr H. F. Shipman, 21 Market Street, Hyde, Cheshire.

Messrs. Hamilton Ward suggested that contact should be established with Mrs Grundy's family. Her daughter, Angela, a fifty-three-year-old solicitor, and her husband, David Woodruff, lived in the village of Harbury, near Leamington Spa, in Warwickshire.

Then, on 30 June, a further typewritten letter was delivered to the office of Hamilton Ward. It was dated 28 June, bore no address, and was signed S. or J. or F. Smith.

Dear Sir,

I regret to inform you that Mrs K. Grundy of 79 Joel Lane, Hyde, died last week. I understand she lodged a will with you, as I, a friend, typed it out for her. Her daughter is at the address and you can contact her there.

No such person as S. or J. or F. Smith was ever traced.

Twelve days after Kathleen Grundy had been laid to rest in her plot in the burial ground behind Hyde Chapel, Angela Woodruff received a letter from Hamilton Ward, notifying her that they were in possession of her late mother's last will and testament, and enclosing photostats of the relevant documentation.

This communication was received as a breakfast table bombshell. Hamilton Ward said that they were not happy about the way that they had been instructed to act for Mrs Grundy, and wanted to talk with Mrs Woodruff about it. Mrs Woodruff was shocked and puzzled, in that order, and most certainly wanted to talk with Hamilton Ward. On 24 July 1998, she walked into Warwickshire Police Headquarters, saw Detective Superintendent Steve Hussey, asked the police to investigate, and set in motion a chain of events, the upshot of which was to lay by the heels Britain's all time premier serial killer.

She did a bit of investigating herself, too. She found that Shipman had said that her mother had requested that she should be cremated. This was completely at odds with everything that Kathleen Grundy had ever expressed as to what she wanted done with her body after her death. Angela Woodruff was now feeling very suspicious. Neither was that suspicion assuaged when she saw what Shipman had written on her mother's death certificate – 'old age'. That is a diagnosis usually interpreted as applicable to cases of people of at least seventy years of age, who are displaying a general, often slow, deterioration in health due to the breakdown of various organ systems, the patient effectively becoming moribund before death. In the case of universally testified to alert and lively, thoroughly *compos mentis*, Kathleen Grundy, that was indeed a questionable verdict.

Mrs Grundy had not, in fact, been cremated, and on 30 July an exhumation order was obtained from the coroner. The exhumation took place on 1 August 1998. A post-mortem was conducted by Dr John Rutherford at Tameside General Hospital, in Ashton-under-Lyne. He was unable to ascertain any cause of death. Tissue samples were despatched to the North West Forensic Science Laboratories for toxicological analysis.

Rumours were soon wriggling uncomfortably about the streets of Hyde, sussurations of suspicion that the police were taking an uncommon interest in the activities of Dr Fred. Indeed they were. The image of the resurrected Kathleen Grundy well in the forefront of their minds, the finger of suspicion now pointing quite firmly Shipmanwards, and, time being of the essence, they proceeded to waste none. With a brandishment of search warrants, the detectives descended upon the doctor's Market Street premises. From a cupboard in his surgery Shipman produced a Brother portable electric typewriter.

'I believe,' he said, a faint smile of condescension flitting across his lips, 'this is what you are looking for.'

It proved to be forensically linked to the will and to both of the Hamilton Ward letters. Shipman said that Mrs Grundy had borrowed the machine from him from time to time, and had later returned it to the surgery. This did not, however, explain how she contrived to type on it the letter to Hamilton Ward informing the solicitors of her death *six days after it had occurred.*

Police simultaneously searching the doctor's home were shocked at the state of the house. It was not just untidy, it was filthy. One woman police constable neatly encapsulated it: 'It was the sort of place where you wipe your feet on the way out.' They did, however, recover from a room at the rear of the house, a C & A white plastic carrier bag stuffed full with a secret hoard of diamorphine.

In a cardboard box in the Shipmans' bedroom ferreting officers uncovered a treasure trove of some seventy gold wedding rings, engagement and dress rings, brooches, earrings, and necklaces, a haul said, perhaps with exaggeration, to be worth in the region of £10,000.

Asked who owned the collection, Primrose claimed it as her own. The police officers were not convinced. 'Her fingers were like Cumberland sausages,' said one of them. 'We couldn't believe she had ever worn such tiny rings.' The jewellery was all photographed and subsequently put into a catalogue for the relatives of Shipman's victims to view.

In March 2005, Primrose instructed her lawyers to claim the jewellery, which was then still in police hands. She is said to have asserted that her husband had told her that they were gifts from his patients, and that he was biding his time, waiting for them to increase in value, before selling them. He allegedly explained to her that they would yield splendid retirement bonus for them.

The suspicion that Shipman was in the habit of stealing from his victims took serious shape. It was hazarded that, within minutes of delivering a lethal injection of diamorphine, he would be creeping stealthily around searching for jewellery or any other cash worthy objects to steal. Trinkets of negligible value would be pocketed as 'trophies' – memorabilia of murder. The money-magnet adornments he kept, with an eye to their transformation into liquid cash were his and Primrose's hostages to future prosperity.

The sideline commerce of his practice is also demonstrated by specific exposed acts of illicit acquisition.

Mrs Joan Melia, aged seventy-three, was an emphysema sufferer and had called Dr Shipman in because of a chest infection. She was found dead on 12 June 1998, sitting upright in a chair, spectacles balanced on her nose, an unfinished crossword on her knees. £20,000 in cash and a pile of jewellery were missing. The doctor had been her sole visitor.

Mrs Winifred Mellor, also aged seventy-three, had died on 11 May 1998. Complaining of a cold and a bad chest, she had had the privilege of an afternoon domiciliary from the good Dr Shipman. Her purse was found empty of her newly collected £50 pension money.

Mrs Joan Dean, a businesswoman who had once dabbled in the theatre and appeared as an extra in the popular television soap *Coronation Street*, died, aged seventy-five, on 27 February 1998, in the wake of a Shipman visit. Missing thereafter was an eighteen-carat Omega watch worth about £1,000 and her £5,000 engagement ring.

A closer inspection by Mrs Woodruff of her mother's will disclosed the names of two people of whom she had never heard – Paul Spencer, who kept a pet shop in Market Street, and Claire Hutchinson – who had witnessed Kathleen Grundy's signature on the will. It was discovered that they had both been sitting in Dr Shipman's waiting room when the doctor stuck his head out of his consulting room and asked, 'Would you two mind witnessing a signature for me?'

Readily they had assented, and followed him, lambs to the slaughter, over to his desk, sitting on the patient's chair near which was an old lady.

They heard him say to her something like, 'Are you sure about this, Kath? Is it okay?'

'Yes,' she had replied.

He had then presented her with a folded sheet of paper. She signed it. What she thought she was signing was a consent form to participate in a survey on ageing, with which Shipman had told her that he was involved. What she was actually signing was her will – and her death warrant.

Then he said, sort of casually, to Paul and Claire,'Just pop your names and addresses there, print and sign it at the bottom, will you?'

The piece of paper was A4 size. It had been doubled over, with the back folded halfway and brought to the front. All that the witnesses could see was the name Kathleen Grundy and her signature at one side.

As soon as the police saw copies of the will and the original letter to Hamilton Ward, they knew that they were looking at falsified documents and forgeries. Clearly, they had all, including the S. or J. or F. Smith letter, been typed on the same typewriter. Most damningly, Shipman's fingerprint was found on the bottom left-hand corner of the will itself. Subjected to scrupulous handwriting analysis, all the signatures – on the letters and the will – revealed them to be forgeries. The old hand had not lost its cunning.

Meanwhile, preliminary toxicological tests had revealed traces of morphine in muscle and liver tissue, and, on 2 September, the news came through that further tests had established the presence of a fatal dose level in the body. That clinched it. On 7 September 1998, Harold Frederick Shipman was arrested. He showed no surprise on hearing that Mrs Grundy's death was being put down to an overdose of morphine. 'That,' said Shipman, 'could well be. She was an addict' – a statement which he sought to substantiate by well-chosen and strategically placed backdated entries in her medical notes.

The arrest was carried out at the police station at Ashton-under-Lyne, where Shipman had attended by appointment at 9 o'clock that morning. His solicitor, Ann Ball, had driven him there in her car. They had arrived at 8.30 a.m., but had not gone straight into the police station. Instead, deep in conversation, they had taken a twenty-minute walk together round the streets. He was obviously anticipating trouble, and registered no emotion on being charged with the murder of Kathleen Grundy, with attempted theft by deception, and with three counts of forgery.

In marked contrast to his brash and contemptuous disregard for the feelings of those whom he regarded as his inferiors – the police and suchlike – he displayed a simultaneous paranoid anxiety for his own well-being and safety, refusing to eat any food offered to him by the police, suspecting that it might be poisoned. He would only accept tea or coffee because it came from a machine that was used by everybody else at the station.

Ten days after Shipman's arrest, his lawyer applied to a judge in chambers at Manchester Crown Court for bail. Substantial sums in surety were offered by the doctor's close friends, but the application was refused. Applications which, on the other hand, were granted, were those which came before coroner John Pollard requesting permission to carry out a series of exhumations.

The first of these was that of Joan Melia. Her exhumation took place at St Mary's graveyard, Newton, on 22 September 1998. The following day the corpse of Mrs Winifred Mellor was lifted from Highfield Cemetery, Bredbury; and, on 23 September, Mrs Bianka Pomfret was taken from her grave in Hyde Cemetery. The bodies of all three were subsequently found to contain traces of fatal doses of morphine.

Lodged now in Strangeways Prison, Manchester, Shipman seemed so seriously down that he was put on suicide watch. The depression soon lifted. He recovered his normal rude equilibrium, and was presently insulting again, with undiminished arrogant self-confidence, left, right, and centre, assuring himself of universal dislike by the offended police and prison officers.

Because of fears that his safety could be menaced by prisoners or prison officers who might have had relatives obliterated by him, Shipman was, in the autumn of 1998, moved from Manchester, first to Preston Prison, and then on to Walton Gaol, Liverpool, where, on 5 October, he was further charged with the murders of Joan Melia, Winifred Mellors, and Bianka Pomfret, charges to which he made no reply; but when the detectives began to interrogate him about the entries that he had made on his computer records, he collapsed, sobbing and gibbering, on the floor.

Two days later, he was put up at Tameside Magistrates' Court. Pale and drawn, wearing a navy-blue, round-necked jumper, he stood swaying in the dock, shaking his head from side to side and sobbing. At the end of the fifteen-minute hearing, he had to be helped from the dock by the two Group 4 security guards by whom he had been flanked. He was escorted swiftly back to Strangeways, whither he had returned from his temporary residence at Walton. He paid a second visit to the Tameside Magistrates on 10 October, for further committal on the charges proffered regarding Mrs Grundy. This time there was no swaying or shaking. He seemed cool, calm, and sufficiently collected to flash a smile and a wink to Primrose, who was sitting hunched in the public gallery. To each of the charges his set reply was a smug 'I treated them appropriately for their medical condition at the time.'

*

It was not until thirteen months after his arrest that, on Tuesday, 5 October 1999, Shipman's trial opened in Court One, Preston Crown Court. The trial had been moved there because it was felt that it would be impossible to find an impartial jury if it were to be held any nearer to the scene of the crimes. It was to last for nearly four months.

A white van drove into the backyard of the courthouse. The prisoner had arrived to face sixteen charges: fifteen of murder of his women patients, their ages ranging from forty-nine to eighty-one years, and one of forging Mrs Kathleen Grundy's will. Harold Frederick Shipman stood accused of the murders of Kathleen Grundy, Joan Melia, Winifred Mellors, Bianka Pomfret, Marie Quinn, Ivy Lomas, Irene Turner, Jean Lilley, Muriel Grimshaw, Marie West, Kathleen Wagstaff, Pamela Hillier, Norah Nuttall, Elizabeth Adams and Maureen Ward.

Richard Henriques, QC, led the prosecution. Tall, formidable, with heavy black-framed glasses, aged fifty-five, he was based in Manchester, was the leader of the Northern Circuit, and had prosecuted in the James Bulger case. His junior was Mr Ian Winter.

For the defence was Nicola Davies, QC, forty-six years of age, slim, fair-haired, always immaculately turned out, she specialised in medical cases, and was an acknowledged adept at the dissection of expert evidence.

The instructing solicitor was Ann Ball.

The trial judge was Mr Justice Thayne Forbes, a very good,

even-handed judge, of whom the best that Shipman could find to say was 'in court you didn't need a Mogadon to get to sleep, you only had to listen to Mr Justice Forbes!'

Primrose arrived early, accompanied by all her children, and they settled themselves on black plastic chairs, forty of which were provided as seats up in the public gallery. Unfortunately, however, their tenure was temporary. After only fifteen minutes legal arguments arose, the resolution of which occupied the court for four days, so that the trial did not get into its swing until the following Monday, 11 October, when Henriques' opening speech lasted for eight hours. Shipman, who had been sitting penning copious notes to his counsel and wrestling with ever-increasing piles of paper, was eventually supplied with a table in the dock, upon which he was able to spread order out of chaos.

As the tale of the doctor's murderous malfeasances unfolded, narrated by a succession of the surviving lame, halt and blind of his list, who, meticulously brushed-up and Sunday-best-dressed, clambered rheumatically into the witness box to tell it; and as the facts and figures mounted, improbable Pelion upon unbelievable Ossa, only the final debit of death made the columns of figures credible.

The prosecution called toxicological experts. Dr Hans Sachs, of the University of Munster, testified to having discovered morphia in hair samples. Julie Evans, of the North West Forensic Science Laboratories, told of her findings of morphia in the tissues submitted to her. A sad little parade of widows, sons, and daughters provided heartbreaking evidence of the deaths of their loved and lost.

The prosecution case breathed to its heavy end after twenty-five days.

Noon had just struck when, on 25 November 1999, the case for the defence opened with Shipman's shuffling from the dock over to the witness-box. Although only fifty-three, he presented the aspect of a little old man. He was looking rather frail and seemed nervous, peering about him through big, round, shiny gold-rimmed glasses. His beard, neatly trimmed, was satisfactorily full, but towards the back of his head he had a large bald patch. He was wearing a light grey suit. He had lost at least two stone, and it hung loosely about his diminished figure. It looked a poor fit. His shirt was white, set off by a sober grey striped tie. His demeanour was totally cold. He gave off no feeling. He refused to take the Bible and swear on oath, preferring to affirm. His voice was low and husky. Mr Justice Thayne Forbes asked him to speak up. Apologetically, Shipman explained, 'I slur my speech sometimes. It's the tablets I'm on.'

During the lunch break Primrose invariably went down to see Fred.

Returning to the witness-box after lunch, Shipman said, in reference to Kathleen Grundy, 'I had a suspicion she was taking an opiate – codeine, pethidine, perhaps morphine – She looked old – going downhill.'

At that day's end, he looked old as he left the court, exhausted and defeated.

Rallied by the next morning, he talked about the backdating of his patients' medical records, and of some deaths that had occurred in his presence, and others within minutes of his departure. When Richard Henriques stood up to cross-examine him, Shipman, pale-faced, sweating and trembling, told the judge that he was feeling unwell. His Lordship granted him a 15-minute break, after which he reappeared in the box, superficially more composed, but patently still uncomfortable. He was to remain there for a further seven days.

On 1 December, the doctor collapsed, weeping in the box, as he was answering questions about the death of eighty-one-year-old Kathleen Wagstaff, who had died in front of him in her first-floor flat in Rock Gardens, Hyde, on 9 December, 1997. Dramatically, Henriques asked him, 'Have you any sadness?'

Obviously, this was a *terra incognita* of sensitivity and sentiment alien to our brave medico. His reply, rendered blank, expressionless, was, 'I'm not quite sure what you're asking me.'

'Did you have any sadness?' came booming back at him the repeated question at the top of the Counsel's voice.

In contrasting flat, quiet tone, devoid of all emotion, Shipman, as though repeating the words of a well-learned catechism, answered, 'You are always sad when a patient dies.'

And, as the court rose, he was led from the box, eyes downcast, fixed on the floor, wringing his hands.

Henriques and Shipman occasionally crossed verbal swords. Discussing the demise of Ivy Lomas, who had had the misfortune to pass away in his surgery at the age of sixty-three, on 29 May 1997, Counsel asked, 'If this lady died at 4.10 p.m., she must have been administered, or administered to herself, diamorphine between 4 p.m. and 4.10 p.m., mustn't she?'

With a carefully engineered sigh shaping his voice, Shipman replied wearily, 'You could put the evidence that way, and, yes, I would agree.'

Henriques, his delivery becoming edged and much sterner: 'Dr Shipman, there is no sensible explanation, is there?'

A long pause. Then Shipman asked, 'Was that a statement or a question?'

Irritated, Henriques snapped back, 'You know very well it was a question.'

Shipman, truly cornered, could only admit, 'I don't know of any explanation.'

'Save for your guilt,' flashed back Henriques.

'That's what you're saying,' retorted Shipman, 'and I disagree with it strongly. I didn't administer anything to this lady, and I had no idea how she got it in her body.'

Again, referring to the death of 81-year-old Mrs Maria West, who had departed this life on 6 March 1995, by visitation of

Shipman, the good doctor said, 'There was no doubt in my mind that the lady had a sudden and lethal stroke.'

'Or a sudden and lethal dose of diamorphine,' countered Henriques.

The seemingly interminable Henriques cross-examination came to an end at last on 10 December. The silence soothed Shipman's every tingling nerve fibre, like a Balm of Gilead.

On Monday 13 December 1999, the evidence now heard, the judge wished the members of the jury a merry Christmas. Faint spirits of Dickensian Christmases past came into the ancient panelled courtroom – the holly and the ivy, the pungent scent of silver-cupped tangerines sidling in on the breath of the austere old place. They would all see each other again, Mr Justice Thayne Forbes announced, on 5 January 2000.

When the first Wednesday of the new millenium broke, Richard Henriques, wigged, gowned and banded, was back on his feet addressing the jury, making his closing speech. Shipman listened, impassive-faced, and scribbled away furiously, making notes on a foolscap pad.

Then it was the turn of the defence. Nicola Davies did all she possibly could, but she was weaving with thin, frayed threads. She presented her client as a dedicated doctor of admittedly idiosyncratic mien, who would regularly go far beyond the modern concept of the call of duty in his old-fashioned style of care for his flock of patients. His concern, she conveyed, was not with paperwork and the clerkly keeping of records, but with the preservation of his patients' well-being and health. His alleged lack of sympathy with the bereaved, and occasional brusqerie and chill of manner, she dismissed as nothing more than the maintenance of 'a calm and professional attitude' in the face of death. Where, she asked, was the motive for murder? What motive had the prosecution even so much as suggested, for the killings, except some amateur psychological babble about a 'power complex'? The expert scientific evidence she dismissed as unsafe, because it was 'fishing in uncharted waters'. She made the best effort of a bad job.

Mr Justice Thayne Forbes began his summing-up on 10 January 2000. The jury must not, he warned them, allow the natural anger, disgust, profound dismay and deep sympathy evoked by the case to cloud their judgment. They must consider the facts dispassionately. They had listened to the testimony of more than 120 prosecution witnesses. And he spent the following two weeks going carefully through all the evidence. Thus intellectually fortified, the jury retired to consider their verdict on 24 January. They deliberated for six days. Then, at 4.33 p.m. on the seventh day, 31 January 2000, they pronounced sixteen verdicts of guilty.

Shipman remained stock-still and emotionless – likewise Primrose.

The judge turned towards the prisoner:

> Harold Frederick Shipman, stand up. You have finally been brought to justice by the verdict of this jury. I have no doubt whatsoever that these are true verdicts. The time has now come for me to pass sentence upon you for these wicked, wicked crimes. Each of your victims was your patient. You murdered each and every one of your victims by a calculated and cold-blooded perversion of your medical skills for your own evil and wicked purposes. You took advantage of, and grossly abused, their trust. You were, after all, each victim's doctor. I have little doubt that each of your victims smiled and thanked you as she submitted to your deadly ministrations. None realised yours was not a healing touch, none knew in truth you had brought her death, death disguised as the caring attention of a good doctor. The sheer wickedness of what you have done defies description. It is shocking and beyond belief. You have not shown the slightest remorse or contrition for your evil deeds, and you have subjected the family and friends of your victims to having to re-live the tragedy and grief you visited upon them.

His Lordship proceeded to pass fifteen concurrent life sentences and a four-year sentence for the forgery, then, breaking with the usual tradition of sending his recommendations about the length of the sentence to the Home Secretary in writing, he told Shipman:

> In the ordinary way, I would not do this in open court, but in your case I am satisfied justice demands that I make my views known at the conclusion of this trial. I have formed the conclusion that the crimes you stand convicted of are so heinous that in your case life must mean life. My recommendation will be that you spend the remainder of your days in prison.

As Shipman was taken down from the dock he did not glance at his wife or sons.

The fifty-seven-day trial was over.

*

On Friday, 14 January 2000, Harold Frederick Shipman had completed fifty-four years on this planet. Across the vista of his fifty-fifth was falling the barred shadow of HMP Frankland, the grim penal stronghold up in the northern wilds of County Durham.

In the wake of his conviction, Shipman's emotional state had degenerated into perilous fragility. The idea of death and dying, translated into personal terms, had begun seductively to haunt his mind. So had the problem of identity.

To quote a letter which he wrote, 'The problem is [that] for thirty years plus I've had the professional mask of a doctor. Now I'm me. Who am I? No idea yet. I find emotionally it's very odd, [I'm] easily upset and unable to hide it – not that I want to. Is this the real me?'

Shorn by the GMC of his title, the now Mr Shipman still flaunted all the accoutrements of his former profession. He made it his business medically to impress both fellow inmates and prison staff. They called him 'the Good Doctor', or, the more timorous among them, 'Dr Death'. His reputation in certain quarters was that of being aloof, haughty, arrogant, and sarcastic, to think himself better by several cuts than everybody else. The police officers who investigated him, the magistrates before whom he appeared and the judge who sentenced him were all ridiculed, and even the grieving families of his victims were superciliously dubbed 'publicity-seeking relatives'.

Harold is said to have stalked the hospital wing, looking for potential patients, grooming elderly prisoners to assume that familiar role. He took care to make himself practically useful. He would wheel sick prisoners from room to room, he would help them in and out of their beds, he would collect their meals and carry them to them. All this unsolicited beneficence led to eyebrow-raising by the less trusting members of staff, who uneasily suspected that he might be thinking of playing God again, was rehearsing the old methodology of his killing behaviour. Peering over his shoulder at one of his letters certainly gives one occasion to pause in allocating him sincerity of motive in his adopted pose of universal helper. He writes, 'The place is full of thieves. I get all the nutters asking me how I did it, how much money did I get, and so on. They are usually frozen out. If I do answer, I tell them to read about it in the papers.'

In other contexts he made real, verifiable contributions. For instance, he learned to read and type Braille, and transcribed the Harry Potter books. He also regularly swept the floors in the hospital wing and worked conscientiously every day as an orderly.

The state of his own health left a good deal to be desired, and he had to be taken to hospital in Sunderland for treatment of a detached retina.

For recreation he read the *Guardian*, and after lock-up at 7.45 p.m. he would make himself a cup of tea or coffee and settle down to watch television until lights out.

Since his arrest Shipman had been making a string of threats to kill himself. That January of 2000, however, although he remained tearful, he gave a firm undertaking that he would not commit suicide for at least five years – because if he were to do so it would affect his wife's pension rights. Even so, such were his periodic black moods that he is known to have been placed on suicide watch at Frankland at least four times – but when, in June 2003, he was transferred to Wakefield maximum security jail, the officers there were never warned that he was a suicide risk.

From the minute he stepped on to its stone floor he was flagged up as arrogant and awkward. He flatly refused to co-operate. At his reception area interview he declined to answer any questions, just turned away, folded his arms, and his sole reply was 'the answer to all your questions is no'.

As prisoner CJ8199, he was then hustled off to Cell 36 of D Wing, where he was one of twenty-seven inmates. The cell was 12 foot by 6 foot, furnished with a bed, table and chair, wardrobe, cupboard, sink, and toilet. He did not decorate it with pictures of the family, but its magnolia walls and orange and green patterned curtains brightened the place up. Providing a prisoner's conduct merited it, he was permitted the privilege of a television set in his cell.

Shipman was thoroughly upset when his radio was stolen and, adding insult to injury, he had no alternative but to buy it back. Surly and dismissive in demeanour, he shunned both his fellow prisoners and the staff. Rumour has it that he was threatened by disgruntled inmates with sexual violence in the shower. Things did not improve. He spent most of his time in his cell.

Actually his fellows' views on him varied. One of them, Geoffrey Shepherd, was to say that Shipman saved his life. Shepherd's girlfriend was dying from lung cancer. He had taken the news hard, and confessed that if she died he would take his own life. That, said Shipman, would be a silly thing, something that his girl wouldn't have wanted him to do, and he threatened to report the suicidal young man to the prison authorities. 'Life is sacred', Shipman told him. Shepherd listened to Shipman's wise counsel and dismissed the idea of suicide.

Another Wakefield prisoner shudderingly recalled how Shipman had threatened to murder him. 'If you don't shut up I'll kill you,' he had said. 'Remember, I'm a doctor. I know where to cut you.'

The Wakefield regime was tough. It meant that Shipman would spend on average fourteen hours a day locked up; at weekends, when the prison was manned by a skeleton staff, it was more likely to be twenty hours out of the twenty-four. Not that he found this any great hardship. He preferred this to mixing with murderers and sex offenders, whom he thought to be 'not worthy' of his company.

Shipman, veritably thy name was delusion!

Just before Christmas 2003, a punishment visited upon Shipman because of his ongoing truculent behaviour meant that his in-cell television set had been removed, permission to wear his own clothes had been withdrawn, his visits had been reduced to two half-hour visits a month, and he was allowed only 25 pence a day to telephone Primrose.

In the second week of January 2004, the punishment regime was lifted, his privileges were restored, and his spirits were further raised by his lawyer's intimation that there could be good, solid grounds for appeal. On the Monday evening, 12 January, he enjoyed a six-minute telephone conversation with Primrose. Monitoring prison officers listening in on the call heard nothing unusual. Nothing to sound any alarm bells. Indeed, he seemed quite cheery that evening, playing cards before retiring to his cell.

It was at some time between 5 a.m. and 6 a.m. on Tuesday 13 January 2004, on the eve of what would have been his fifty-eighth birthday, that Fred Shipman hanged himself. At 6.20 a.m., when the duty prison officer slid back the cover on the Judas spyhole of his cell door, he saw his body, suspended by a noose made of his bed sheets shredded into strips, hanging from the bars of the window of his cell. Shipman had pushed the window open, secured the sheet rope, stepped up on to a heating pipe some 2 feet above the floor, and jumped, pulling the orange-and-green curtains around him as he did so, to prevent anyone looking in from seeing and saving him. Prison staff cut him down and attempted to resuscitate him, but at 8.10 a.m. a doctor pronounced him dead from strangulation, and at 11.07 a.m. his body was conveyed to a mortuary in Sheffield, where a post-mortem was planned.

Shipman's suicide was no real surprise. The idea of suicide had been continually swishing about in his mind. In 2001 he was writing, 'There is no possible way I can carry on, it would be a kindness to Prim.' And on his birthday that year he wrote, 'Prim and the kids have to go on without me, and when it is the right time. Got to keep the façade intact for the time being.' Then, in March 2001, 'I'm looking at dying, the only question is when, and can I hide it from everyone?' On Good Friday 2001, he wrote, 'If I was dead they'd stop being in limbo and get on with their life perhaps, I'll think a bit more about it. I'm desperate, no one to talk about it to who I can trust. Everyone will talk to the Pos, then I'll be watched twenty-four hours a day, and I don't want that.' By 26 June 2001, 'As near suicide as can be. Know how and when, just not yet.' 14 January 2002: 'Fifty-six today, cards from everyone – very, very sad day, not what life is about at all. Prim not very good, it must be dreadful for her.' Practically a year later, on 7 January 2003: 'A new year, a visit from Prim. ... if this year doesn't get anywhere, I know it is not worth the effort. I have to lock down this overwhelming emotion or else I'd be on a suicide watch or drugs.'

Ever since his arrest he had expressed the belief that all prisoners serving life sentences should be given the option at least once every five years of taking their own lives. A prison officer is alleged to have told Shipman, 'Go and hang yourself – if you don't know how to do it, I'll show you how.' He knew how, none better, and the following year, 2004, he made a quick, clean job of it.

Hours after the news of his death had been broadcast, the word 'JUSTICE' was scrawled twelve times across the metal shutters of his Market Street surgery.

At an inquest held by West Yorkshire Coroner David Hinchliff on 11 April 2004 at Leeds Crown Court, an official who had searched Shipman's cell at Wakefield Prison stated that he had found three ligatures with different types of knots under his pillow. The relatives of his victims were angry that Shipman 'took the easy way out'. They had hoped that one day he would make a full confession. Primrose apart, the only ones to benefit from his death were the tax payers. His keep had been costing them £27,783 a year.

*

So gross, not to say grotesque, was Harold Frederick Shipman's behaviour that there have been those who have harboured serious doubts as to his sanity. He has indeed been suspected of having play-acted with an exempting insanity angle in view. I do not accept this, for it is, I am sure, axiomatic that a man of Shipman's self-conceit would never elect the stigmatised anonymity of a bed in Broadmoor rather than the opportunity of lording it over the lesser criminal fry as a doctor in prison. There he would be able to – and, as we have seen, indeed did – play the beloved physician all over again.

That self-conceit, Shipman's pride in his achievements, was not unjustified. He had, after all, entirely by his own efforts, come a long way from a distinctly unpromising working-class beginning, with all its inherent restrictions of opportunity, to the eminence, both social and intellectual, of being a looked-up-to doctor. Not unnaturally, he was jealous of that hard-won position, and that jealousy made him aware of, and conservative in regard to, the privilege and respect which he felt to be his rightful due. This unfortunately tended to manifest as an often crudely expressed affectation of superiority, an intolerance of 'fools'.

The very last adjective that one would apply to Shipman is 'normal'. But normalcy was the currency in which he contrived to deal. He lived a superficially normal family life, with a wife and four children. Normality was the key characteristic of the lifestyle which he displayed among his medical colleagues and patients. He exhibited no conspicuous evidence of eccentricity. Even so, his psychology was a puzzle. There was never any suggestion of psychosis. That he was at core a psychopath – impulsive, bereft of 'the agenbite of inwit', that is to say the stabbings of conscience, oblivious to suffering caused to others, devoid of compassion, immune from feelings of guilt, entertaining no regret – is irrefutable.

Dr Richard Badcock, the psychiatrist who, in the early summer of 1999, interviewed Shipman in Strangeways on behalf of the prosecution, concluded that, as Wensley Clarkson records in his *The Good Doctor*, 'Shipman was a classic necrophiliac, a man obsessed not with having sex with the dead, but with the act of inducing death, and controlling and observing the moment when life leaves the body.' This aspect of controlling, this question of addiction to power – *vulgo*: a control freak, crops up in other psychological evaluations: 'He was extremely self-controlled, calm, unflappable, desensitised and distanced from his victims, who, at his bidding, as it were, became just dead bodies.'

Dr Julian Boon, who provided a psychological report on Shipman after he was arrested, examined a series of letters which he had written from prison. They confirmed, he said, the profile of a man who revelled in the ability to control people: 'His comment that he feels inadequate when he is not in charge absolutely encapsulates Shipman. He is interested in exercising control over people and I think he ultimately got an enjoyment over controlling that point between life and death. His supreme arrogance was such that he thought he could get away with anything. He thought he would always be believed because he was a respected doctor, a pillar of his community. He found that not everyone was beguiled by his lies. In the end, the loss of power and authority that followed was impossible for him to live with.'

Shipman's own GP, Dr Wally Ashworth, sincerely believed him to be a control-obsessed personality. 'He was a little man with a big woman. He was dominated at home. Then he came to work. He was controlling and a perfectionist, a bloody hard worker. But not very intelligent. I have seen other doctors with God complexes and I think that's what Shipman had.'

Perhaps. Perhaps not.

Martin Fido, in *To Kill and Kill Again*, recalls 'the more mechanical approach to the supposed "epidemic" of serial murder in the late twentieth century', proposed by Joel Norris, who suggested that the serial killing phenomenon might be physically based in a damaged limbic lobe of the brain, either innate or the result of head injury; or it might be consequent upon the ingestion of excessive quantities of lead and cadmium, which occur in poor diet. Parallel genetic research was 'concurrently suggesting that the presence of an extra Y chromosome in men might be statistically related to an inability to control violent or lust-driven urges'.

A widely favoured psycho-diagnosis was that of personality disorder. But Shipman stolidly refused to co-operate with psychologists because he felt superior to them. 'What,' he asked, 'has a twenty-two-year-old psychologist got that I didn't already know? I have been there and done it. I can't be told what to do by a young psychologist straight out of university.'

But the most persistent notion is that Shipman's psychological problems arise like ghosts from the deathbed of his mother. Like a picture projected by one of those old-fashioned magic lanterns, there kept coming back before his mind's eye the terrible night in 1963 of his mother's passing. He saw the bed upon which she had lain – wasted, ivory pale, heartbreakingly frail. He felt again the cold tears of the rain coursing down his cheeks as he ran and ran through the black wetness of the Nottingham night, putting street after street between him and the awful tableau that he had left behind him in the little house in Longmead Drive. He remembered the coming of the doctor, bearing his syringe-load of relief from the nagging bite of the savage teeth of pain that chewed relentlessly at his mother's dearly loved flesh. He was haunted; nightmare and reality, anguish and relief, mingled in a needle-sharp-nosed glass tube.

The puzzlement of psychology was followed by the bafflement of motivation.

The dreadful lingering death of his mother, his addiction to opiate drugs, the megalomaniacal wielding of the power of life and death, all have been put forward as the suggested source of Shipman's destroyer's obsession.

None of it really makes sense.

It is perhaps instructive to measure him against a long line of members of his peer group, medical killers, the majority of whom have been nurses, of both sexes, or care assistants, and operating as a rule within an institutional setting, a hospital, a clinic, a nursing or residential home. Against such a background one encounters the Münchausen Syndrome by Proxy, that is, the bid for recognition of power, or the effort to win sympathy, drawing by either route the recipient of such zealously courted notice into the emotional Klieg light. The self-aggrandisement tactics of the afflicted young Grantham nurse, Beverley Allitt (1993) and those of Genene Jones, the Texan paediatric nurse (1987) are prime exemplars of this psychological phenomenon.

Neither can one safely exclude the murder for pleasure principle.

The fact remains that none of the classic motives – murder for gain, for revenge, for elimination, for jealousy, for the lust of killing, from conviction – seem to fit Shipman's homicidal proclivities, unless it be perhaps murder for the lust of killing. Hence, his crimes have been spoken of as being without motive. But there is no such thing as a motiveless murder; however warped or meaningless and unrecognisable to normal perception, motivation is always a part of the lethal equation.

Expert opinions as to motivation are as mixed as were psychological evaluations.

Professor Robert Forrest, Professor of Forensic Toxicology at the Medico-Legal Centre, connected with Sheffield University, says, 'I think he did it simply as a matter of convenience, getting rid of an awkward patient by killing her rather than transferring her to another GP. I think that quite a significant number of the people he killed were murdered quite simply because he did not wish to continue caring for them, for whatever reason.' Forrest goes on to say that the driving force seems to have been a form of necrophilia, not wanting to have sex with the dead, but wanting to cause and have control over the moment life leaves the body.

Wensley Clarkson (*The Good Doctor*) neatly nutshells it: 'Some of those patients were getting on his nerves; they needed tidying away.' He made away with patients whom he regarded as a nuisance, or who had annoyed him.

Detective Superintendent Bernard Postles, for all his wide experience of crime, was at a loss. 'It appears,' he said, 'that he just got the compulsion to kill. We looked at greed, we looked at revenge. We examined the possibility that the victims were all women draining his drug fund. But although some of them made visits to him, this was not the case. Anger? He wasn't annoyed with these people. The clue to the motive is his attitude that he is superior and wanted to control situations.'

Some psychiatrists were convinced that Shipman was motivated by low-level necrophilia, the obtaining of sexual satisfaction from being in the mere presence of death; possibly a lust for control, the act of playing God. Other psychiatrists thought that Shipman's arrogance was a mask for low self-esteem, and that, probably angry and chronically depressed for most of his adult life, he nurtured a deep-seated need to control people and events.

Dr Anthony Daniels stated in an article in the *Sunday Telegraph* of 21 July 2002, 'The snuffing out of human life seems to have gratified him in an almost orgasmic way: for his manner changed immediately after he had carried out murder. Before it, he was the kind, considerate, normal doctor: afterwards, he was the cold, arrogant, unfeeling psychopath. The act of killing, then, must have caused a seismic shift in his whole being.'

Dr Theodore Dalrymple, writing in the *Sunday Telegraph*, opined that: 'The contrast between a beloved mother who died in agony before her time [she was only forty-four], and old ladies who had long outlived her, but who were continually (and ungratefully) complaining of something or other, might well have been very galling to Shipman. It is in the nature of old age that people should suffer from multiple ailments, most of which are not life-threatening, but for which they naturally seek alleviation. Dr Shipman, perhaps, couldn't stand the contrast between them and his mother: he decided to punish them.' (It is perhaps of note that Dr Anthony Daniels and Dr Theodore Dalrymple are actually one and the same, Dr Dalrymple being one of Dr Daniels' pseudonymous literary *noms de guerre*. 'I chose a name that sounded suitably dyspeptic,' says Dr Daniels, 'that of a gouty old man looking out of the window of his London club, port in hand, lamenting the degenerating state of the world.' Dr Daniels, born in 1949, is a retired prison doctor and psychiatrist. His father was a Communist business man of Russian ancestry, his mother, born in Germany, fled to Britain as a refugee from the Nazi persecution of the Jews).

Dr Badcock further commented, 'Such power can give a sense of omnipotent invulnerability. It can become quite seductive, especially if the person begins from a point where they feel inadequate. It is quite a potent buzz.' He was reaching for 'complete powerfulness – complete ability to make the world go the way you want it to'.

Dame Janet Smith, the High Court judge who chaired the Shipman enquiry, said that she believed the catalyst for Shipman's regime of murder was an early fascination with drugs and his wish to 'push the boundaries regarding their use'. In her sixth report she puts it admirably:

> His first killings were of victims who were terminally ill or already close to death, overdoses which relieved pain even as they terminated life, interventions which he could convince himself were in the ethically twilit territory between limiting suffering and straightforward euthanasia. He appears to have been introduced to the thrill of power which comes from dispatching life in circumstances where moral borders are hazy. The ease with which Shipman could succeed in these initial killings gives pause for thought to anyone concerned at the erosion of the boundaries between medical treatment and clinical killing. Power over life and death clearly gave Shipman a pleasure in exercising dominion over others. And that pleasure must have proved intoxicating, as powerful as any drug, so the habit became 'a form of addiction.'

That Shipman had an addictive personality is indisputably demonstrated by his reliance upon pethidine, which, as a young hospital doctor, he may have taken in order to get some sleep. Long hours and a merciless work schedule at Pontefract could well have seduced him into taking advantage of the easily available narcotic. That the pattern of addiction was early imprinted is borne out by the testimony of Terry Swinn, one of his school friends and a fellow cross-country runner, who reveals that Shipman became obsessed with the pungent smell of Sloan's Liniment, an ointment used to ease aching muscles, became addicted to sniffing it and enjoying the same sort of feeling of relaxation and well-being as other addicts derived from sniffing glue. Shipman's strong streak of addiction surfaces in his structured killing behaviour, a series of ever more intensive waves as the buzz from each becomes gradually less. It is typical of addictive behaviour that the subject demands more and more opportunities to become possessed of, or by, the object that feeds the addiction. The killings increased from the occasional single strike during his days at Pontefract and, possibly, Todmorden and Donneybrook, to one every couple of months, then one a month, to the final frenzy of a possible six or seven a month. A case of familiarity breeding attempt! Shipman would pause at certain junctures, not from stabbings of remorse, but from flashes of fear of detection. Returning, inevitably, to the habit, he would often begin a new phase in the modus that he had originated when he started the whole process, with the despatch of patients who were in any event terminally ill. In the well-chosen words of Dame Janet Smith, 'It was as if he were entering the pool at the shallow end to see if he could still swim.'

The dynamics of the Shipmans' marriage are not immediately obvious. It will be remembered that the contract was entered into under what seemed resemblant to Helen-of-Troy-like bad auspices. Indeed, in a moment of rare candour Shipman confided to district nurse Kate McGraw, a confidante with whom he seems to have developed a bond of communicative sympathy, that Primrose was not the girl that he would have married had he been able to explore other options. Primrose's pregnancy was a mistake. 'I was a bright boy,' he told Katie, 'I should have known better, shouldn't I?'

There can be small doubt that he found sex with Primrose of minimal interest. It is likely that after the birth of their fourth child, Samuel, on 4 April 1982, transactions of the bedroom sort were of rare occurrence. It has been said (*vide*: Clarkson. p. 243,) that he 'regarded the act of sex itself as messy and difficult and to be avoided because he couldn't control it and be successful. Sex was one of the few times when he lost control of his surroundings.'

That Fred's erotic tendencies went on occasional walkabout has been uncovered. There was the odd evening when, after the imbibing of a pint or two at an anonymous pub well outside the catchment area of his patients, he would drive 30 miles north to Bradford, to cruise those same incarnadined streets as Sutcliffe, the Yorkshire Ripper, raked, ball-peen hammer in hand. This I know to be so, for a retired Bradford police officer let it slip that the good doctor's name was several times booked for kerb crawling.

A half-whispered accusation of thwarted sexual intent wreathes sinister about the Shipman head with regard to his offices, good or otherwise, towards his young patient, twenty-five-year-old Mrs Elaine Oswald. She came to his surgery on 21 August 1974, complaining of a severe pain in her left side. He made a lightning flash diagnosis of a possible kidney stone, and the more leisurely formulation of a therapeutic dosage of the opiate analgesic Diconal, two tabs, and home to bed, where, he insisted, he would call upon her after morning surgery to take a blood sample. 'Leave your front door unlocked so that I can walk in without disturbing you,' he carefully instructed her.

Mrs Oswald went home and rang her husband, and her boss at the Department of Social Security, to let them know of her illness. 'I curled up in bed with one of my novels,' she afterwards testified. I was just getting drowsy when Dr Shipman called "Hello", and came upstairs. I sat up, we chatted and he told me he had just picked up his wife and child. They were waiting outside in his car. As we talked, he took blood from my arm.'

And that was when Elaine Oswald passed out.

According to what Shipman later told her, she had stopped breathing for five or six minutes, although her heart had not stopped. He had given her cardiac massage and the kiss of life. All that she could remember was 'coming to on the bedroom floor, bruised, battered and bleeding from the mouth, surrounded by Shipman, two paramedics, and Shipman's wife and child, who were watching the proceedings'.

Accompanied by Shipman, she was then whisked off by waiting

ambulance on the 8-mile drive to The Victoria Hospital in Barnsley. Every time her eyes closed, someone in the ambulance had slapped her face. At the hospital, Shipman allowed it to be thought that she had overdosed herself on the painkillers, an unfair indignity which was enhanced by being forced to submit to, quite unnecessarily, having her stomach pumped. Dr Shipman shifted the ultimate blame on to 'allergic reaction to Diconal'.

Dame Janet Smith took a somewhat different view. She thought that Shipman had come up with a 'spurious excuse' to pay a home visit to Mrs Oswald, as 'the appropriate test would have been to analyse a urine sample. In any event, either type of sample could easily have been taken at the surgery'. Whether or not Shipman did take such a blood sample does not clearly emerge, but he definitely did inject Mrs Oswald with a drug substance. Dame Janet believed it likely to have been pethidine. Whatever it was, it rapidly produced unconsciousness. Because of all the lengths to which he went in trying to revive her, Dame Janet was sure that Shipman had not purposed to kill Elaine; she thought it far more likely that he had hoped to involve her in some sexual activity.

There was possibly – there is no real justification for pitching it much higher – a significant degree of *tendresse* between Fred Shipman and Dr Brenda Lewin, the sole female doctor in the Todmorden group practice. She was fifteen years older than Shipman and beset with problems of her own which circulated the orbits of alcohol. She was also married to an invalid. Dr Michael Grieve, head of the practice, passed opinions but not judgments.

> Fred and Brenda had a very interesting relationship. In some ways they were both tragic people. Thinking back on it, they obviously both recognised something in each other. They enjoyed a very close relationship. They were always going into each other's offices and closing the door. Fred only ever seemed to open up to Brenda. ...

Brenda sympathised with Fred in many ways. It says a lot about both their characters.

One doctor at the practice said, 'It was as if she was the only one who truly understood him as a person.'

Another of the practice doctors felt sure that the couple were romantically involved. 'I saw them out together one evening in a local restaurant. They didn't see me, but they seemed very animated with each other.'

Whatever chinks of extramarital romance may or may not have filtered fitfully into Fred's austere life, Primrose remained constant, loyal and true. How much did she know, or guess? All or nothing at all? It is impossible to say. Primrose is the wedded enigma. She kept her emotional encroachment dry, within her own envelope of space. And she kept her space inviolate, to the end and beyond. What fantasies she constructed, what realities she defensively deconstructed, there is no knowing. But for her, it was Fred and Primrose versus the world.

All those friends who, in the time of adversity, refused to see her husband as a wronged man, she dropped forthwith from her life. Primrose did not deal in half measures. Her devotion to Fred was stubborn. She frankly worshipped the man described by a mutual friend as 'her moon and stars'. She had been at his side since she was sixteen – some thirty-eight years.

Fred's attitude to her was bizarre. While exercising full control, mental and physical, over her, he yet blamed her for anything that caused him annoyance and for everything that went wrong in their life. When, pre-trial, he was lodged in Strangeways, where he insisted that everyone, staff and inmates, called him 'Doctor', Primrose not only visited him daily at 2 p.m., but also penned sheaves of letters to him.

They are ungrammatical, somewhat lacking in clarity, and difficult to interpret.

> My dearest Fred,
>
> Only 216 days to go [until the start of his trial] good idea, keep my maths going. I have done everything this morning when I should have done the paper work, sorted out the clean sock (*sic*) made bed …
>
> My dearest Fred,
>
> I am sat at the dining table the rain is coming down like stair rods. I hope it is better with you. You will not notes (*sic*) you are with yet another women (*sic*) this is getting silly I must get on with the paper work. Love you and the pain you feel is just how I feel I am coping. But that is all – do not get upset we have an hour a day.
>
> All my love,
>
> Primrose.

Another letter from Primrose refers to her husband's alleged victims.

> Well, I am very sorry or them as you happen to be my husband and I love you very much and am not thinking of leaving you. Funny what sets me off. I need all my friends and supporters but that has given me thought. I wonder if other women have looked at it that way.

It was, incidentally, during his enforced residence at Strangeways that Shipman, to his great delight, rubbed shoulders with royalty. He was picked out as a suitably respectable 'prisoner' to welcome VIP visitors, and among them was Princess Anne, paying a visit to the prison as royal patron of the prison welfare organisation, the Butler Trust, with whom he chatted and shook hands. The Princess later commented that she had found the serial killer polite and well-spoken. After she had left the jail, Shipman's comment was, 'It was nice to meet a normal woman again. Pity she looks like a horse!'

A practical measure of Primrose's loyalty was the lengths to which she went to ensure that it would be possible for her to pay regular visits to her imprisoned husband. After Shipman's removal to Frankland High-Security Prison, Primrose took a three-bedroomed cottage near the Yorkshire village of Walshford, just a couple of miles north of Wetherby, where she grew up. Frankland was a two-hour, 60-mile drive up the A1 in the red Mini Metro, which she had bought second-hand after her red Ford Sierra had been crashed by joyriders.

The cottage, cement-rendered brick, cramped and ramshackle, stood a mean ten or twelve feet from the thundering highway of the North Yorkshire A1 dual carriageway. The brown paint peeled from the front-door, which was, in any event, made all but unreachable by cascades of untrimmed ivy. What might once have been a pretty cottage-garden had become a wilderness entanglement of triffid-effusive weeds. Described by the author Geoffrey Wansell as 'like a witch's house in a terrifying fairy-tale', it was certainly run-down and beyond the periphery of seedy. The place was enclosed, folded in upon itself. Guarded by high trees, high hedges, rampant weeds, and long grass, spattered with abandoned plastic sacks, rusting car exhausts, and a litter of jettisoned flowerpots, the cottage defended itself with sealed-firm front door, tight-drawn curtains and terminally-down blinds. There could be no mistaking the implicit 'No Visitors Welcome' sign that hung invisibly in the air.

The châtelaine of this grisly abode was a large, dowdy and dumpy, unsmiling woman with lank grey hair, a world of anguish away from the giggly girl on the cheery red omnibus, mourning the loss in life of the bearded and bespectacled little doctor, her husband, who himself bore scant resemblance to the sharp dresser with the mop of curly black hair, who had set off his stocky, well-built figure with a fancy waistcoat of mustard-yellow. Those dread droll sculptors, the years, had wrought spectacular metamorphoses.

When Fred was transferred to Wakefield Category A Prison, he and Primrose used to meet in a room set aside for maximum security inmates. Observers reported that the couple would kiss and hold hands, chatting happily and behaving as though they hadn't a care in the world.

Primrose Shipman's vigil ended in January 2005. To all appearances Fred had done his best for her in the end – fiscally, anyway. The circumstances were, if he were to die between ages sixty and sixty-five, his widow's one-off lump sum payment would drop by 20 per cent each year. And after sixty-five, there would be no lump sum. To achieve the maximum benefit, a policy holder would, therefore, have to die before age sixty. Shipman took good care to shuffle off his mortal coil well before the literal deadline. He gasped his last on 13 January – lucky for some! – aged 57. Primrose received a pension and a lump sum the following June.

On 19 March 2005, Shipman was cremated at Hutcliffe Wood Crematorium, Sheffield. Primrose had wanted him buried, but she is said to have been advised by the police against burying her husband in case the grave was attacked. At a cost of £26 per diem, by 15 January 2005, Primrose had spent £9,000 keeping her husband's body in cold storage at the Medico-Legal Centre, in Sheffield. Family wrangling over his last resting place had kept him on ice.

April brought the Shipman inquest, held by David Hinchcliff, the West Yorkshire Coroner. On the 22nd, a Friday, at the conclusion of a ten-day hearing, the jury decided that Harold Frederick Shipman had killed himself to ensure that his wife would be financially secure. Home Office pathologist, Dr Philip Lumb, testified that Shipman had died only minutes after setting up the ligature and there had been no signs of struggle. Primrose Shipman told the court that her husband had been worried that he had left her and the family in the lurch financially. His pension had been withdrawn, although it would be reinstated if he died before reaching sixty. On the telephone he had told her 'see you tomorrow.' Despite being in poor physical shape – gout and arthritis – he was not suffering from any mental condition, but was always worried that his wife did not have enough money and said that she had been forced to move into a smaller house.

The jury ruled that Shipman was neither bullied nor goaded into taking his own life, neither was there any evidence of third party involvement.

Dame Janet Smith was appointed chairman of the Shipman Inquiry, which was set up in June 2001, and opened in Manchester Town Hall. Dame Janet spent three years on the Inquiry investigation of Shipman's alleged murders between 1970 and 1974, and produced a six-volume report, totalling over 2,000 pages, which took a year to complete. She heard the evidence of 190 witnesses in sixty-six cases. She considered 14,000 witness statements, scanning more than 37,000 pages of evidence. She examined 888 cases, and issued written decisions in 494 of them. She found that Shipman murdered 215 of his patients –171 women and forty-four men – found real suspicion in forty-five more cases, and, in a further thirty-eight cases, there was too little evidence to form a judgment.

She found Mrs Shipman to be a straightforward and honest witness, who, when asked if she still possessed any documents relative to the inquiry's investigations, said that she had delivered them up. They had proved of considerable assistance to the inquiry, and had helped Dame Janet to reach decisions on a number of individual deaths, where, without them, she would have been unable to do so.

Said Dame Janet, 'Although Mrs Shipman might not have realised the potential importance of these documents, and the extent to which they might damage her husband's interests, I consider that a dishonest woman whose only concern was to protect her husband would have withheld or disposed of the documents and said that they had been destroyed long ago.'

Primrose had said more than a hundred times that she could not remember crucial details of her life with the doctor. Her memory, she stated, had again and again failed her, and she confessed her inability to recall a specific incident, or could summon up only a vague recollection of it.

Summing up, Dame Janet announced,'My overall conclusion ... is that Shipman killed about 250 patients between 1971 and 1998, of whom I have been able positively to identify 218.' It was her opinion that in his early years Shipman had been very interested in drugs, and willing to test the effects of those drugs whatever the results. She had thought that in the early years he killed by the reckless administration of drugs rather than with the calculated intention to kill that he was to display later.

After her husband's suicide, Primrose went back to the Wetherby area and tried to make it up with her mother, but just a few weeks before she died, Edna Oxtoby, who was by then in a nursing home, but who owned her own very substantial house in Wetherby, re-wrote her will, leaving the house to a neighbour. She did this knowing full well that her daughter was at the time in fairly dire financial straits, and Primrose was left not a penny.

Echoes of the Shipman affair still resonate from time to time.

In August 2006, it was reported that a survey of the Small Practices Association had found that one in three GPs was saying that they had stopped carrying diamorphine in their medical bags while on home visits. And one in four had stopped stocking it in their surgeries. This was not a good thing, for, in consequence, some patients were inevitably experiencing delay in receiving the pain relief medication which they needed.

On a lighter note, in January 2007, the forty-seven-year-old paedophile, Roy Whiting, who murdered eight-year-old Sarah Payne, claimed to be scared witless by eerie noises and strange goings-on in the cell, D 336, allocated to him at Wakefield Prison. This, it may be remembered, was the cell in which the good

Dr Shipman hanged himself. Whiting in a major state of funk, complained to the prison governor, to his psychiatrist, and to various members of the jail staff. Shaking in every limb, he told one and all that he was too terrified to sleep there. He said that he was convinced that the ghost of Dr Shipman had returned, and the closer it got to the anniversary date of Shipman's suicide, the worse the haunting seemed to get.

As a matter of fact, many prisoners in Wakefield tend to believe that cell D 366 is jinxed. Another inmate, Jasbir Singh Raj, aged thirty-two, was found hanged there in April 1987. But so far as Whiting's haunting is concerned, prison officers felt pretty sure that he was being targeted not by the spectre of Shipman, but by non-sex-offenders who despised him and his terrible crime and were deliberately making spooky noises to torment and frighten the nonce. Indeed, one of them confessed with glee at the time, 'prisoners in the neighbouring cells are winding him up, making strange noises when he is asleep. The 'straights,' as they are called, left a noose in there for him to find, which didn't help!'

And, as recently as August 2010, the supernatural has again been invoked. The ghostly scene this time is No. 21 Market Street, Hyde, locus of The Surgery, now reverted to its original function as a shop, that of appliance superstore Oakland Domestics. Says Colin Marsland, its manager, 'The back area is where the consulting rooms were. People sometimes shiver when they walk through. They talk about ghosts and things.'

Did Shipman, like so many other serial killers, ultimately *intend* to be caught? So lacklustre was his forgery of Kathleen Grundy's will, so amateurish, that even the police saw it as a cry for help. So abysmal was the planning and execution for a man of Shipman's proven intelligence, that it is tempting to think that he actually *wanted* the ruse to fail.

The facts which emerge from the investigation of Shipman and his background fail to supply any remotely satisfactory answer to the overwhelming question: why did he kill and keep on killing? Could it perhaps be that in the case of Shipman, as in those of other intransigent repetitive killers of his ilk, we are faced with an as yet generally unrecognised psychosis – Serial Killer Psychosis (SKP)? The condition appears to present a sufficiently consistent diagnostic symptomology to establish it as an entity:

1. Cruelly treated or deprived in childhood.
2. Early display of sadistic behaviour towards animals.
3. Abnormal interest in death.
4. Loner, even in matrimonial setting.
5, Absolute lack of regard for suffering, even delight in it.
6. Inability to stop killing.
7. Total absence of remorse.
8. Prevailing feeling of being better than everybody else, approaching a paranoid attitude.
9. Removal of trophies.
10. Absence of introspection about why he is doing it.
11. Arrogance when caught and put on trial.
12. Capacity to carry on with normal life.

'Let us do evil, that good may come,' somewhat paradoxically instructs the Bible (*Romans* 3:8). Without doubt, Dr Shipman's nefariousness has contributed to the better ordering of medical practices and the security of the patient's future.

It is because of him that a much closer eye is being focused upon the matter of death certification. In *The Detection of Secret Homicide* (1960) by J. D. J. Havard, both a doctor and barrister-at-law of the Middle Temple, it was revealed that every year more than 100,000 people were being certified dead without their bodies being seen by doctors. Many others were certified dead while very much alive. A doctor reported death from haemorrhage of the lungs, based on the information that the man had had a cough and had been found dead in bed with some blood round his mouth. It later transpired that the man had actually cut his throat from ear to ear. Another doctor certified as death from coronary heart disease that of a lady who had died of corrosive poisoning, after drinking concentrated hydrochloric acid. As in the previous case, the evidence would have been clearly visible if the body had been viewed after death. A certificate of death from heart disease was given by a doctor who, although he had not seen his patient for some months, had been expecting his death for a long time. In fact, the man had shot himself through the heart. The pistol had fallen into an open drawer which had later been shut by someone without noticing its presence.

The handling of dangerous drugs was also flagged up as a matter that required to be more rigorously monitored.

The establishment of single practices, unpoliced by partners, is further being discouraged.

The divinity, the quasi-religious infallibility of doctors, has, since the advent of Shipman, undergone a timely and healthy reappraisal.

2

A DEATH IN BROADMOOR

Murderers come frequently to Broadmoor, the old-time criminal lunatic asylum, re-christened in these gentler days Broadmoor Hospital. But murder itself is a rare visitant, not always identifiable. Never doubt it, though, it has arrived, mysteriously, behind those high, red-brick Berkshire walls, beyond the bland, flat face of the main gate's timeless clock. So, too, has death at its most enigmatic.

It was a quiet night insofar as any night is ever quiet in the crowded and tormented fastness of Broadmoor's wards and cells. Suddenly, just after 1 p.m. on Thursday, 8 August 1963, the clangour of the alarm bell fragmented the uneasy stillness in Block 4.

Medical staff rushing into Ward 3 found a young patient, John Berridge, lying unconscious on his bed. A fellow inmate, Gordon Gylby, was crouching anxiously over him.

'I thought he was having a fit,' he explained. 'He came over sort of queer. When I turned him on to his side to ease him a bit, he took a few deep breaths and then went all quiet. I think he's dead.'

Gylby was right. And within hours, the Broadmoor authorities were to be faced with one of the most baffling mysteries in the long and bizarre history of their institution.

Suicide by cyanide poisoning.

Suicide? How could such a thing be possible in what was unquestionably one of the most carefully monitored special hospitals in Britain? To begin with, how could Berridge have got hold of cyanide? As was later stated at the inquest, they did not even keep cyanide in the Broadmoor dispensary. Nevertheless, a lethal dose of the substance was subsequently recovered from the body of John Berridge.

Did someone smuggle it in to him from the outside? A possibility, for visitors were not searched. But who would willingly supply him with the means to destroy himself? That is, if it *was* suicide – and the official view was that it most likely was, since the dead man was a known suicide risk, and was under close and constant supervision.

But there was one man, Berridge's closest friend and fellow patient, Sidney Henry, who believed he knew the true answer to the riddle. Henry, thirty-eight at the time, was himself an interesting character. For one thing, he claimed – and was supported in his claim by a former male nurse who knew him well – that he was sane. He had, he said, faked insanity for purposes of his own, rather overplayed his hand, and ended up in Broadmoor. (He was, however, eventually discharged with a clean bill of health in February 1964.)

Naive Henry was not. No ingénu, he had heard plenty of crazy tales during the long, lonely nights in Broadmoor. Talk, talk, talk. There isn't much else to do but talk when the day has died and the raucous noise of the rooks in the tall dark trees has faded away until another dawn. Most of the talk is the maunderings of disordered minds, but Henry, listening at first with half an ear, became gradually, unwillingly, both ears cocked, convinced that Berridge was telling the truth.

Serving in the RAF, Berridge had been posted to Butzweilerhof Airfield, West Germany. He had been approached there by a tall man of about forty-five, who, speaking perfect English, said he was a Communist agent and would buy any information.

'He wanted to know things like squadron strengths, the kind of bombs we stocked at Butzweilerhof, and anything I could find out about a secret radio-fuse for detonating H-bombs at predetermined heights. He also wanted to know about a bombing test we'd carried out involving smaller nuclear weapons. Well, I did what he asked. It was easy money. I also gave him impressions of all the keys to the bomb dump. Then one night, back in South Wales on leave, I did the most stupid thing I've ever done. I confided in my father, and he threatened to expose me.'

Back to the world of resoundingly concrete fact: at 6 a.m. on 25 April 1959, John Berridge took a 12-bore shotgun, went into his father and mother's bedroom and shot them as they slept.

*

Found guilty but insane at Pembrokeshire Assizes, he was sentenced to be detained at Her Majesty's pleasure, and sent to Broadmoor. Like many an insane killer before him – Ronald True and Christiana Edmunds spring to mind – Berridge might have ended his days at a ripe old age in Broadmoor. But he was only twenty-three when he died by cyanide.

Sidney Henry told me, 'A few days before his death, John got a parcel, the first I'd ever known him to receive. And later he said: "I've got a phial of cyanide in a bag of sugar that came in that parcel." I tried to persuade him to throw the stuff away, even pretended I'd grassed him, but before I'd worked out what to do, he'd taken it and died.'

Henry was adamant that it was the Russian Secret Service, who, knowing Berridge's suicidal tendencies, had posted to him the poison which would seal his lips forever.

'I remember, too, he'd had two or three letters. Usually we shared our letters, but he'd hidden them away. I think they told him to expect the parcel with the cyanide and what to do when he got it.'

There is not, of course, and now never can be, any sure solution to this enigmatic death in Broadmoor. It may very well have been suicide. But, a nice point: does suicide shade into murder if someone deliberately slips the easy means into the ready hand?

Remember the lush bushes of Broadmoor, and how richly the bruised leaves of the laurel furnish the lepidopterist's killing bottle.

Remember, too, that Broadmoor is full to the gunnels with killers for pleasure, such as Master Graham Frederick Young, who, in July 1962, at the age of fourteen, was, for his own and everybody else's good, despatched (under Section 66 of the Mental Health Act 1959) from the Bailey to Broadmoor by Mr Justice Melford Stevenson, who tried him in respect of the murder by poison of his stepmother, and took into the reckoning three other alleged poisoning attempts. Released prematurely in 1971, Young was to become the celebrated thallium poisoner, an absolute master of the art of venenation.

3

THE LADY WAS FOR BURNING

He is said to have been a dapper little man. He wore a bowler hat. He materialised like some evil northland boggart out of the blackness of the winter's night, importing with him the lethal Will-o'-the-Wisp flame with which, cruelly and senselessly, he incinerated a harmless young woman ... and then melted back into the shrouding darkness whence he came.

The trouble is that in searching for the killer of Evelyn Foster, daughter of the family who owned the buses and ran a taxi service in the pleasant Northumberland village of Otterburn, who died a most mysterious death one bitter January night in 1931, we do not have a single substantial clue as to the manner of creature that he was.

Tuesday, 6 January 1931. Twelfth Night. The dead end of Christmas. A clear, star-flecked sky, like a cold sarcophagus lid, gleaming over the sabre-toothed heights of Northumberland. Chugging and steaming across rough, tussocked moorland, frozen stiff as corrugated iron and magpied with great splotches of frost that glittered grittily in the cold blaze of moonlight, the little country bus, one of Joseph Foster's, was returning shortly before 10 p.m. from Newcastle to home base, Foster's Garage, Otterburn.

There were no passengers aboard, only the driver, Cecil Johnstone, and his conductor, Thomas Rutherford. They had just passed through the small sliced crag of moorland backbone known as Wolf's Nick, when they saw the eerie orange glow. Drawing closer, they spotted the source of the fire. A burning car.

Johnstone recognised it. The Hudson Super-Six TN 8135. It belonged to his boss's twenty-nine-year-old daughter, Evelyn Foster.

Then, from somewhere out of the smoky darkness, came a thin, rustling moan. It was Evelyn Foster – transformed into a human torch – burning against the ice.

They wrapped the poor charred body in an overcoat and carried her gently to the bus. Over and over again she kept whispering, 'It was that awful man. Oh, that awful man.'

The young woman had a strange tale to tell. She had, she said, been hailed by some people in a stationary car as she was passing through Elishaw, on her way back to Otterburn, after having driven three passengers to the village of Rochester in her hire car.

A man got out and came across to her. He had, he explained, after missing the Newcastle bus at Jedburgh, been lucky enough to get a lift as far as Elishaw, and he could, he understood, pick up a Newcastle-bound bus at Otterburn.

No, said Evelyn. It was now 7 p.m. and the last bus from Otterburn had long gone. But what she could do was to drive him to Otterburn, and take him on from there the 24-mile drive to Ponteland, where he would get a Newcastle bus.

Arriving at Otterburn, she had dropped the man at the village inn, the Percy Arms, where he said he would go in and have a drink, while she went to the garage to fill up the petrol tank. She found him waiting for her by the bridge, beside the Percy Arms. He clambered into the front seat next to her, and off they went.

They had just reached Belsay, some 6 miles from Ponteland,

when the man suddenly ordered, 'Turn here and go back.' As he spoke, he was creeping along the seat towards her. He seized the steering wheel, drove the car off the road and over on to the moor. She protested. He dealt her a stinging blow to the eye, shoved her roughly over to the side of the car and, pinning her there, headed back in silence in the direction of Otterburn.

At Wolf's Nick he stopped, and began to attack her – hitting, kicking, finally knocking her into the back of the car, where, as she later told her mother, he interfered with her. She lost consciousness. She awoke to find him pouring the contents of a bottle or tin over her. Then – a great swoosh of flame – and she was burning.

*

At half-past seven the following morning, in her own bed, Evelyn Foster died. Her last words were, 'I have been murdered, Mother, I have been murdered.'

With every confidence, the Northumberland police began combing the frost-bound wilderness for the man in the bowler hat. But clue after clue melted away like ice water.

Oddly, the barman at the Percy Arms swore that no stranger had come in that evening. Professor Stuart McDonald, the pathologist who carried out the post-mortem on Evelyn Foster, said that he had found no indication of the dead girl having been raped. She was, in fact, a virgin.

At the inquest, held in Otterburn's War Memorial Hall, where, a mere three weeks before, Evelyn had attended a Boxing Night dance, the coroner, Mr Philip Mark Dodds, sought to impose his view that the girl had set fire to herself. But the jury would have none of it. Steadfastly, bleakly, and strongly resistant to the coroner's plain direction, they returned a verdict of wilful murder against some person or persons unknown. The villagers greeted the verdict with cheers. Contrastingly, the Chief Constable of Northumberland, Captain Fullarton James, went on record with the flat denial that the man Evelyn Foster had described had ever existed.

The case of the burning girl had been concluded – but not resolved. The mystery is still alive. So many questions remain, glowing unanswered in the grey moorland air.

One among half a dozen theories pleads special consideration. Formulated by the late Jonathan Goodman, author of a book upon the case, it would fix the guilt of the burning of Evelyn Foster upon a man named Ernest Brown. He was a thirty-five-year-old groom, working for Frederick Morton at an isolated farm, Saxton Grange, near Tadcaster, in Yorkshire. Between Brown and Morton's wife, Dorothy, there developed a passionate liaison, which, on her side, turned sour, and on his, escalated into a frenzied jealousy.

One September night in 1933, Brown murdered Frederick Morton, by shooting him and then incinerating his body in a car. What possible linkage could there be between the Lothario of Saxton Grange and the pyromaniacal killer of Wolf's Nick? Briefly, both Evelyn Foster and Frederick Morton were accused of self-immolation. Evelyn testified that her assailant had an accent like that of Tyneside, and Brown had spent part of his childhood in Newcastle. Brown used to attend horse and cattle sales around the country, so could well have been in the vicinity of Otterburn. Finally, as he stood, pinioned and hooded, on the scaffold at Armley Gaol, Leeds, Brown spoke three muffled words – 'ought to burn.' Or was it, perhaps, one word, 'Otterburn.'?

Whatever, time has not bulked out the killer of Evelyn Foster. He has remained what he was then, the invisible man, his entire existence encompassed in a few flame-lit hours around Otterburn. All that there is to mark his terrible visitation is a black marble stone in the graveyard of St John's Church, and a clutch of rapidly thinning memories.

4

STILL LIFE: THE MURDEROUS BRUSHWORK OF WILLIAM HEPPER

The wicked old *chèr maître's* hand of Salvador Dalí himself could hardly have bettered the macabre surrealism of the scene.

A dingy one-room flatlet. Centre-canvas an artist's easel, bearing upon it the half-painted portrait, head and shoulders, of a captivatingly pretty young girl; shiny, almost-black hair; dark, straight eyebrows, over wide, intelligent eyes; a full, well-shaped mouth. The paint on the canvas still tacky. Beside the easel, a seedy divan-bed. Splayed upon it the young model. No longer young or lovely. Timeless now, frozen in the ugly moment of sudden, premature death. Naked, save for a pair of rumpled socks. Discoloured. Bruised. Seeping a dried scab run of blood. Decay setting in. Popping eyes. Swollen lips. Jutting tongue. Lank hair. Bloodied face. Empurpled throat. A stilled life. Throttled and raped. A hideous and pitiful reality, drawn, fashioned, and finished by that same artistic hand which had created the fantasy, the make-believe beauty, of the unfinished pretty picture.

Every picture tells a story. Behind this one lies a tale of ... well, it is not possible to be quite sure. It may be one of cruelty and cunning, of an evil self-indulgence; or it may be the sad outcome of an action conceived in innocent kindliness, which, touched by the goblins of mischance and sadness, went all unexpectedly and tragically wrong.

If one looks to pinpoint the first link in the ill-starred sequence, the juncture of circumstances where it all started would have to be when, on Christmas Eve, 1953, eleven-year-old royally named Margaret Rose Louise Spevick – Margot as she was generally and affectionately known – tumbled from a wall and broke her arm.

Margot, an only and much loved child, lived with her father, a civil servant, and mother in Embankment Gardens, Chelsea, and attended a secondary school in nearby Victoria. Her special friend there was twelve-year-old Pearl. She also lived in Chelsea, in a flat in Ormonde Gate, just a few minutes' walk away from Margot's. The two little girls were often in each other's homes, and Margot got to know Pearl's father, William Hepper, very well. She liked him as much as he seemed to like her, and she used to call him Uncle William. Both Uncle William and his wife were also on the friendliest of terms with Mr and Mrs Spevick.

Naturally, Uncle William was very sorry to hear of poor Margot's accident, and when, some three weeks later, her arm seemed to be on the mend, he wrote – on Sunday 17 January 1954 – a little note to Margot's mother, Mrs Elizabeth Spevick, in which he invited Margot to come and spend a fortnight's convalescence beside the seaside with him in the family flat which he owned at Hove, near Brighton, in Sussex. There was, he said, an old nurse sharing the flat, and she would be able to give Margot medical attention should she need it.

He wrote also to Margot, telling her, 'I want to paint a nice canvas of you (16 x 20 inches), which I want to exhibit here together with another portrait of a very pretty Greek-Jewish girl. I will pay you three shillings per hour when sitting. If you could sit two hours a day during seven days that will be enough. There is an old nurse sharing this flat that could look after you in case you need medical attention or to replace bandages, etc.'

Mrs Spevick wrote thanking Uncle William for his kind offer, but added that, although Margot's arm was out of plaster, she still had to attend the doctor for exercises.

Back came another letter. No problem. The exercises could be arranged daily at a local Brighton hospital.

And, on Tuesday 2 February, before the Spevicks had really made up their minds one way or the other, Uncle William turned up in person at Embankment Gardens and, kindly and charming as ever, persuaded them to let Margot return with him to Hove the following day.

So it was that, on Wednesday, 3 February, off the pair went, hand-in-hand, for the much looked-forward-to seaside holiday. On Thursday, 4 February, Margot's mother received a postcard from her daughter. 'Enjoying myself. Having a splendid time. Love.' And that same Thursday, accompanied by a solicitous Uncle William, Margot attended at the Royal Sussex County Hospital, in Brighton, to make an appointment to have her arm looked at. On Friday 5 February, the Spevicks were delighted to receive another postcard, this time from Uncle William. 'Dear friends, we are writing sitting on a deck-chair at West Pier Head. It is like a summer day. Margaret is happy about it.'

It had been agreed that Margot's mother would go down to Brighton on the Sunday – 7 February – to collect her daughter and take her back to London. She would catch a train from Victoria. Margot and Uncle William were to be at Brighton station to meet her.

When Betty Spevick arrived there wasn't a sign of them. Had they got the train time wrong? Had they been delayed? She waited patiently. Half an hour. An hour. An hour and a half. Two hours. Still no sign of them. Some sort of silly mistake. A misunderstanding, no doubt. What was even sillier, she couldn't go off to see what had happened to them, because she hadn't brought Uncle William's Hove address with her, and for the life of her she couldn't remember it. There was nothing for it but to trail all the way back to London, check if by any chance they had returned to Embankment Gardens or Ormonde Gate. And, if not, ferret out the address of the Hove flat, and catch another train back to the south coast. *What* a stupid muddle!

And that, at this stage, was all that Betty Spevick thought it was – a stupid muddle!

She went round to Ormonde Gate. Rang the bell. Knocked. Waited. No reply. No one there. Dead quiet. Still as the grave. Totally empty and lifeless. Next, down to Embankment Gardens, by the riverside. No, they had not put in an appearance there either. But now she had the address. Of course, that was it – Western Road. Flat 14. A bus to Victoria station. Back on the Brighton train. Soon now they'd all be together, laughing over the silly mistake.

Fear, real fear, first fixed its grip on her heart and stomach, set her scalp and spine tingling, when, hammering ever more desperately on the door of Flat 14, she realised that here, too, was only lifeless silence and its echoes.

Bang. Bang. BANG ...

Disturbed, made curious, by the unusual Sunday evening noise and turmoil, Mrs Holly, tenant of another of the adjacent flats, creaked open her door and inquired what the matter was? Could she help?

Pleased and relieved to have at least some human contact, an ear into which to release the overspill of the pent-up torrent of her anxieties, Mrs Spevick told her story. Mrs Holly invited her into her flat, wrote on her behalf a note to the caretaker of the flats,

Mr David Bishop. He was out for the evening, but would find it awaiting him as soon as he returned.

Over the inevitably offered, and equally inevitably accepted, cup of tea, disquieting things began to emerge. The seaside holiday flat, of which Uncle William had boasted so grandiloquently, turned out to be nothing more than a single-roomed flatlet, with no one but Uncle William living there. Had they known that, Margot's parents, who had regarded Uncle William as a reliable and trusted family friend, would never have let their little daughter go to stay with him.

Another cup of tea, dear? Time dragged. Lead rather than sand draining from the upturned glass. Sugar? Terrible alternations of bright, hopeful, cheerful chatter and heavy, aching, hollow spaces of darkness and aridity deep down inside – all under the glaring alien light in the meaningless landscape of Mrs Holly's welcoming yet alien parlour. The waiting room, the reception area to ... what?

It was getting on for midnight. At last Mr Bishop returned. He read the note. He came up and tapped at the door. Explanations were furnished. He fetched his pass-key. Mrs Spevick had missed the last train back to London. Did he think that, in the circumstances, she could stay the night in Uncle William's flat?

Mr Bishop opened the door.

This is where we came in.

It is, too, where the police came in.

*

MEDICAL FILE

Patient: William Sanchez de Pina Hepper.

Born: 14 August 1891, in Huelva, Huelva Province, Andalusia, South West Spain.

Father: British. Born in Gibraltar. Died in a mental hospital in Madrid.

Mother: Spanish.

HISTORY: Patient is married and has five children. Has lived in Gibraltar, Spain, Portugal and England. Representing a Yorkshire woollen firm, built up a successful business in Lisbon as a wool merchant. In 1928 joined the American Consulate, and for eleven years, until 1939, supplied the Americans with details of airfields, naval bases, and all sorts of background information concerning Portuguese political and economic life.

Patient states: 'One of my achievements at this time was my discovery of a plot to overthrow the Spanish Republic before the Civil War broke out in 1936.' He further says that once the Civil War had started he worked full-time for the United States Intelligence Service, spying on General Sanjurjo, head of the Spanish Fascist Party, whose headquarters were in Lisbon, and supplying details of his plans.

Patient states: 'My information about all these events was so accurate that the Secretary of State in Washington, Mr Cordell Hull, rated my reports 'excellent', but I received no reward for my work other than praise. I was never a politician, simply a socialist pacifist and a champion of human rights. While the Civil War was on, a stream of refugees from Franco's invading forces fled to the frontier hills between Spain and Portugal and, using my official position, I became the key figure in an escape route.'

He also claims to have rescued, from a frontier jail, an American political prisoner who was due to be shot. Not long after this incident, he was arrested by the Portuguese authorities, accused of spying, and given ten days to leave the country.

Patient states: 'To go to Spain would have been certain death for me, so I decided to come, with my wife and four children, to England, feeling that it was the last free country in Europe. A refugee from Spanish and Portuguese Fascism, I landed at Tilbury, jobless and penniless, in June, 1939, on the eve of World War Two.'

He made for London. He was to work there for the London County Council, the American Red Cross, and, finally, the BBC. During the London blitz, he found a job looking after bombed-out people in a rest centre. In 1944, he became a 'night translator-typist' in the BBC's Latin American service.

Patient states: 'I worked at night and early one morning, as I was being taken home from the BBC to Chelsea, I was in a bad car smash. The car ended up like an accordion. I was thrown out of the vehicle, my skull was fractured, and I was in hospital for more than a month. That accident had an important effect on my life. My health became bad. I suffered from severe headaches, and sometimes lost my memory. For a time I returned to the BBC, but after several relapses I had to give up and was never again able to do a full day's work. Fortunately, I had always loved painting. As a child I would sketch from nature at the seaside and I was so enthusiastic that when I was ten years old my mother sent me to evening classes at an art school.'

Of family life, patient states: 'Often I told my mother and sister that I would never marry because it was impossible to find a woman who would live up to my idea of what a wife should be. When I first met Patra, my wife, I tried to dismiss her from my mind. It was impossible. I was too much in love. And within three months of our first meeting she had become my bride. The British Consulate-General in Madrid had just asked me to become secretary at his Consulate, so I was a good match and our wedding was an important event. But though we had five children (the fifth, Pearl, was born in London in 1942), and one of them graduated with highest honours, I cannot pretend that we were happy. Throughout our married life I have been tortured by jealousy. Friends I trust have told me it was all nerves and imagination and that my wife has always been loyal and true.'

Seen by Dr Hugh Gainsborough, Physician, St George's Hospital, London, in November, 1951.

Observations: The patient was suffering from asthma. He displayed lung changes possibly due to tuberculosis. In 1952, patient wrote a letter to me in which he outlined the history of his relationship with his wife. He referred to her confessions of infidelity and his reactions. I am not disposed to believe these accusations of his. Referred him for psychiatric examination.

Seen by Dr Desmond Curran, Consultant Psychiatrist at St George's Hospital, London, in February, 1952.

Observations: Case referred to me by Dr Gainsborough. I consider this patient presents as a case of paranoia. It seems, however, impossible to certify him as insane, since for all I know patient's wife may have had an affair with a Spanish marquis who has been murdered.

*

When, that February Sunday night, they arrived at the scene of the crime, naturally, the first thing that the Hove police wanted to know was all about the missing Uncle William. It might, of course, turn out that he was completely innocent, had had nothing to do with the death, but, for the time being, he was the obvious – the only – suspect. His name, they were told, was William

Hepper. Actually, he spelt his surname variously, D'Epina or de Pina. Hepper was the Anglicised form. An eccentric, a wanderer, whose family saw him only at unpredictable intervals, he would turn up unexpectedly, and leave again abruptly, without a word of warning or farewell. He and they alike victims of the so-called 'artistic temperament'.

Shortly after the police, the doctor arrived. He examined the child's body and formed the opinion that she had been dead at least twenty-four hours. He noted that her clothes – frock and underwear – lay in a pile, neatly folded. On top of them, her books and a jigsaw puzzle. On top of that, Hepper's rent book, paid in full to date.

Preceded by a sudden whirlwind of police movement, local top brass Superintendent Joseph Nicholson, in charge of the Hove Division of the East Sussex Constabulary, and Detective Inspector Reginald Bidgood, head of Hove CID, erupted into the small, and by now overcrowded, room. Under their direction, a number of photographs of Hepper were collected from walls, shelves, and drawers. Interviews were conducted with the other tenants of the Western Road flats and the caretaker, and from them a description of the man they urgently wanted to help them with their inquiries was rapidly put together.

> *Aged between 50 and 60. Height: 5 ft. 10 in. Of medium build. Grey hair. Brown eyes. Sallow complexion. Long angular face. Of foreign appearance, but speaks with a cultured English accent. Inclines forward when walking.*

This description was widely circulated.

An instant and extensive hunt was launched. Hepper's photograph was shown to railway staff and taxi drivers. Ports, especially the Channel port of Newhaven, were checked to see if the wanted man had passed through. A watch was put on airfields. Hepper's description went to Interpol in Paris, to be broadcast throughout European police networks. Sûreté men in Paris made discreet inquiries among the members of the French capital's Spanish community, while back at Western Road detectives were seeking a lead from a cache of old letters from women friends, which they had discovered in a shabby deed box in the flatlet. Incidentally, the various women were subsequently traced, through several Lonely Hearts' clubs, and interviewed, but the interviews yielded nothing.

On the afternoon of Monday, 8 February, a Sussex force detective made fourteen separate journeys on buses whose routes lay along Western Road, hoping to jog the memories of conductors or passengers who might have seen Hepper. Other detectives in London scoured the various Chelsea clubs and other haunts of artists, and kept Hepper's house at Ormonde Gate under round-the-clock surveillance, just in case he should return there.

That evening's newspapers, describing him, because of his known habit of peering forward, as the 'Stooping Artist', carried Hepper's photograph. It was also shown on cinema screens. More than six thousand police on night patrol in the Metropolitan area were put on alert. They kept a sharp eye on bombed sites, waste grounds, wrecked buildings, empty houses, cinema queues, cafés, and amusement arcades. The Flying Squad ran spot checks on lodging houses, and other less salubrious boltholes that were known to them.

Despite everything, by Tuesday, 9 February there was still no news of the so eagerly sought artist's whereabouts. That day two important conferences took place at Scotland Yard mooting the possibility of asking for the co-operation of BBC television to put Hepper's face on the small screen. In fact, the Yard had first requested the help of television in a murder hunt when, in the previous September–October, they had been trying to track down a twenty-seven-year-old labourer from Eltham, south-east London, William Pettit, wanted for the stabbing to death of a woman in

Chislehurst, Kent. As was forthrightly pointed out at the first of these two conferences, the results of the television publicity in the Pettit case had hardly been encouraging. However, at the second conference an urgent request from the Chief Constable of Sussex being accorded due weight, there was a consensus in favour of making an approach to the BBC.

It was not until after seven o'clock that evening that a picture of Hepper was delivered to Lime Grove Studios, but, at peak viewing time, immediately following the TV newsreel, for two minutes – from 8.15 to 8.17 p.m. – there stared out of the screens in the houses of an estimated three-million-plus people, the motionless, glazed and static face, grey-whiskery, sinister, unsmiling, half-averted, of the unspeaking likeness of a possible child-rapist and killer, while the voice of the then popular television personality, Donald Gray, intoned, 'Here is a special announcement. This is a photograph of William Hepper. Police are anxious to trace this man, who it is believed can assist inquiries in connection with the death of an eleven-year-old girl at Hove.' He then read a description of Hepper, ending, 'He walks quickly and is very active, head usually inclined forward, cultured English speaking voice. When last seen he was wearing a brown overcoat, half-belted, brown brogue shoes, and black or blue socks.'

Within minutes of that grey fox face fading from the screens, telephones began to ring – and went on ringing. Sightings poured in from Hastings and Horsham, Canterbury and Margate, Southend and Southampton, Bristol and Birmingham, Liverpool and London. From, indeed, all points of the compass. All well-intentioned. All false alarms. No better than the Pettit fiasco, nodded the departmental wiseacres.

But there were inchings of progress. Back at Hove, inquiries were revealing that Margot Spevick had last been seen alive two days previously – Thursday, 4 February – by both Mrs Holly and a Major G. R. K. Davey. Mrs Holly had seen Margot and Hepper together when she called at Hepper's flat that evening; Major Davey, who worked on a Brighton newspaper, had also visited Hepper at about 8 p.m. on the Thursday. Margot, he said, had then been sitting in an armchair reading a book, while he and Hepper talked. 'He told me that he was going to Gibraltar and that he had been to a travel agency to inquire about fares.'

Another useful discovery made at the scene of the crime had been the fact that the mantelshelf of the room where the dead girl lay had been laden with a long row of medicine bottles, pillboxes, and packages of drugs of various kinds. Clearly, Hepper was, hypochondriacally or otherwise, treating himself for quite a variety of conditions. A doctor, who, at the police's request, examined this therapeutic haul, declared that Hepper apparently departed with such celerity that he neglected to take with him adequate supplies from his medicinal armoury. It looked, for instance, as if he had no more than three days' supply of sodium amytal – for chronic insomnia – and he would need to procure refreshments with some urgency. Consequently, chemists all over the world were put on red alert.

As the unproductive hours slipped by, the officers of law and order exchanged ever more dejected glances and depressing looks. The suspect held a perfectly valid British passport, didn't he? He could easily 'go Spanish', couldn't he? What guarantee was there that he wasn't already hundreds of miles away, out of the country? A palpable air of gloom descended ... like an old-fashioned pea-souper.

It was a telephone call that brought the good news from Gibraltar to Hove. William Hepper had been found. Miraculously the fog of despond evaporated. The clue that led to his capture had come from the Rock. And it was a kinsman of his who had delivered Hepper up. Hepper had written to this man, his uncle, as, indeed, he had written to all the rest of his relatives, in both Spain and Gibraltar. Asking for money, because, he said, he had lost all he had in the course of a journey from England. In some of the letters Hepper even went so far as to say that if he did not get help he would take his own life. And with many of them the threat worked. A considerable number of letters, containing in all quite a substantial sum of money, subsequently arrived addressed to him. But this uncle of his living in Gibraltar was an extremely religious man. He had read of the terrible thing that his nephew was alleged to have done in that Hove flatlet, and decided that he could not be forgiven by his fellow men. With the distressing picture of the murdered child before his eyes, this man felt that the blood of the child ran thicker than the blood of kinship. Therefore, he did not send the ten pounds requested. Instead, he got in touch with the Chief of Police in Gibraltar. 'Because of my religion, and because of what I feel about what this man has done, I have brought you this,' he said, and handed over the begging letter from Hepper. It bore at its head the name of the Pension Espana, a small hotel in the little northern Spanish frontier city of Irun.

The news was instantly transmitted to Scotland Yard, and immediate action was taken through Interpol. A 'find and detain' message was flashed to police headquarters at Irun. At Hove, a local magistrate hurried down to the police station at midnight, to sign a warrant for Hepper's arrest when he was located in Spain.

At around two o'clock on the afternoon of Wednesday, 10 February, Don Federico Inglesias, Chief of Police in Irun, accompanied by three of his detective officers, strolled nonchalantly and inconspicuously into the Pension Espana. Here, in Hepper's own words, is what happened:

> I was sitting on a seat opposite the post office waiting for my lunch time, when I noticed four men like detectives go into my hotel. I suspected that they were looking for me because they mentioned my name. A minute or two later, I went into the hotel. The owner told me there were four policemen waiting for me. I said: 'Let them pass into my room, please.' The officers came in and they asked me

> my name. Then they said: 'Will you please come to our office for the question of documents?' I went across to the police station with them, and half an hour later I had an attack and fainted on the floor.

Hepper spent the night there. The following morning, after breakfasting on black coffee and a couple of aspirins, he was whisked away, surrounded by detectives and provided with an escort of armed motorcycle police, the eleven or so miles to the nearest large town, San Sebastian, the seaport and watering place to the west, on the Bay of Biscay. While the British vice-consul in San Sebastian was busily trying to make arrangements for the Civil Governor to be requested to issue a warrant for Hepper's extradition to Britain, there was also being delivered in the sealed diplomatic bag to the British Embassy in Madrid the warrant signed by the Hove magistrate. Also winging its way to Spain was a second warrant, holding an application for extradition under the terms of the Anglo-Spanish Extradition Treaty 1878, which had been issued by the chief magistrate at Bow Street.

Cheerfully unaware that all this was going on, Signor Hepper was, under questioning in San Sebastian, coming up with a garbled story of how he was a translator for the BBC in London, and how, because he had been ill, they had insisted that he should go away to Spain or Portugal for a holiday. However, he had lost the money they had given him for his vacation. He vaguely remembered someone in London lending him money, but he had left his case, containing all the cash he had as well as his papers and clothes, in a taxi in Paris. Unimpressed, Spanish police officers asked him straight out if he knew Margaret Spevick. Yes, he told them, as a friend of his daughter's. She was often in his family home in London at weekends. He said that the child was never with him in Brighton, and added that he had always seen her when she was in company of either her parents or his daughter. Then, without favour or finesse, they lobbed the big question at him. Did he know of the death by strangulation of little Margaret, discovered in the very room and the bed he occupied?

Hepper, bland-faced, roundly denied having any knowledge of such a dreadful occurrence.

Very well, then. Did he know of any person who could possibly have been involved in this appalling business? He wrinkled his forehead. He rubbed the side of his temple, gave a half-shrug of the shoulders. Well ... the room he occupied in Hove was frequented by many artist friends and neighbours who went to his studio to see his works, and – yes – the door always remained open.

Was he, they asked, disposed to appear voluntarily before the English courts to make a statement? Slowly, sadly, he shook his head. Regretfully, he felt that his state of health would not permit him to do so. The due time having passed during which international rules and regulations had been observed, Inspector Bidgood, from Hove, accompanied by Spanish-speaking Sergeant Everard Lane, of Scotland Yard, arrived by air in Madrid, and, having completed the necessary formalities, travelled to San Sebastian to see Hepper. They asked him for an explanation of the death of Margaret Spevick. 'That is impossible,' he replied. 'I cannot remember since I lost my memory in Brighton, until I came round a few days ago.'

After Bidgood and Lane had returned from Spain with preliminary papers, the same magistrate who had originally signed the midnight warrant for Hepper's arrest sat alone behind a desk in police-guarded Room No. 25 in Hove Town Hall. Apart from his clerk, the only others present were a representative of the Director of Public Prosecutions and Superintendent H. J. Nicholson. One by one, seven men and four women were admitted to Room No. 25. Each made a statement on oath. Each statement was carefully and laboriously written down by the clerk. Each signed his or her statement. The signed, sworn statements were then delivered to the Home Office. After careful scrutiny, they were passed on to the Foreign Office. Then, after further examination, they were despatched, via the Spanish authorities in London, to Madrid.

The remains of the murdered child were lowered into a grave dug from frozen ground.

Hepper sat in his stuffy cell – writing scores of letters.

To the British Vice-Consul ... saying that he had been living in an unconscious mental state for a considerable period, and from which he was only now just awakening. 'I hardly remember anything. The last thing that I do remember is that the BBC sent me at home in Brighton the passage-money to spend a holiday in Southern Spain, but I remember that I lost the money, possibly while sleeping in a cinema.'

To the British Consul-General in San Sebastian ... demanding to know the reasons for his arrest and asking for news of his wife and children.

To his daughter, Maraquita ... asking for sleeping tablets, because of 'something hot running in my head'; saying that his wife had been to see him at Hove, and that when he opened her purse he found in it a letter from her lover. 'I struck her and she gave me one with a bottle. I hit her again and we fought body to body. I believe I left her unconscious on the bed. I tried to revive her with smelling-salts, then, as I love her with madness, although she was unconscious, I caressed her. In the morning I decided to flee to my beloved country.'

To the Spanish Ambassador in London ... 'First of all, I have to inform your Excellency that I am a Spanish subject one hundred per cent, although I had previously believed, until a few years ago, that I was a British subject because my father was from Gibraltar and had registered me as such in the British Vice-Consulate in

Algeciras when we were living there. Exactly two years ago, I was called by a secretary to the Home Office in London to be told they had verified that I was Spanish and that I had no right to use the British passport that I had used all my life. I now desire to legalise my Spanish position and to live in Huelva with my family.'

Plainly, Hepper was now attempting to adopt the only course of salvation open to him; that is, to 'go Spanish'. This left him with the awkward fact to explain away of his lifelong carrying of a passport which described him as a British subject.

Many of the letters which Hepper had written in jail had not been posted. The Spanish police handed them over to the British authorities. Despite the wide variety of people to whom they were addressed, in all of them one statement was repeated. It was the statement which Hepper had made over and over again to anyone who would listen to him in prison. 'I had a horrible nightmare. I cannot get it out of my mind. It was a dream of murdering someone, probably my wife.'

In his letter, quoted above, to the Spanish Ambassador in London, Hepper verbalised unequivocally his position. 'What I now desire is to be put at liberty and to be sent to Huelva, close to my relatives, in order to live there tranquilly and to establish myself with a studio, and be able to paint, which is the only thing I am able to do without causing damage to my brain.' This, without doubt, had been Hepper's plan all along. When, in response to his begging letters, his relatives had sent to him at Irun, as he was sure they would, money, he intended to flee to Huelva and over the border into Portugal. Hepper, it seems, still thought that he was in with a chance of making a successful break for it. What he did not know, was that almost a month before he sat down in his San Sebastian prison cell in mid-March to scribe that lengthy epistle – ten foolscap sheets of it – to the Spanish Ambassador, the machinery of Fate had already been set in motion against him.

The Hove police and Scotland Yard had been anxiously consulting between each other and with the Home Office, who, in their turn, consulted with the Foreign Office. The upshot was the recognition by one and all that there was an undeniable snag as regards the matter of Hepper's nationality. In the minds of the police and senior civil servants considering the case for extradition, there was little doubt that he could make a valid claim to be Spanish. But would Spain let him go?

Protracted high-level discussions both in and between London and Madrid proliferated. A lot of this diplomatic chit-chat was really no more than that. Mere formality – on the Spanish side. What had tipped the scales, perhaps slightly out of kilter, was Hepper's record. Not the single conviction for larceny against him in 1916, but the much more heinous offence of being on the politically losing side. The Spanish authorities, appreciating from the outset that they were certain to be met with a request for Hepper to be extradited, had made it their business as a matter of priority to take an extremely careful look into his previous history in relation to Spain. What they saw did not please them at all. Namely, that from an office in Portugal, he had, during the Civil War, established an escape route for anti-Franco Spaniards. Indeed, so embarrassing to the Portuguese Government had his activities become that he was eventually arrested, kept for a week in a political prison, and then given ten days to get out of the country.

In frank terms, his record of anti-Franco plottings of nearly twenty years before was about to settle his hash. Franco's Spain would not, and did not, forget. However, as befitted so truly great a country for outward show, they demonstrated the nicety of going through all the legally required forms and formalities, the ritual fire dance, the imprimatured flamenco. The Spanish hierarchy moved with measured and dignified tread towards the reaching of the foregone, and long fore-decided, conclusion. Then, protocol having been fastidiously observed, Spain felt not the slightest hesitation in rendering up Signor Hepper into the hands that would bear him away to stand his trial. Britain was welcome to him. Let England have his bones.

Considerable delay resulted from Hepper's refusal to be flown back to Britain – a course to which the Spanish authorities were perfectly amenable. But, playing for every moment of time, in the hope that the longer that passed the more was the likelihood that he might be permitted to stay in Spain, Hepper adamantly would not fly. But it was no use. When you've got to go, you've got to go, as they say. And Hepper had to go.

It was in the third week of March, 1954, that Spanish police officers escorted William Hepper to the western Spanish seaport of Vigo, where the liner *Alcantara* lay in waiting, and, at the top of the gangway, handed him over to Bidgood and Lane. Passengers and crew members watched him stumble aboard and saw him led below to the sick-bay quarters, which had been allocated to the prisoner and his two escorts. During the voyage to England, Hepper proved himself a better sailor than the detectives. With the ship rolling pretty badly and Bidgood and Lane feeling somewhat sorry for themselves, Hepper sat merrily down and wolfed all three of their dinners, complaining the while to the nauseated policemen that he had not been properly fed in the Spanish prison. The part of the voyage that Hepper definitely did not enjoy was having to be locked up at night in a padded cell. He was always very anxious to be let out again when morning came.

The *Alcantara* docked at Southampton on Tuesday 23 March. Police cars were waiting. At the wheel of one of them sat Superintendent Nicholson. Hepper, with his escorting officers, was first off the ship. He was wearing a battered Panama hat and a crumpled suit. A seedy, pathetic-looking figure, he was led over to Nicholson's car, and, with the superintendent driving, they set off at a cracking pace for Hove.

A large crowd, composed largely of women and girls, was waiting outside the police station there to see him arrive. Inside was one of his daughters and her husband, a well-known West End pathologist. They were allowed to talk briefly with him. That night, Hepper was formally charged with the murder of Margaret Spevick. He was arraigned at Hove Magistrates' Court on Wednesday 24 March. Asked by Mr Arthur Jolly, the chairman of the magistrates, the purely formal question, 'Have you anything to say?' he replied, 'Well. all I can say at this stage is that I didn't do it.' It was noticed that his usually impeccable English pronunciation was now heavily accented.

'You do not want to ask any questions?' inquired Mr Jolly.

Hepper lifted his head. 'I have no questions to ask. The only thing I have to say is ...'

The clerk of the court, Mr A. E. Thompson, interrupted him quickly with a cautionary word of advice. 'I shouldn't say too much at this stage.'

But, in a husky voice, Hepper persisted '... I lost my memory and I lost my consciousness.'

The only evidence given was that of his arrest as he boarded the liner at Vigo.

Charged with the murder of Margaret Rose Louise Spevick, he was remanded in custody until the following Wednesday, 31 March. His appearance had been brief – no longer than eight minutes. After being given lunch at Hove police station, he was driven to Brixton Prison, where he was to be held during the remand.

Back in Hove, before the Magistrates' Court for the third time, on 25 April, Hepper was asked if he could account for the body of Margaret Spevick having been found in his flat. He said that he could not. He was then committed for trial to the coming Sussex Assizes in July.

*

William Hepper appeared at Lewes Assizes before Mr Justice Austin Jones on Monday 19 July 1954. He pleaded not guilty to the charge of murdering Margaret Rose Louise Spevick between 3 February and 7 February 1954.

He was defended by Mr Derek Curtis-Bennett, QC. Prosecuting was Mr N. F. Levy, QC.

Inspector Reginald Bidgood, after giving evidence of the finding of Margaret Spevick's body at the Hove flat, was cross-examined by Mr Curtis-Bennett. He agreed that, with the exception of the single conviction for larceny thirty-eight years before, Hepper was a man of good character. He agreed, too, that when he returned to England in 1939 after eleven years abroad, he was recommended by the American Ambassador to the Court of St James' as suitable for work with the London County Council and the Red Cross. Mr Curtis-Bennett asked Bidgood if, when working in the American Consulate in Oporto from 1928 to 1939, Hepper was 'doing very dangerous investigations in Portugal?' Bidgood replied, 'I know he was assisting Spanish refugees.'

Mr Maxwell Turner, for the prosecution, read a further extract from the mammoth letter which Hepper had written to the Spanish Ambassador in London in mid-March. 'When I entered here [San Sebastian Prison], I was in a serious condition, and since I left London I was no more than an automaton that did not know what it was doing, nor what it was saying and writing. Consequently, I am going to make a confession in writing to your Excellency that, with the help of God, will clearly reveal, so all may understand, the motives which incurred [*sic*] in my transforming myself from a cultured and mild, as well as industrious, youth into almost a madman. On the night of my wedding I bore an enormous disillusion. She [his bride] was not what I believed before. I continued to love my wife madly as on the first day, but she treated me so coldly.'

The letter went on to say that when he was injured in a car

crash and was 'near to death', his wife, believing he was about to die, revealed to him that she had never loved him. He said that she had told him, 'My heart always belonged to a man whom I loved with passion. I always hated you.' He said that she admitted that she had not always been faithful. 'I have not always received from you the consolations necessary for a young and beautiful woman.' Wrote Hepper: 'This put my head in a whirl. She had waited to tell me it for thirty years, believing that I was about to die.'

Commenting on the suggestion, rising from the letters which the prosecution had read out, that the prisoner thought that it was his unfaithful wife he was attacking in the Hove flat, Mr Levy told the jury, 'You may come to the conclusion that he did think, under some curious sort of delusion, he was attacking his wife and not this little girl. He appeared to be saying that he thought the person he left on the bed was his wife. It may be he was inventing this for the purpose of trying to cover up the consequences of what he knew he had done.'

Referring to Hepper's claim in his letter to the British vice-consul in San Sebastian that he was in a confused state from which he was just awakening, Mr Levy said, 'You may well think that by this time Hepper was taking the view that it would be safer to claim complete loss of memory for everything that had occurred.' Medical evidence attested that the child had been strangled, and that she had been sexually interfered with, but, he added, 'this may have taken place during a period of unconsciousness.'

In his opening speech for the defence, Mr Curtis-Bennett told the jury that the defence had 'two fangs'. He said: 'You will see that my defence is quite plain – 'I never did this'. We say that whether this man did it or not, you are looking at a man who, certainly between 3 February and 7 February, probably long ago, and probably now, is mad in the eyes of the law.' Hepper, he continued, had never at any time made any confession. He had always said either, 'I did not do it', or 'It is impossible', or 'I cannot remember'. It was, said Mr Curtis-Bennett, the submission of the defence that his client was suffering from a disease of the mind known as paranoia; that is, a form of chronic insanity which often presents delusions of grandeur or fantasies of being the subject of persecution. It frequently manifests promptings in the sufferer to write letters to grand or important people.

Before Hepper gave evidence on the second day of the trial, his counsel emphasised that in his submission the accused was insane and had harboured prolonged delusions against his wife. In the witness box, Hepper effectively confirmed this, telling the court of a Spanish marquis who was killed by a group of outraged husbands, of whom he was one, because of the attentions he paid to their wives.

> Mr Curtis-Bennett asked him: 'Are you fond of children?'
> Hepper: 'Yes, very fond.'
> Curtis-Bennett: 'Have you ever had any desire to do anything wrong with one?'
> Hepper: 'No, sir, it is inconsistent with my qualities.'
> Curtis-Bennett: 'Did you kill this little girl, Margaret?'
> Hepper: 'Not at all. I could never do it.'
> Curtis-Bennett: 'You have heard the evidence that someone had interfered with the little girl?'
> Hepper: 'I couldn't do it. It is inconsistent with me in every way. I am impotent since about eleven or twelve months. It is inconsistent with my capabilities, and God knows it is impossible.'

Hepper went on to say that he had taken the child, with her parents' permission, to Hove. When they reached his flat, he had found a letter awaiting him there. It was from his sister. In it, she asked him to go to Spain as quickly as possible because his brother was dying. He translated the letter and he and Margaret both cried because it had spoilt their stay at Hove for the painting of the picture. 'I gave the girl a spare key to come into the room and leave when she liked. I gave her a ten-shilling note to go home, as I was going to Spain.' He had had a bad attack of asthma the following night [Thursday 4 February] and went to the seafront leaving Margaret reading a book. He did not remember seeing her after that. When he returned to his room, he went straight to an armchair, had some tablets and a glass of brandy and fell asleep. 'Then I had a terrible dream. I saw my wife coming into the room with a man I know very well, and I got up from the chair and followed almost in the dark to the corridor outside my room ...'

> The Judge [Interrupting]: 'Whom did you follow?'
> Hepper: 'The man. My wife stayed in the room. The man disappeared in the dark. I went back into the room and had a discussion with my wife and accused her of infidelity.'
> The Judge: 'This is still a dream, isn't it?'
> Hepper: 'Yes, my lord.'

Hepper went on to say that in his dream his wife struck him on the head with a bottle. 'Then we had something like a fight, and she fell on the floor, suffering from pain. Later, I woke up and found nobody in the room. It was about six o'clock in the morning [Friday 5 February]. I took the first train to Victoria, where I buy a ticket for as far as Paris. I don't remember reaching Spain.'

As he was entering the dock and his name was called on the third day of his trial, Hepper suddenly collapsed and fell to the floor. He was attended by a doctor, who told the judge, 'I can't find any physical cause for his collapse. His pulse is normal. He's just lying down and won't speak to me, and won't even co-operate to the extent of taking smelling-salts.'

Mr Curtis-Bennett went across and spoke to his client. After about twenty minutes he took his place in the dock, and sat holding the back of his head with his right hand.

The previous day Hepper had spent nearly three hours in the witness box. Now he was recalled for cross-examination by Mr Levy. Counsel began by trying to clarify the arrangements which had been made for the little girl to stay with him. Hepper denied that he had told her mother that there was a nurse available, even when a somewhat surprised Mr Levy told him that a nurse who lived in the flats at Hove agreed that she had made arrangements to take in the child.

> Mr Levy: 'Do you know why she should tell falsehoods about you?'
> Hepper: 'No.'
> Mr Levy: 'You knew that Mrs Spevick would never have agreed to let her child go if she knew she had to sleep in that room with you?'
> Hepper: 'The child never did.'

He also said that the reason he was at the seafront for a long time on the Thursday 4 February night, was because he had lost his memory.

> Mr Levy: 'When you went off at six o'clock on the Friday 5 February morning you had still lost your memory?'
> Hepper: Yes, but I remembered the letter about my brother because it was in my suitcase.'

Seven doctors were called for the defence.

Dr Hugh Gainsborouh, of St George's Hospital, told of first examining Hepper at the hospital in November, 1951, and of his decision that he ought to be seen by a psychiatrist.

Dr Desmond Curran said that he was in private practice at 6 Devonshire Place, London, W1, and consultant psychiatrist at St George's Hospital. He told the court of seeing Hepper in February 1952, and submitting a report of that interview to Dr Gainsborough. Dr Curran said that when he saw the accused in

1952, 'I believed he was in a paranoiac state, but not certifiably insane.'

> The Judge: 'You think such a person suffering from paranoia may be mentally responsible?'
> Dr Curran: 'Yes, for certain things.'
> The Judge: 'You take the view they are better treated in hospital rather than prison?'
> Dr Curran: 'Yes, my lord.'

Dr Curran, incidentally, was the specialist who had, the previous year, given expert testimony in *R.* v. *Christie* – in which case, interestingly enough, Mr Derek Curtis-Bennett, QC, also led for the defence and Mr Maxwell Turner appeared as one of the Crown counsel.

Dr Alexander Wilson Watt, a mental specialist at the Royal Sussex County Hospital, said that he did not believe the story that Hepper had told him about his wife. He said that he was quite prepared for him to 'deny tomorrow what he said yesterday'. Nevertheless, two examinations had confirmed that Hepper was suffering from paranoia. 'Hepper just left that room and that child, dead or alive, as you would leave an article of furniture, a chair or a table. He had no more thought for it in his mind than an inanimate object of furniture. It is my belief that on the night of 4 February and the morning of 5 February, he was the prey of his delusions.'

Mr Levy suggested that Hepper might have fled from a sense of guilt.

> Dr Watt: 'Not a sense, but a feeling, of guilt.'
> Mr Levy: 'You are making rather a fine distinction.'
> The Judge: 'If he dreamt he strangled his wife, and awoke and found she was not there, why should he go away with a feeling of guilt?'
> Dr Watt: 'I cannot give you or myself an explanation of this.'

> Mr Levy: 'There is one simple explanation: that he knew he had murdered a little child and wanted to escape when nobody was about.'

Hepper was shaking his head violently. 'No, no, I had to go to Spain to see my brother.'

The precise itinerary of that alleged flight from justice had by now been established. And a very rational escape route for an 'insane' man to have planned it seemed. The first train to Victoria. The earliest available train thence to Newhaven. The 10.39 a.m. boat to Dieppe, connecting with the Paris train. From there, a third train 400 miles south-west to the town of Hendaye on the French–Spanish border. Arriving in the early morning of Saturday, 6 February, he had immediately applied for an entry visa to Spain. He then took a tram to Irun, where, at around noon, he booked into the modest Pension Espania. He had spent five days there – 6–10 February – waiting for the solicited donations from his relatives to arrive, passing himself off as an ordinary tourist.

Small wonder that, with such impressive evidence of rational planning capacity manifest, Mr Levy felt that he must put it to Dr Watt whether it had never struck him that Hepper's memory defects might have been simulated.

Replied Dr Watt, 'I think a man would have to be much more clever than that man to keep up such a simulation consistently. I cannot think that he was acting.'

Called on the fourth and final day of the trial – 22 July – Dr John Matheson, Principal Medical Officer at Brixton Prison, was, perhaps predictably, to rebut evidence of insanity. He stated that he had had Hepper under close observation for more than three months while he was in the prison hospital awaiting trial. Not only had he interviewed him six or eight times, but he had also interviewed members of his family, and he had formed the opinion that Hepper was not, at the time of the crime or at the present time, insane in law. Neither had he found any evidence of paranoia.

> Mr Curtis-Bennett: 'You heard the doctors I called and it was pretty plain from them that in 1952 this man was abnormal?'
> Dr Matheson: 'Certainly. I think he is still abnormal, but paranoia gives a defect of reason because of a disease of the mind.'

Detective Sergeant Richard Arnold, of Hove, was questioned by Mr Levy regarding a statement which he had taken on 17 March 1954, from a Miss Lines, who had a flatlet in the same building in Western Road as Hepper. Arnold testified that he was absolutely positive that Miss Lines was mistaken in saying that she had seen Margaret Spevick on Friday 5 February. He agreed with Mr Curtis-Bennett that if anybody had seen Margaret alive on that Friday, it would mean that Hepper could not have committed the murder.

In his closing speech for the defence, Mr Curtis-Bennett was careful to re-emphasise that if the statement made by Miss Lines was true, it meant the end of the case. The fact that Hepper made a journey to Spain to see his dying brother was not evidence that he fled. Doubt after doubt had, he said, been stirred up, and it would not in this case be safe to convict. He put it that what, at worst, the jury should do was to say that his client was guilty by reason of insanity. But the main defence was that it was not true that Hepper committed the act at all.

In the final speech for the Crown, Mr Levy said that it was an inescapable conclusion that the child was violated and murdered by Hepper and by no one else, and in going to Spain he was fleeing from justice. On the question of insanity, only one doctor had said that Hepper was suffering from a mental disease, and he had based his conclusions on what the accused had told him.

Mr Justice Jones' summing-up lasted for two hours. He told the jury that it was necessary to consider the circumstances in which the girl went to Brighton with Hepper and lived alone with him. In view of the fact that she was violated, they might think that the person who murdered her was the person who had intercourse with her. As regards Hepper's evidence about the letter from Spain relating to the dangerous illness of his brother, the Judge observed, 'I think it is a fact that in none of his letters or written statements does he refer to that letter, which has never been found. I think you will be wise to check the evidence against his statement in the witness-box. You may think he made it up, and that no such letter was received. If so, you may derive some assistance in coming to a conclusion as to whether the rest of his evidence was accurate.'

Referring to the postcard which Hepper sent to the Spevicks from Brighton on Thursday (4 February), Mr Justice Jones remarked, 'When he wrote that postcard ... he never said a word about going to Spain.' That is an important matter. And he went on to point out that the time of about half-past eight on the Thursday night was a very crucial period. Hepper had said that he went to the seafront, leaving Margaret reading, and that he never saw her again, inviting the conclusion that the girl went out on her own somewhere. 'Do you believe,' he asked, 'that this man travelled in a sort of dream all the way from this country to the Spanish border?'

The jury – ten men and two women – pondering all the circumstances of the crime, which included the fact that Hepper had received severe head injuries in a car accident, and the expert medical witness' testimony that he was 'the prey of his delusions', had an anxious time and were obviously worried.

Outside County Hall, holidaymakers in bright summer clothes, their open-necked shirts and shorts and sandals, waited for the verdict. Inside, the court was oppressively packed.

After an absence of one hour and twenty-five minutes, the jury returned.

They found Hepper guilty.

Standing in that same dock where Field and Gray, Patrick Mahon, Norman Thorne, Sidney Fox, and John George Haigh had stood before him, and likewise listened to the pronouncement of their doom, Hepper was asked if he had anything to say.

'I think,' he said, 'it is quite unfaithful – I mean incorrect. I did not do it.'

A sentence of death was passed.

*

There was no appeal.

But it is known now that the Home Secretary of the day, Sir David Maxwell Fyfe (subsequently the Earl of Kilmuir), carefully considered a mass of medical testimony relating to Hepper's mental state. One piece of evidence to which he gave most particular attention was the report, written almost two years to the day before the murder, in which Dr Curran had opined, 'I consider this patient presents as a case of paranoia. It seems, however, impossible to certify him as insane.'

On 9 August 1954, it was officially announced that there would not be a reprieve.

Fiat justitia?

The case of William Hepper is a disturbing one. Once the natural anger provoked by its grossness and brutality, directed as it was against, and claiming the life of, an innocent and helpless child, has abated, it sits a little uneasily upon the conscience. Did we, not for the first time, in our revulsion judicially murder a madman? Was Hepper a paranoid schizophrenic? Should a padded, rather than a condemned, cell have been his just portion?

Certainly, many of those who actually saw him in court husbanded grievous misgivings as to his sanity. Moreover, a number of doctors unequivocally pronounced him a psychotic. Even so notoriously unsympathetic and cynical an observer as a prison medical officer described him as 'abnormal' – whatever, scientifically, that can be taken to mean.

Those who knew him, and they were not many, for he was

essentially, as one would expect, a loner, described him as having always been a compulsive liar, exhibiting a braggadocio which compelled him to make everything connected with himself much grander than it was. To disentangle the cats' cradles fabricated by involuntary liars is difficult. To distinguish them from delusional constructs of the diseased mind is equally taxing. Undoubtedly he had plenty of scope to exaggerate and embroider upon his adventures and achievements as a spy, suave master-outwitter of Generalissimo Franco's minions. Yet the evidence is that he did not gild the lily. The dangers he risked, the good work of rescue he accomplished, were, and were presented as, plain facts.

It is not easy to derive any significant data from his mode of living because information concerning it is sparse. There is no doubt that he was of a genuinely artistic turn of mind and talent. Painting was the main and absorbing interest of his later years. He exhibited his works at open-air shows on the Thames Embankment and at Brighton. A psychological glimpse is afforded by the reported testimony of a fellow-artist at Brighton who attained to a mild degree of friendship with Hepper. He said:

> apart from painting, [Hepper] seemed to have no other interest in life and never joined in the social life of the art set. He specialised in flower studies and would spend hours arranging single specimens of different flowers until he had the exact composition he wanted. Some of his fellow-artists thought his tones were too hard and too brilliant, but his work always sold well. During a discussion on art, he said, 'You will never find my paintings in the Royal Academy or in any of the Bond Street galleries. It is the pavement and the seashore for me because there you will find the greatest painters; you don't find them in fashionable salons.'

Joanna Gomez, of Hove, posed for her portrait by Hepper. He had, she said, started to paint the portrait from a photograph, but said that he could not finish it without seeing her in the nude, because he could not paint skin tones from a photograph. 'I agreed to pose and, accompanied by a woman friend, I sat three times for him. He was always very nice to me.'

Was Hepper sexually abnormal? Certainly the raping of a child is not a normal channel of sexual satisfaction, but there was no police record of his having previously committed any type of sexual offence. It may be that he had long fantasised over the commission of such an act, and coolly and deliberately, of lust aforethought, engineered the circumstances for the translation of the fantasy into excitatory fact in that sordid little flatlet by the throbbing sea at Hove. It could equally well be that he had had no such plan or intention in mind when he invited Margot Spevick to stay with him, and that it was an impulse rape brought about by proximity and opportunity, and that the murder, rather than being an integral part of a perverted sexual scenario, was the result of it; the method of silencing the potential accuser, the betrayer of his rich secret.

Going towards the theory that the impulse came over him is the fact that the child was found naked with her clothes neatly folded, which would indicate that he was painting her in the nude at the time. The neat folding of the clothes might, of course, mean no more than that the girl, on her best behaviour as taught, had first undressed, and then folded them herself, before going to bed. Or, probably less likely, because he panicked afterwards, it could suggest that Hepper stripped her, and, at some stage subsequent to his act, himself obsessively, as with flowers, either to imply natural sleep, or finding work for idle neurotic hands to do, had so imparted neatness and order to them – and the post-coital shambles.

Although the portrait was a head and shoulders, we have the previous evidence of Joanna Gomez, that, even when contemplating what was surely not in her case a nude portrait, he found nudity a prerequisite. All one's instincts, reinforced by the circumstance that the child was found still wearing a pair of socks, tell one that the little girl was required to stand, foot-warming socks apart, defenceless, in the nude. However, tempting as this construct may be, it can be argued that the timing is wrong, in that he must have killed in the late evening or night, after the visit of Major Davey, when the 'painter's light' would not have been right. Conversely, against the sudden impulse presumption, he might have planned to pounce upon the child while she was posing – an exciting situation for him – in which event the fact that the light was inadequate would have been immaterial, as painting was not the object of the exercise. Too much must not be made of the socks 'clue' in this context. One must resist the temptation to read into their retention anything more, perhaps, than a straw indicative of the rapist's impatience to fulfil his fell purpose.

The fact that it was not raised in his defence, ought not to put out of court Hepper's own description of his condition as that of an automaton. There is, or was, a specific and not much used defence of automatism. It did not apply only to murder. From the lawyer's point of view, it was a notoriously difficult defence to run. At the best of times there is, like the presumption of innocence, a presumption of sanity; the difference is that the burden of proof of insanity is placed squarely on the accused. There is, moreover, a wide gulf between legal and medical concepts of insanity.

The definition of legal insanity was laid down in 1843, when Daniel M'Naghten, intending to shoot Sir Robert Peel, mistakenly killed his secretary in his stead, and was acquitted of murder on the grounds of insanity. The judges, at the request of the House of Lords, supplied answers to a number of questions submitted to them, and it was those answers which provided what came to be known as the M'Naghten Rules governing the legal definition of insanity. The crux of them was that a defence of insanity could only be established if '*at the time of committing the act, the party accused was labouring under such a defect of reason, from disease of the mind, as not to know the nature and quality of the act he was doing, or, if he did know it, that he did not know he was doing what was wrong.'*

Did a defence of automatism imply insanity? In the past two types of automatism were distinguished. Automatism caused by a disease of the mind – that is insane automatism. And automatism due to some other cause, such as a blow on the head or somnambulism – that is non-insane automatism. Normally, an accused wishing to plead automatism would be reluctant to claim that it was of the insane variety. That would be to risk incarceration for an indefinite period. Since Hepper pleaded not guilty, it may be safely assumed that, had automatism been offered, it would have been non-insane automatism. The vexing question to be considered is, when a plea of non-insane automatism is made, can the court or the prosecution raise the issue of insanity, even though insanity is not pleaded by the defence?

No, it cannot, said Mr Justice Barry in *R.* v. *Charlson* (1955). In this case the accused, a devoted father, had suddenly struck his ten-year-old son on the head with a mallet and thrown him from a window. Evidence was given that there was a possibility the defendant was suffering from a cerebral tumour. Medical testimony affirmed that a person so afflicted would be liable to an outburst of impulsive violence over which he would have no control. Barry J. directed entire acquittal because the defendant was not guilty if he was 'acting as an automaton without any real knowledge of what he was doing'. The judge did not go into the question of the distinction between mental (diseases of the mind) and physical (diseases of the brain) diseases.

Two years later, in *R.* v. *Kemp* (1957), Mr Justice Devlin reached a very different conclusion. The facts of this case were that the accused made a completely motiveless and irrational attack on his wife with a hammer. It appeared that he was suffering from arteriosclerosis, which was causing a congestion of blood in his brain. As a result, it was claimed, he sustained a temporary lapse of consciousness, during which he made the attack. Relying upon the decision in *Charlson*, it was urged that the defendant was suffering from a non-insane automatism, arising not from any mental disease, but, as in the instance of the cerebral tumour, from a purely physical one. But Devlin J. rejected the argument, holding that the defendant was suffering from a disease of the mind. The law, he said, was not concerned with the brain, but with the mind – in the sense that 'mind' is ordinarily used, that is the mental faculties of reason, memory, and understanding. He said that, whereas the doctors were agreed that the defendant in *Charlson* was not suffering from a mental disease, in *Kemp* they disagreed.

Lord Denning, in *Bratty* v. *A.-G. for Northern Ireland* (1963), doubted *Charlson*, and upholding the decision in *Kemp*, said that the old notion that only the defence can raise the issue of insanity had gone.

In fact, Hepper's bad luck held. Had he come to trial a bare three years later, his neck might well have been saved under Section 2 of the Homicide Act 1957, which allowed the defence of diminished responsibility:

> Where a person kills or is a party to the killing of another, he shall not be convicted of murder if he was suffering from such abnormality of mind (whether arising from a condition of arrested or retarded development of mind or any inherent causes or induced by disease or injury) as substantially impaired his mental responsibility for his acts or omissions in doing or being a party to the killing.

In *Byrne* (1960), the so-called 'Birmingham YMCA Hostel Murder', in which Patrick Byrne, a sexual psychopath, strangled a girl, decapitated and mutilated her body, Lord Chief Justice Parker said in his Judgment of the Court of Criminal Appeal:

> 'Abnormality of mind' which has to be contrasted with the time-honoured expression in the M'Naghten Rules "defect of reason", means a state of mind so different from that of ordinary human beings that the reasonable man would term it abnormal. It appears to us to be wide enough to cover the mind's activities in all its aspects, not only the perception of physical acts and matters and the ability to form a rational judgment whether an act is right or wrong, but also the ability to exercise willpower to control physical acts in accordance with that rational judgment.

Thus was the defence of irresistible impulse made legally possible.

*

At eight o'clock on the morning of Wednesday 11 August 1954, three days before his sixty-third birthday, maintaining to the last that he knew nothing about the murder, Hepper was hanged at Wandsworth Prison.

There were only forty or so people outside to keep the death vigil and watch the posting of the execution notice. But someone left a large bunch of pink gladioli on a ledge at the main entrance to the jail. Attached to it was a card. On it was written:

In memory of Sanches de Pina Hepper.

Judge not that ye be not judged.

It was game, set, and match for the spy who came in from the Francoist reign in Spain, lost his memory and got his cover story lethally wrong.

5

THE TUNNEL VISION OF PERCY LEFROY MAPLETON

Striding one June afternoon to catch the London train at Brighton Station, young Edward Marshall Hall, the celebrated barrister to-be who was to become famous as the 'Great Defender', passed on his way to the platform a youth, white-faced, bloodstained and dishevelled, who had apparently been attacked by robbers on his journey down from town, being solicitously assisted to the stationmaster's office. It was one of life's extraordinary path-crossings. The youth's name was Percy Lefroy Mapleton.

On the morning of 27 June 1881, things had come to a head for twenty-two-year-old Arthur Lefroy. An orphan, survivor of a hand-to-mouth childhood, he nurtured high artistic hopes of a career as a writer but endured poor prospects. Not to put too fine a point on it, he lacked talent.

Since his return from Australia two years before, he had been lodging – 8*s* 6*d* per week B&B – at No. 4 Cathcart (now Clarendon) Road, Wallington, near Croydon, the home of his cousin and her husband, the Claytons.

A scarecrow-thin, beak-nosed, incipiently-moustached, chinless lad, he had recently changed his name from Percy Mapleton to the – he thought – 'sharper'-sounding Arthur Lefroy, and squandered his days dreaming in his leafy suburban bedsit of success as a playwright, poet, novelist, actor, or journalist.

Donning each night his most prized possession, full evening-dress, he would go up to the West End to haunt stage doors, striving to rub shoulders with real actors and actresses, to several of whom, including the celebrated Violet Cameron and Kate Santley, he had despatched romantic *billets doux*.

His efforts had contrived a few successes – the odd walk-on part, occasional publication of article or short story in some obscurish weekly. But now, his resources dwindled to zero, the time had come for desperate measures. With a few swindled shillings he redeemed a pawned pistol and bought a one-way ticket to Brighton.

On Monday morning, 27 June 1881, Isaac Frederick Gold, a sixty-four year old retired East London businessman, set out, as he did every Monday morning, from his home in Clermont Terrace, Brighton, for London. There he would collect the previous week's takings from his corn chandler's shop in East Street, Walworth, and any dividends accruing on his and his wife's investments.

Mr Gold was a bit of a miser. 'Close even with me,' as his wife expressed it. He suffered – like Miss Gilchrist in the Oscar Slater case – from the phobic burglar-under-the-bed syndrome, locking the bedroom door nightly. He nourished, too, a paranoid fear of the probing talk of strangers. On the train he would ritually avoid conversation by taking off his hat, putting on a skullcap and pretending, with closed eyes or a handkerchief over his face, to be asleep.

On the afternoon of the aforesaid 27 June, shortly before 2 o'clock, Arthur Lefroy was pacing the platform at London Bridge Station, peering into the compartments of the 2.10 Brighton train, trawling for a well-heeled victim. Sitting alone in a first class smoker was prosperous-looking Isaac Gold. Lefroy, primed with knife and pistol, therein joined him. Gold feigned sleep. He was to have a rude awakening ... to a personal nightmare.

At 3.30 p.m. the train pulled in to Preston Park Station. That first class carriage door burst open and out tumbled a wild-eyed, bedraggled, blood-smeared figure, a watch chain, attached to a watch, hanging out of his left boot. It was Percy Lefroy Mapleton, aka Arthur Lefroy.

Escorted on to Brighton, Lefroy told there a tale of being attacked as the train entered Merstham Tunnel. He had heard a shot, been knocked out by a blow to the head. When he came to, his attacker had vanished. The watch and chain in his boot were his. He always hid his valuables thus on train journeys. He had, he explained, come to Brighton to keep an appointment with Mr Nye Chart, lessee of the Theatre Royal.

Patched up at the Sussex County Hospital, Lefroy was accompanied back to Wallington by Detective Sergeant George Holmes. But there had been developments. Mr Gold's body, punctuated by fourteen knife wounds and a bullet in the neck, had been found in Balcombe Tunnel. His watch and chain were missing.

Eluding Holmes, Lefroy made his escape. In the person of Mr Clark, engraver, newly arrived from Liverpool, he took a room at the Widow Bickers' – 32 Smith Street, Stepney. However, a drawing of him was published in the *Daily Telegraph* and displayed on a wanted poster offering £200 reward for his capture. He also made the mistake of sending a telegram to a man named Seal, who shared his room at Cathcart Road and worked at a City office in Gresham Street, asking for money. Someone, somewhere, somehow guessed – and whispered. On 7 July, the fugitive was arrested.

From Lewes Prison he wrote to 'My darling Annie,' requesting from her a saw file concealed in a meat pie, and a tiny bottle of prussic acid, in a cake. Regretfully, Annie told her 'Ever dearest Percy' that she was unable to accede.

A cruel contemporary conundrum: Why had Lefroy a supreme contempt for money? Answer: Because he threw Gold out of the window and then ran away from the coppers.

Tried at Maidstone Assizes in November, Lefroy's defence line was that of the alleged involvement of a third man, who attacked him and murdered Gold.

Before his trial, Lefroy begged in vain for the retrieval of his evening dress from pledge, that he might wear it in court. Someone however presented him with a brand-new top hat. The devotion which he lavished upon that hat was bizarre. Each day it was gently deposited upon the ledge of the dock in front of him, and every so often he would pick it up and lovingly polish it with his sleeve, showing more concern for it than for his own fate. So extraordinary was his demeanour that there were many, including his counsel, Montagu Williams, who thought him as mad as a hatter. More seriously, the evidence of his violent mood swings suggests the very real possibility that he was a true psychotic, a manic depressive.

After a fair but lethal summing-up by Lord Chief Justice Coleridge, the jury pronounced Lefroy guilty. Playing to the last curtain the role of the wronged, he bowed and enunciated in his best histrionic mode, 'The day will come, Gentlemen, when you will find, too late, that you have murdered me,' and vanished, bearing his silk hat tenderly away to the condemned cell with him.

For all his bravado and words, what the thrasonic Lefroy bequeathed to posterity was a full confession – his fiat justifying the last rites performed by deft ropesman Marwood.

6

NURSE BERRY AND THE DANCING HANGMAN

The female of the species is, opined Kipling, more deadly than the male, and there is no more appropriate adjective than 'deadly' to attach to the bustle of Mrs Elizabeth Berry.

The story that brought her to the dock, standing trial for her life before England's most feared judge, Mr Justice Hawkins – known to the criminal fraternity as as ''anging 'awkins' – was not a pretty one.

It had begun on New Year's Day, 1887, in Oldham, Lancashire, where the thirty-one-year-old Widow Berry was a nurse at the workhouse infirmary. Nurse Berry had spent Christmas with her sister-in-law, Mrs Ann Sanderson, at Miles Platting on the outskirts of Manchester. For the last five years Mrs Berry's daughter, Edith Annie, now aged eleven years and eight months, had lived with her Aunt Ann, Nurse Berry contributing £12 of the £25 per annum salary which she received towards Edith's keep.

The Christmas holiday had been a very jolly few days, and when the time came for her mother to pack her bags and set off back to

Oldham, Edith begged her to take her and a school friend to spend a bit of extra time together at the Oldham Workhouse infirmary. Although at first reluctant, her mother eventually yielded to Edith's persistent pleading, and on Wednesday 29 December 1886, the three of them bade Mrs Sanderson farewell, and caught the train to Oldham.

A letter which Edith posted off to Aunt Ann told her how much she and her friend were enjoying their stay with her mother. The next communication that Mrs Sanderson received from Oldham was a very different one. It arrived on Monday 3 January. It was a telegram. 'Come at once. Edith is dying.'

According to Nurse Berry's account, the first intimation that all was not well with Edith came on the Saturday morning, 1 January, when she felt too ill to eat any breakfast; and later, while her mother was in the kitchen preparing sago for her patients, she was violently sick. Shortly after that, Elizabeth Berry was seen trying to persuade her daughter to swallow down a glass of milky-looking fluid. When, at midday, Dr Patterson arrived, paying his usual daily visit to the workhouse, she asked him to take a look at Edith, who, she said, had eaten something at breakfast that had made her ill. He duly examined the child, diagnosed a stomach upset, and prescribed a mixture of iron and quinine.

As the day progressed, the vomiting continued, and Edith's condition worsened. Dr Patterson saw her again in the evening. He found her no better, and was frankly puzzled to account for her symptoms. However, when he saw her for the third time at midday on the Sunday, 2 January, he thought the girl was looking a little better, and told her mother that in his opinion she was on the mend.

It was at this juncture that Nurse Berry showed the doctor a blood and vomit stained towel, which, he noticed, gave off a distinctly acidic smell. Deciding to give his patient some additional medication, he asked Nurse Berry for the key of the infirmary dispensary, which was next to her room, and the only key to which she held. The doctor had it in mind to administer a bicarbonate mixture. He wanted to add some drops of creosote to it, but finding the dispensary bottle of creosote to be empty, he wrote there and then an order for a fresh supply and instructed Nurse Berry to dissolve eight drops in water and give Edith a tablespoon of this 'tar water' every two hours.

That Sunday evening the child was again violently sick, and Dr Patterson observed red marks around her mouth. They had been caused, Nurse Berry told him, by some lemon and sugar she had given her. Not satisfied, thinking it more likely that the child had been given a corrosive poison, Dr Patterson consulted with a second doctor. He agreed. By the next day, Edith's pulse was barely palpable; she vomited back any medicine they tried to administer; she was steadily weakening, and her lips were covered with blisters. She died at 5 o'clock on the morning of Tuesday 4 January.

This sudden, swift decline of a previously healthy child did not sit well with Dr Patterson.

In fact, the circumstances of little Edith's death led him to believe it to be likely that her mother had poisoned her. He suspected that Nurse Berry had given her the contents of the dispensary bottle of creosote on the Saturday, and another massive dose, from the second bottle which he had ordered, on the Sunday. It distressed him to think that had he not given her mother a second supply of undiluted creosote, the little girl might have survived.

Mrs Berry offered no objection to the carrying out of a post-mortem. Three doctors who performed the examination disclosed that the body displayed no signs of natural disease. The stomach and intestines exhibited marks of blood, and the throat appeared black and corroded. Death was due to an intake of corrosive poison, quite possibly creosote which had an acid content, and which aforesaid poisonous substance had disappeared, as a probable consequence of prolonged bouts of vomiting – the result, that the presence of poison could not be proved by toxicological analysis.

Although a death certificate was issued stating acute inflammation of the stomach and bowels as the cause of death, rumour began to weave its sinister skein, and, hardly surprisingly, suspicion crystallised around Elizabeth Berry, who, after all, had had sole access to the infirmary dispensary.

And that suspicion grew sufficiently in strength to convince an inquest jury to deliver a verdict of wilful murder and send her for trial on the coroner's warrant.

Elizabeth Berry was arrested and charged with the murder of her daughter. The Oldham magistrates had meanwhile concluded their hearing with the statement that, due to lack of motive, Mrs Berry had no case to answer.

She made her bow in the Assize Court dock in St George's Hall, Liverpool, on Monday 21 February 21 1887. The trial lasted four days. The prosecution alleged that the prisoner had poisoned the girl in order to obtain £10 on a life insurance policy, and, at the same time, to rid herself of the £12 per year upkeep cost of her daughter, which sum did amount to practically half of her total annual income. Of potential significance may be Nurse Berry's previous response when asked if Edith was insured, and she had replied, 'Not a penny. I shall have to pay for the burial out of my own pocket.' As a matter of fact, she had received £10 from a burial society in April 1886, and had at that time tried to insure her own life and that of her daughter for £100, this amount understood to go to the survivor when the first of the insured died. Although she had failed to pay the premium on this transaction, there are some grounds for believing that she fully expected this sum to be paid out to her.

Counsel for the defence averred that Mrs Berry had been a kind and affectionate mother, and said that the suggestion that she would kill her own child for money was a monstrous proposition. Mr Justice Hawkins, in the course of his summing-up, pointed out that the prisoner had made several false statements relative to the child's health and the insurance upon her.

The jury took little time to reach their verdict. Within ten minutes, Elizabeth Berry had been sentenced to death for what Hawkins J. described as a 'cold-blooded, merciless, and cruel murder'. What the jury did not know, although it would have been known to the trial judge, was that the suspicions surrounding Edith Berry's death had led the police to further investigate the death, in February 1886, of Mrs Berry's mother, Mrs Finley. She, like her granddaughter, Edith, had died suddenly, and permission had been sought and granted by the Home Secretary for the body to be exhumed. Once again, the examination did not rule out poisoning, and the symptoms surrounding both deaths were disconcertingly similar. Mrs Berry had on that occasion also profited from an insurance payout, albeit small, but the circumstances were sufficiently weighted with suspicion for the issue of another coroner's warrant charging her with wilful murder.

There were other rumours, too. Her husband, Thomas Berry, had died in the summer of 1881, and her son, Harold, had followed his father into the grave in the autumn of 1882. Thomas had succumbed after a long illness. Harold had been taken ill and passed away after a trip to the seaside. After both events Elizabeth Berry was said to have benefited, but since she was already detained under sentence of death, there was no point in further pursuance of the accusations. Incidentally, it was immediately after Harold's death that she had placed Edith with Mrs Sanderson.

It has been reported that to the very end Mrs Berry continued to protest, even to the prison chaplain from whom she was receiving spiritual consolation, of her innocence. It has been alleged that she admitted her guilt in a memorial sent to the Home Secretary, in which she used the words, 'I must have been mad if I did it', and mentioned tea as the medium in which the poison was given. Her execution date was fixed for 14 March 1887.

From the time that she received her death sentence, Mrs Berry's health seems steadily to have declined; she became withdrawn, apathetic, expressing a desire not to see any visitors, occupying the handful of hours that remained to her in penitent mode – meditating, praying, and in the performance of devotional exercises.

Something of her state of mind is revealed by her demeanour when, two days before the carrying out of the sentence of the court upon her, she was visited by her solicitor, who was to take final instructions from her in the matter of settling her worldly affairs. Attired in prison garb – a blue serge dress, white collar, and white cap – she was seated behind a steel mesh partition. No sooner did she see the solicitor than she crumpled up in a swoon, and it took two doctors two or three hours to bring her round. Later in the day the solicitor saw her again, and this time she was able to conclude the necessary arrangements.

Now comes the strangest of codas to this strangest of stories. When James Berry, the Victorian hangman, arrived at Liverpool's Walton Gaol in the late afternoon of 13 March 1887, he was received by the governor, who gave him a peculiar smile.

'I did not know you were going to hang an old flame, Berry,' he greeted him.

'What do you mean?' asked Berry, who thought the governor must be joking, on account of the condemned woman's name being the same as his.

'She says she knows you very well,' he replied. 'You'd better go and have a look at her tonight. I'll make the necessary arrangements.'

Later, Berry gazed curiously through the narrow slit in the cell door and recognised the woman inside as someone he had met in the past. Describing her as 'a woman of not unpleasant appearance' whose 'chief charm about her was her beautiful chestnut tresses', he went on to recall how he had once met her in a crowded ballroom while having some refreshment. She had approached him, asking if he was alone, and then, with a coy glance and a smile, enquiring if he would dance with her. With his arm around the waist of a young woman of charm and vivacity, who chatted gaily to him about herself and her work as a nurse in Oldham Hospital, he had trodden 'the mazy dance'. Then, after sharing refreshments together and another dance or two, they had discovered that they were travelling home in the same direction, so he had invited her to join him in his cab.

The following morning, Berry was early at her cell.

'I never liked to hang a woman. When I opened the door of her cell she looked up and nodded to me. "Good morning, Mrs Berry," I said. She came forward instantly and held out her hand.'

'Good morning, Mr Berry. You and I have met before.'

'Where was that now?' he asked, pretending to have forgotten.

'Oh, at the ball in Manchester, given by the police,' she said. 'Surely you can't have forgotten.'

'Oh, yes, I remember. It is a long time ago, and I did not realise that I was to officiate at the execution of a friend of mine.'

'No, I suppose you didn't,' she said.

'Well, I'm very sorry to have to do it,' he said.

She looked at him and with a toss of her head said, 'You've no doubt heard a lot of dreadful things about me, but it isn't all true what people say about one.'

'Well, I've heard a great deal about you,' he agreed, 'but you must pull yourself together and die bravely.'

'Oh, I'll go bravely enough,' she said with a shudder. 'You need not be a bit afraid of me, Mr Berry. You don't suppose I'd want to give you any trouble, do you?'

'I hope you won't give me any trouble.'

'You'll be easy with me. You won't give me any pain. You'll be gentle with an old friend, won't you?'

'I shall not prolong your life a single minute. Have you made your peace with God?'

She made no reply, and Berry besought her to make the most of what time remained to her. He went outside and caught hold of the arm of one of the warders. 'That woman is one of the biggest cowards in the world,' he said.

*

Shortly before eight o'clock Berry returned to the condemned cell to pinion her. She was wearing a black silk dress.

'Now, Mrs Berry, I've come back again. Is there anything I can do for you before you leave the condemned cell?'

She shivered and shrank back.

'Would you like a drink of water?' asked Berry.

She shook her head.

'All right, then. Time is getting on. Don't be afraid. I'm not going to hurt you.'

After Berry had pinioned her, the governor of the gaol led the way, followed by the chaplain, reading the prayers for the dying, with the rear brought up by three doctors. The distance from the cell to the scaffold was not more than sixty yards, and along the roadway sand had been sprinkled freely. It was the depth of winter. Snow had fallen on the ground and Berry was afraid that she would slip and fall. The condemned woman walked firmly until she turned the angle of the building and saw the gallows … a cry of terror left her lips. 'Oh, dear!' she wailed, reeled over and was just about to faint when Berry rushed up to her. 'Now look here, Mrs Berry,' he said, 'You remember what you promised me in the cell.'

Her only reply was a deep groan.

'You promised me that you would give me no trouble. What do

you call this?' He had caught her arms to keep her from falling. 'Let me go. Let me go, Mr Berry, and I will go bravely.'

She staggered along supported by two warders, and as she looked at the scaffold again a wave of terror overcame her, and she shouted 'Oh, God forbid! God forbid!' The warders helped her along, and she repeated the responses to the chaplain's prayers in a faint voice. But at last the ordeal was too much for her, and she fainted.

They lifted her on to the scaffold and held her up while Berry completed his preliminaries. She recovered consciousness while Berry was busy and resumed her responses to the prayers, calling out to her Maker at intervals to have mercy on her. And just as Berry was about to draw the white hood over her head, she exclaimed, 'May God forgive me!' and she repeated the words again as Berry pulled the lever.

No sooner had Elizabeth Berry gone crashing down than one of the wardresses came over, and, in bitter tones, said, 'There goes one of the coldest-blooded murderers – the worst species of womankind to carry out the deeds she has carried out.'

Early that morning of the execution, a heavy hailstorm, accompanied by a clap of thunder and a flash of lightning had passed over the gaol. There followed a fall of snow. The flakes thinned and ceased shortly before the hour fixed for the hanging, but the snow lay thick. The air was like liquid ice, and a bone-stripping wind scoured the tree-bare, stony ground of the prison yard. Outside the massive prison gates, kept at a distance by a modest cordon of police, a small knot of people had gathered; mainly men on their way to work, and a sprinkling of cold-pinched women. Sympathetic souls, they hoped, perhaps, for the granting of a last minute reprieve. But the tolling of the prison bell sounded a tocsin of dashed hope, and the black flag, struck from the pole, bore fluttering witness to the ceased fluttering of Elizabeth Berry's heart.

7

THE OLD CURIOSITY SHOP MURDER

There was undeniably something Dickensian about Hugh George Walker. Seeing him, in his rather old-fashioned Sunday best suit and well-brushed bowler, making his way to St Peter's church, in the Liverpool suburb of Aintree, he was every inch a Dickens' character. And, with Dickensian appropriateness, he was the proud proprietor of 'The Old Curiosity Shop' – at least that was what his neighbours in Aintree called his place of dwelling and sporadic commerce – No. 98 Warbreck Moor.

There is a touch of Sherlock Holmes about his story, too. You will recall how, in 'The Adventure of the Silver Blaze', Holmes calls Watson's attention to the curious incident of the dog in the night-time. But, Watson protests, 'The dog did nothing in the night-time.' 'That,' replied Holmes, 'was the curious incident.'

In the sad case of Mr Walker, the dog, or rather dogs, did, as we shall see, plenty in the night-time.

When death, in the shape of the pale-faced man, came to Hugh George Walker he was eighty-two years old, a widower. A small, frail man, anguished by arthritis, who walked with a stick and looked even older than the burden of years he carried. He had, before his retirement from the world of daily grind, been the master tailor at Fazakerley Cottage Homes, where he had taught generations of orphanage children the intricate art of the needle, professional stitching and cutting.

He lived after his retirement on his own in a large, detached Victorian house, where he set up in business as a second-hand dealer, with a Jackdaw-of-Rheims-like stock-in-trade assortment of bright bric-a-brac and ponderous antiques – much of it little more than junk. Cellar to attic, room after room of the rambling house was piled, floor to ceiling, with the re-sale detritus of vanished lives.

Mr Walker lived on the first floor. The ground floor had been turned into a tangled jungle of a shop. Slap-bang in pride of place, the centre of the window, his trade mark as it were, hung an eye-catching old birdcage, a plumed stuffed bird perched rakishly in it; a powerful symbol amid the hotchpotch of seedy merchandise.

A gradually developing eccentricity on the part of the increasingly eremitical Mr Walker, had been a slow-burgeoning reluctance to part with or sell anything. Nine times out of ten, his door was to be found tight-shut. His would-be customers had to hammer at it vigorously to attract the old man's attention, and, after a longish wait, be reluctantly admitted.

On a January afternoon in 1953, a young man came, directed by evil destiny, to knock for admission to Mr Walker's somewhat bizarre premises. The young man's aspect was not precisely engaging, but his manner was – at any rate, so thought Mr Walker. After poking around for a while, the young man made a purchase. He handed over one shilling and sixpence for a pick-up arm that had been wrested off an antique gramophone. In conversation, he conveyed to Mr Walker that he was a dab hand at fixing broken clocks and watches; tinkering with them was indeed something of a hobby with him, and asked if he had any work for him, repairing any of his timepieces.

Now it so happened that Mr Walker was harbouring upstairs a recalcitrant grandfather's clock, and this seemed to him a heaven-sent opportunity to have it brought to order. He accordingly intimated that he would be glad if the young man would care to match his skills against the aged mechanical rebel. The young man would, and agreed to return next day for that purpose.

The amateur clock-mender materialised, like a pantomime demon, at Mr Walker's shop door at around 2.30 p.m. on 9 January. That Friday, Mr Walker's sister, Mary Eliza, came across from her home in Gloucester Road, Tuebrook, to see her brother. She saw, too, the young man. She did not warm to him. Some sort of sixth sense seemed to switch on. What's more, she did not at all like the knife which she saw dangling in a sheath from his waistband.

The young man was there again when Mary Walker visited her brother on the following Monday, 12 January. Walker, who had obviously taken a shine to him, had allowed him to go upstairs on his own to a room over the shop and work unsupervised on the grandfather's clock. Miss Mary did not at all approve. She noticed, too, that the man seemed very familiar with her brother, laughing and joking with him, and calling him 'Pop'.

Mary Walker was not at Warbreck Moor on Tuesday 13, but the young man was. He opened the shop door in answer to the knocking of two lads, Ronald Cole and Allan Lake. They wanted to purchase some valves for a wireless set. He told them to come back the next day.

The pallid young man turned up at Mr Walker's seedy antique emporium once more on Wednesday 14 January. It proved to be his last, his fourth and final, visit. After he had gone, the grandfather's clock remained unticking. And Hugh George Walker ceased to tick, too. Not that anyone knew that at first. The darkness and silence surrounding his brooding old house was simply interpreted to mean that he had set off somewhere for a brief break.

But there were those who knew – a nine-year-old black Scotch terrier and a three-year-old red and brown little mongrel. They had somehow managed to get locked out of their home, and all night long whined and howled and barked outside the shop door. Their instinct, which humans are not privileged to possess, conveyed to them a sense of danger, a sensation that all was not well. They woke the neighbours, were roundly cursed, but loyally continued sending out their warning and distress calls. They kept it up for two days.

At about 10 p.m. on 14 January, a Mrs Lawson saw a thoroughly upset terrier barking frantically, clearly in distress, outside Mr Walker's door. A good Samaritan, she rang and knocked for twenty minutes before she gave up, thinking that he must have gone away overnight. There was, therefore, she thought, nothing she could do about it so far as the disturbed dogs were concerned.

Mrs Lawson was far from being the only one who, over the course of two days and nights, passed the dogs by, and, ignoring at length their obvious distress, unwillingly turned the other way. (One is, incidentally, happy to interrupt the narrative, briefly, to report that Mr Walker's two faithful hounds, after being fed, watered, and lodged in a local dogs' home, where, fit and well, they had been kept together and played together, they were, in the following May, found new homes near each other, and far away from the scene of their bereavement and ordeal.)

On the evening of Thursday, 15 January, a Mrs Marion Owen, who lived at 21 Hall Lane, the next street to Warbreck Moor, recognised that the dogs were trying to tell her something. She had been in the habit of giving them the odd bone, and one of them, it is not recorded whether it was the terrier or the mongrel, went round to her door. She saw at once from its demeanour and the distressed state it was in – both the dogs were terribly hungry

– that something seriously wrong had upset the animal, and was sufficiently sensitive to follow its lead to Mr Walker's front-door. There was no answer to her persistent knocking, no sign of life about the place. She did not like the look of things one little bit. He might have been taken ill or had a bad fall. At 9.30 p.m. she telephoned the local police.

Sergeant Hosker, accompanied by a constable, came over from Rice Lane police station. Having satisfied himself that there were reasonable grounds for Mrs Owen's anxiety, the sergeant decided to force the lock of the front-door of No. 98. Shining his torch into the darkened hall, he saw by its light a figure lying spread-eagled on its back at the foot of the stairs, and quickly realised that Mr Walker was dead, murdered. His head was surrounded by a pool of blood, spicules of shattered skull-bone spattered the floor and starrings of squirted blood stippled adjacent walls.

At 10.20 p.m. Sergeant Hosker wirelessed his report of the murder to Rice Lane. They, in turn, contacted Chief Superintendent Herbert Balmer, head of Liverpool CID. As soon as he arrived on the scene, Balmer ordered the cordoning off of the area, and called in Dr Charles St Hill, of Huyton, the Home Office's chosen pathologist. He drove up at 12.30 a.m., conducted a cursory examination of the body and its surroundings, stated his opinion that the time of death would have been between twenty-four and forty-eight hours previously, and had the body removed to the city mortuary for a full examination. He began work there at once, and by 3 a.m. had concluded the post-mortem.

His findings: thirty-two blows to the head; skull and left cheekbone shattered. All the indications indisputably those of a brutal, prolonged and murderous attack.

The forensic expert, Dr J. B. Firth, Director of the North Western Forensic Science Laboratory of the Home Office at Preston, and his specialist team arrived just as dawn was breaking, and set at once about a microscopic examination of the scene of the crime.

They turned up the probable murder weapon, the head of an axe with a broken wooden shaft, lying immersed in an enamel bowl of bloodstained water in the first-floor kitchenette. The other piece of the shaft was found on the hallway floor. It looked as if it had been broken off by the savagery of the attack. An additional important discovery was that of a set of bloody footprints on the hall floor. They had been made by somebody wearing crêpe-soled shoes.

From the testimony of Mary Walker and the two schoolboys, Ronald Cole and Allan Lake, Balmer was able to cobble together a fair working description of the man they were looking for 'to help them with their inquiries.'

He was 'a travelling watch and clock-mender, aged about thirty, with thin, pale features, a long, pointed nose, with a distinct whitish wart at the side of his left eye. About 5 feet 8 inches tall, and last seen wearing a fawn gabardine raincoat'.

Miss Walker provided some useful additional facts. She had noticed that her brother's silver pocket watch, which he always used to carry in his front waistcoat pocket, was missing. It was valuable, and had moreover been of great sentimental value to him. She remembered that the knife that the wanted man had worn at his belt was single-edged, and carried in a brown leather sheath, which was pinned together with five metal rivets. The point of the knife protruded a little from the bottom of the sheath. She also remembered that the axe that killed her brother was one that he had used to break up large lumps of coal for the fire. She recalled, too, that the pale young man had said that he wanted to buy a big old wireless set from her brother. He agreed to pay him £2 for it, and said he would borrow a pram to carry it away with him.

Mary Walker's information about the suspect's planning to take the wireless set home in a pram, suggested to Balmer that they were looking for someone who lived within walking distance of the scene of the crime, and, between 16–18 January, detectives carried out a daunting programme of door-to-door inquiries. But, as so often happens in these cases, it was pure chance that snapped the net shut around the killer of Hugh George Walker.

On the morning of Monday, 19 January, Iris Tucker was sitting in her home at 2 Park Gardens, sipping her breakfast cup of tea and flicking through the newspaper, when she suddenly received the shock of her life. Interested, like pretty well everyone else in Liverpool, in the sensational Old Curiosity Shop Murder, she read with horror the description of the wanted man. Detail for detail, it coincided exactly and irrefutably with that of her boyfriend, John Todd. Moreover, the mentionings of watch-mending, the sheath knife, the old wireless set, and the pram, put the absolute seal upon her horrified realisation that the murderer had to be her own beloved.

Iris, twenty-two years old, had met Todd eighteen months before when she had been working as an usherette at the Bedford Cinema, Walton, where twenty-year-old Todd had been the cinema fireman. They had become fond of each other. Every single evening since their first meeting, John had called at her home, just to see her and confirm that all was going well with her, for because of ill-health she had had to leave her job at the cinema, where she had worked for five years.

Unable to keep such appalling news to herself, Iris had immediately told her father about it. Come to think of it, he had never warmed to his daughter's boyfriend, hardly ever even spoken to him, and, after reading the newspaper account and listening to what Iris had to tell him, Walter Tucker had gone straight out to the nearest telephone box and rung the police.

Within minutes, Detective Chief Inspector Morris, Detective Sergeant Metcalfe, and Detective Constable Hall were on their way to Roxburgh Street, Walton, where Todd, an unemployed labourer, lived with his mother. Of course, he denied everything. They still arrested him, and, at 7 p.m., at Rice Lane, charged him. His response was, 'No. Only I know I didn't murder him.'

As a matter of fact, the police had already had dealings with Todd. The previous Friday evening, 16 January, following an appeal put out by the police for people who had recently visited Mr Walker's shop to come forward in order to be eliminated from their inquiries, and perhaps to prove able to yield some useful clue as regards the identity of the unknown killer, Todd, prompted by his mother, had presented himself at Rice Lane, where he signed a brief statement telling of his recent purchase at Walker's of a gramophone pick-up arm, and went on his way.

When Todd paid his customary evening call on Iris at 7.40 p.m. on 14 January, the fatal Wednesday, she had noticed that he was not wearing his habitual sheath knife, and asked him where it was.

'I won't be wearing it any more, love,' was his cryptic reply.

On the day after his arrest, 20 January, John Lawrence Todd was arraigned before the Liverpool Stipendiary Magistrate, Mr Arthur MacFarland, at Dale Street Police Court. He was represented by his solicitor, Mr Harry Livermore.

The prosecuting solicitor, Mr A. E. West, said that Todd had made and signed three different statements to the police. The first was that made on the occasion of his voluntary visit to Rice Lane police station on 16 January. The second had been made on 20 January, the day of his arrest. In it he had affirmed that he had been to Mr Walker's shop only once before, and that had been with his mother, some two or three years previously. (It was, incidentally, to what was now Mr Walker's house that Todd's mother used, as a girl, to go for dancing lessons.) Later on 20 January, Todd made his third statement. In this he told of how, on the afternoon of 14 January, Mr Walker had tripped over and fallen on the floor in the hallway of his house, just before opening the door to let him out.

As Todd stood in the Magistrates' Court dock, Hugh George Walker was at that very time being buried in Everton Cemetery. Todd was to make two further brief appearances at Dale Street, before being committed for trial at the next session of the Liverpool Assizes.

That trial opened at St George's Hall on 8 April 1953, before Mr Justice Cassels. Todd was defended by Miss Rose Heilbron, QC. Prosecuting was Mr Edward Wooll, QC. Todd pleaded not guilty.

Opening the prosecution case, Mr Wooll told the court that the police had discovered a heavily bloodstained fawn raincoat in Mr Walker's house. Todd had denied that the coat belonged to him. He claimed that he had lost his raincoat on 7 January, a week before the murder. He said that he had left it in a hut at Sandon Dock, when he went to look for the shore captain, hoping to land a job. He had actually gone, on the evening of the day of the murder, to the house of a neighbour, a Mr Humphries, an ex-policeman, to ask him what he should do about his lost coat, and was advised by him to speak about it to the officer on duty at Sandon Dock gate, but he did not do so. He subsequently admitted that he had not lost his coat at all. It was indeed the one found at Mr Walker's. He explained the blood on it, on his navy-blue suit, and his crêpe-soled shoes, by his account of Mr Walker's accident.

> As I was leaving on the Wednesday, the old man tripped and fell against me. His nose hit my shoulder and started bleeding. His nose rubbed down the front of my raincoat as I tried to get my hands under his arms to try to stop him falling down, but I did not succeed. I then helped him up to see what had caused him to trip. I saw a type of adze or axe on the floor. I picked up the head, as the handle was broken, took the head up to the kitchenette, and put it on the bottom shelf of the food cabinet.

This, said Todd, happened between two and half-past on the Wednesday afternoon. The old man, who had recovered from his fall, told him: 'You've got blood all over you. Leave your coat and I'll get it cleaned, and you can collect it on Friday when you collect the stuff' – the 'stuff' being the old wireless and some clocks. Mr Walker had said that he was expecting a visitor, with whom he would be going away until Friday.

Dr St Hill had taken scrapings from underneath Todd's fingernails, and found them to be stained with human blood. Todd's facile explanation was that the blood could have got there when he was scratching some irritant sores on his leg.

At the end of his examination, Miss Heilbron asked her client, 'Did you kill Mr Walker?'

Todd replied firmly, 'I did not kill Mr Walker.'

Dr J. B. Firth went into the witness box to testify to the finding of blood on the inside of both pockets, on both trouser legs, and in the seams of the jacket cuff of a navy-blue suit. The blood was group O, which was the same group as that of Mr Walker. Similar blood was found on the raincoat, and on the upper part, but not on the soles, of the pair of tan-coloured, crêpe-soled shoes.

Iris Elizabeth Tucker, pale, with long dark hair, and wearing a smart green coat, went into the box. She informed the court that on 9 January Todd had said that he had been to a second-hand shop to mend some clocks, and that the shopkeeper was small and only came up to about his waist.

On 13 January, he had said that he would bring her 'some clocks and an old-fashioned wireless.' He would carry them to her house on a pram.

On 14 January, Todd had said that he could not get the things as 'the old man had gone away until Monday.'

She remembered that when they met on 17 January, he was wearing a blue suit. But it was a different one from that which he usually wore.

In his evidence, Walter Tucker said that he had met Todd in the street shortly after the murder, and he had asked him if there was anything in the paper about it. Tucker had told him, 'Yes, there's plenty. They're looking for a man discharged from the army suffering from a spinal injury and carrying a sheath knife.' As Walter Tucker well knew, the description fitted Todd to a 'T'.

Todd said, 'Anyone who can do that to an old man wants hanging.'

The best reply that Tucker could manage was a grunt.

David Harrison, a jeweller and watchmaker, with a shop in Liverpool's Paradise Street, stated that he recognised the silver hunter watch which the police had found in Todd's possession as one that he had repaired for Mr Walker in September, 1951. He was absolutely certain of it. Todd, however, insisted that it was his watch. He said that he had got it some eighteen months before at the Bedford Cinema from a man named John Arthur.

Addressing the court on Todd's behalf, Miss Heilbron, finding herself pretty well bereft of straw, told the jury of ten men and two women, 'Todd comes to you not as a man with petty convictions or grave convictions against him, but as a man of sterling character, and if ever a character could be weighed in the balance, I am sure you will take that into account. Todd is a very ordinary young man living with his mother.'

The judge, summing up, said, 'No man is to be convicted on a charge such as this merely because he told lies, but you are not to leave out of your consideration the reflection as to why he told lies ... If you are satisfied that his was the hand that struck those thirty-two savage blows on that defenceless old man's head, and thus battered the life out of him, you will return a verdict of guilty.

They did.

John Todd displayed no sign of emotion when the foreman announced the jury's finding. He stood unflinching to attention as the black cap was placed by the chaplain on the judge's head and sentence of death was solemnly pronounced upon him.

The hanging was carried out on 19 May 1953, at Walton Gaol, my old friend, the late Albert Pierrepoint, despatching him with his customary expeditiousness.

One cannot but feel mystified by the crime. What was the point of it? Surely it cannot have been the acquisition of an old and well-worn silver watch? What on earth can it have been that so suddenly released in the normally peaceable breast of a hitherto decent young man such a whirlwind of savagery upon a timid and harmless old man?

8

SUPPER WITH THE MURDEROUS WAITER

According to the calendar, the man sitting across the table from Edgar Lustgarten and me in that upper room of Stone's Chop-House, in London's Panton Street, was old. But with his raven-black, marcel-waved, fastidiously brilliantined hair, and neat, black Ronald Colman moustache, he looked not only anachronistically young, but also extraordinarily like a film star of the Hollywood heyday. And, indeed, his name had once, like that of one of those now forgotten celluloid shadows, blazed famously the length and breadth of Britain; not for acting ability – although perhaps it should have been – but as the notorious Brighton Trunk Murderer.

For this supper-table fellow of ours was none other than Toni Mancini aka Hyman Gold aka Jack Notyre. Nor was Mancini his name. The son of a Deptford shipping clerk, he was really Cecil Lois England, but bedazzled by the lives and styles of the Italo-American gangsters of Chicago, of which he had widely read in the newspapers, he became Toni Mancini, unsuccessful hood manqué.

Fresh out in August 1933 from a spell inside following his latest disastrous enterprise in petty theft, he got a menial bread-and-margarine job at a crumby eating-house in the Leicester Square hinterland. It was here that he met Violette Kaye aka Mrs Violet Saunders, *ci-devant* vaudeville toe-dancer, now, at forty-two, foot-slogging the streets.

He, with his dark, Italianate façade and studiously projected Valentino-Novarro aura, caught her fancy. He was twenty-five. She invited him to share a new life.

So they ventured forth, the erstwhile *soubrette* and the fledgling *souteneur*, to set up shop together in the shoddy underworld Greeneland of Pinkie and *Brighton Rock*. She established her seedy clientele. Things settled into a flyblown pattern. She paid the rent, bought the food, doled out pocket money to Mancini. He danced attendance upon her, did the household chores, including the cooking, warmed her bed, made himself scarce when she brought gentlemen home with her to occupy it. On clientele-free evenings, he, an expert dancer, too, escorted her to the dance-halls.

Then Mancini got himself a job. Nothing spectacular. Just as a waiter-cum-washer-up at the Skylark Café, underneath the arches, at shingle level, just below the point where West Street meets the promenade. And the trouble started. Violette grew jealous. There were rows. Bitter words tossed back and forth. Vicious remarks, the white flames of mutual anger cooled, to be subsequently brooded upon.

A final crescendo, a public row in the Skylark, over a waitress. That was on Thursday, 10 May 1934. The next morning, Mancini announced that Violette had left him – which was true. But she had not gone to Paris.

Tidings of the basement drama enacted at 44 Park Crescent came about as the result of Brighton Trunk Murder No. 1. A light-brown, canvas trunk, containing a headless, legless female torso, discovered in the left luggage department at Brighton Station, set in motion a massive investigation into all cases of missing women.

This led to the finding of a big, black, evil-smelling trunk, which had been abandoned by Mancini in his last lodgings in Kemp Street. Police opened it. Inside was the body of Violette Kaye.

Mancini was arrested as he trudged aimlessly along the Sidcup bypass, near Blackheath. He was put to his trial, as Jack Notyre, at Lewes Assizes in December 1934. His defence was handled magnificently by Norman Birkett. According to Sir Bernard Spilsbury, a depressed fracture of the skull was the woman's cause of death. Produced by a blow delivered by Mancini, said the Crown. The result of a drunken fall down the steep area steps, said the defence.

In the witness box the man the press nicknamed the 'Dancing Waiter' made a very plausible showing. The jury, told by Birkett to 'stand firm', took two hours weighing the pros and cons. When they delivered their finding, Mancini appeared, in the elegant parlance of posterity, to be 'gobsmacked'. 'Not guilty, Mr Birkett, not guilty!' was all that, in startled amazement, he could say.

*

There is an epilogue.

Forty-two years went by. Hugging his secret to himself, Mancini worked for a time in a sideshow, touring fairgrounds. Then he went to sea. He settled ashore in Liverpool. It was in November 1976 that he stepped back into the black limelight with a confession in the *News of the World*: 'Before I die I want to set the record straight. The verdict was wrong. I did kill Violette Kaye.'

And over the supper table that April night in 1977, Lustgarten and I heard the tale from Mancini's own lips.

> After the scene Violette made in the Skylark, I came home filled with an awful anger. I found her lying on the bed drunk and under

the influence of morphine. She glared at me and shouted "Come here, you. You belong to me, d'you hear?" Suddenly I hated her. I was disgusted by her. I turned to go to the kitchen, felt a blow on the shoulder. She launched herself at me like a wild cat, clawing and scratching at my face and eyes. I struck out at her. She reeled backwards into the fireplace. I went to pick her up and she spat full in my face. That's when things went blank. Next I knew, she was limp in my arms, head lolling back, blood coming from her nose and mouth. I realised she was dead. I thought that I was banging her head on the floor. I'd been banging it on the knob of the fender.

I crouched there for some time, nursing her head in my arms. I was in a daze. Couldn't think straight. And I knew the police wouldn't believe I hadn't intended to kill her. I lifted her on to the bed. Suddenly I had to get out of that room. I walked down to the sea. And that was when I decided the only thing to do, the only way out, was to hide the body. I put her in the corner cupboard we used as a wardrobe. I spent the night cleaning up the flat. A few days later I bought that big black trunk, and ... '

At that moment, most timeously, the waiter set down three large brandies beside our coffees.

9

DENTIST IN THE CHAIR

Arthur Warren Waite was every other inch a charmer. Those 'other', non-charming inches? Pure, unadulterated psychopath.

The infant Arthur drew well in the chromosome lottery. A child of fortune, the good fairy at his crib side had handed out a generous package of gifts. A fine, healthy physique, sharp intelligence, slender good looks, athletic prowess, charm of manner ... but he was also touched with what were to prove fatal consequences, by the wand of the bad fairy, who bestowed upon him a single quality which was to destroy all the others – psychopathy.

Although, so it has been said, he was actually born in Canonsburg, a small township some 20 miles south-west of Pittsburgh, Pennsylvania, all sources agree that Waite was reared in the bustling Michigan city of Grand Rapids.

His parents were by no means well-to-do, but they were good and dutiful folk, anxious that their boy should do well. He was encouraged in every possible way and provided with the very best education that they could afford. After attending Grand Rapids high school, from which he graduated satisfactorily, his parents, at some sacrifice, managed to send him to the dental college at the

University of Michigan, Ann Arbor, whence he emerged in due course a fully qualified dentist.

Having no expectation of an inheritance of any significant kind, his degree in dentistry his sole asset, Waite was faced with the prospect of earning a living in the profession for which he had been trained.

Now it so happened that at that time it was the beneficent custom of two Ann Arbor dental graduates of yesteryear, Messrs Wellman and Bridgeman, who had since done surpassingly well for themselves, having set up a veritable dental empire in South Africa, to cast a warm eye homewards and kindly select their assistants from among the newly qualified, otherwise prospectless alumni of their alma mater, and this was to provide Waite with his first chance in his new professional life. Since, however, under the British colonial law then obtaining in South Africa, no one was permitted to practise dentistry there without holding a certificate from a British university, Waite had first to go to Scotland. A bargain of some sort, perhaps not unconnected with an anonymous act of enlightened generosity on the part of the South African dental magnates, had been struck on behalf of their protégés between Messrs Wellman and Bridgeman and the dental school at the University of Glasgow, whereby certificates would be granted to the laureated Michigan dentists applying for employment by Messrs Wellman and Bridgeman after only a few weeks of cursory lecture attendance and examination.

This not very strenuous postgraduate ordeal behind him, and in consequence thereof now styling himself a dental *surgeon*, Waite arrived in Cape Town at the beginning of 1910 to embark upon his five-year-contract life as a journeyman dentist on the Wellman–Bridgeman circuit, in their chain of dental offices throughout Cape Colony.

Starting off in one of the firm's Cape Town offices, his subsequent extensive travels involved brief periods of drill-and-forceps duty in the various towns, villages, kraals, and mining settlements of the Cape of Good Hope, before, in 1913, being given charge of a branch office in Durban, Natal.

Then something went badly wrong. His contract with Messrs Wellman and Bridgeman was cut short. He had, it would seem, been filling not only clients' teeth but even more liberally his own pockets with dental gold. There were tales of missing stocks, tooth-marked for the inlays and bridges of Cape Colony. Within weeks of the outbreak of the First World War, his baggage comfortingly lined with twenty thousand dubiously acquired dollars, he sailed back to the United States.

The man in his late twenties returning from South Africa in the autumn of 1914 was a completely different proposition from the callow, sallow, lanky lad who had left Grand Rapids half a decade before. Handsomely sun-tanned, tall, well-proportioned, athletic, clean-limbed, clear-eyed, clean-shaven, a successful dental surgeon, crack tennis player, perfectly groomed, unfailingly urbane, speaking with a British accent, and calling himself now *Doctor* Waite, he hit Grand Rapids like a superman from another planet.

Displaying all the sophistication and *savoir faire* of the far-travelled get-up-and-go man, an adept practitioner of the wit-spangled conversation of the *homme du monde*, the cosmopolitan, who seems able to talk easily, entertainingly, informatively, authoritatively on practically any subject under the sun, he proved an irresistibly attractive companion to men and women alike; although, it has to be admitted, his superlative attraction was to women, and most especially to women older than himself. He exerted, effortlessly, the gigolo effect. He inspired faith and accepted trust. His broad, toothy smile never, but never, faded. He was always, through thick and thin, the smiler.

But Arthur Warren Waite was like one of those teeth which he must often have come across in the course of his 'open wide, please' days – perfect, bright, shining white on the outside, but inside, deep down, hidden, rotting with decay. The dazzled Rapids natives looked and marvelled but did not see. Small wonder that Grand Rapids, eyeballing only the toothsome man, the beamish orthodontist, received this errant son with open wide pleased arms.

If Grand Rapids viewed Arthur Warren Waite with optimism, that gentleman assuredly returned the compliment. And in so doing he bethought himself of a young woman named Clara Louise Peck. The memory was practical rather than romantic. The two had known each other since they were children and had in fact attended school together before Clara had been hied off to the Chevy Chase School in Washington, and then to Columbia University.

One must, I fear, however unwillingly, interject at this point the unpalatable fact that the dazzlesome Arthur Warren Waite was a gentleman to whom money was dearer than all else in his universe; dearer, indeed, as was sadly to prove the case, than the deepest family ties. It was a divine article of his creed that you cannot pay too great a price for money, provided, of course, that others foot the bill. And not only was Waite a young man with an overweening love of the multi-coloured dollar, and a ruthless determination to acquire lots of them, but he was the original get-rich-quick guy. For, despite his name, the one thing that Arthur could not, would not, do, was wait. He was a young man in a tearing hurry to, by hook or by crook, make himself a millionaire.

Clara Peck's position in the Arthur Warren Waite scheme of things will become clear when it is confided that she was the only daughter of John E. Peck, millionaire drug manufacturer. One has no wish to be ungallant, but, indisputably, Clara was not a beauty. Rather a heavy-featured girl – lips somewhat too thick, nose undeniably too flashy, chin decidedly too solid – three years younger than Waite, she was no swan. Nor yet your total ugly duckling. But beauty, it is said, lies in the eye of the beholder, and in this case the beholder's eye was firmly fixed upon Miss Peck's beautiful inheritance. A Peck was not to be sniffed at as a marriage partner, for the dowry would be munificent and the legacy magnificent.

Waite, it must in fairness to him be allowed, worked hard at the wooing of Clara. Whatever his other trifling faults, in initiative he was not lacking – at least where self-promotional interests were involved. He got himself invited to a reception at the Peck mansion. He was assiduous in his attentions to his prospective heiress. He smiled ... and smiled ... and smiled. So nice and good-natured.

He followed the Pecks to Florida, for the winter 1914/15 holiday, where, at Palm Beach, he took part in a number of tournaments, bewitching the Pecks by the sheer ferocious brilliance of his performances on the tennis courts. For all the shop-window layout of the engaging young man's sterling qualities, it was far from being a quick and easy courtship. The Pecks, acutely aware of the perils of fortune-hunters, harboured a bushel of suspicions. Gradually, though, with skill and cunning, the indefatigable charmer smiled, and smoothed and smarmed his way into the beguiled family's confidence. They even began to like him. He did not drink or smoke. They never heard him swear. He seemed so genuinely devoted to Clara. He was such a brilliant doctor. (Somehow he seems to have made them believe that he was not just a dentist, but a medical man also, and not just a medical man, but a highly skilled surgeon. All of which speaks volumes for the sagacity of poverty and the ignorance of wealth!)

Clara and Arthur became officially engaged.

On Thursday 9 September 1915, at Fountain Street Baptist Church, in one of the grandest of Grand Rapids weddings, the Reverend Alfred W. Wishart officiating, Clara Louise Peck became Mrs Arthur Warren Waite.

Phase One of the Master Plan successfully completed. Now he *had* something to smile about.

*

The Waites' honeymoon was, for people in their position, oddly brief: just a few days in Detroit, albeit at the deluxe Pontchartrain Hotel, on Washington Boulevard, overlooking the river.

It came as quite a surprise in a number of quarters that, after his return from honeymoon, Waite did not open up a practice in Grand Rapids. But no, he said, opportunities for advancement in his profession were much greater in New York, and it was to that city that 'Dr' and the new Mrs Waite now headed. There they found awaiting them, on Riverside Drive, one of Manhattan's most glamorous addresses in those days, at No. 435 on the 116th Street parallel, a sumptuous, seven-room apartment, which, rent free and lavishly furnished, was old John Peck's present to them. He had also made his daughter an allowance of $300 (at that time about £60) a month. Far from being grateful, Waite was angrily disappointed. He regarded apartment and allowance as a pittance, measured against the high-stacked columns of the old man's cash. He had calculated on an outright gift of $50,000.

A couple of months before the wedding, Waite had enrolled himself at New York's Cornell Medical School, paying on registration an advance fee of $225, which, having presumably blown the $20,000-dollar gold tooth haul on rich living in the year since his return from South Africa, he had only managed to raise by cashing-in a small insurance policy which had somehow or other survived the spend-spend-spend spree. Now, securely wed to money, the impulse to serious, disciplined medical study had evaporated, and, informing the school that he was leaving the city, he obtained a refund of $200.

'Dr' Waite did not immediately engage offices in which to pursue private practice in New York. He was, he explained, very fully stretched as a staff consultant in surgery – dental and otherwise – at several hospitals.

He had other fish to fry, too.

The personable young 'doctor' had made an instant impact on

the circles of Upper West Side society to which his new wife had introduced him, and was much in demand among the lion-cub-hunting hostesses of New York. 'Young Dr Waite. He's lovely!'

His chutzpah with a tennis racket served an added attraction, and when, after winning a number of prominent amateur tournaments, he became Metropolitan Indoor Tennis Champion, his stock rose to dizzy heights; the fashionable columnist Franklin P. Adams, and other similarly celebrated tennis addicts, unstintingly hailing him with praise as 'the best player on the local courts', and his wife visibly swelling with pride. 'He's Metropolitan Amateur Champion,' she wrote triumphantly to her parents. 'Isn't that wonderful?'

To all outward appearances, Arthur Warren Waite was now a well set-up, passing fortunate young man, blessed with a nice, devoted wife and a millionaire father-in-law. His mother-in-law, Mrs Peck, adored him. In her bedazzled eyes, her precious son-in-law could do no wrong. Mr Peck, too, was immensely proud of him, regarding him as a brilliant and dignified addition to the family, and was prepared to stump up all the financial support that might be necessary to put Arthur in a position to carry out any research work which he thought would help him to advance his great calling. It was like being presented with a blank cheque. And Mr Peck's spinster sister, Clara's maiden Aunt Catherine, who, by the by, had given each of the couple $3,000 (nearly £1,000) as a wedding present, had also fallen completely under the spell of the medicinal enchanter. So utterly did she trust him, and so highly did she value his advice, that on one of his many fond and dutiful little visits to her at the Park Avenue Hotel, where, lapped in comfortable elegance, she lived, she was easily persuaded to let him bear away $40,000 (£15,000) of her money to invest for her. On some subsequent visit she unhesitatingly handed over power of attorney to him, thus giving him access to most of her liquid assets. It was on this money that Waite was living, pretending that the wherewithal to maintain Clara and his grand style of life, came as the harvest of his quite exceptional medico-dental skills.

Clara, it must be clearly understood, devoutly believed that her husband was in practice as a doctor. Had he not taken her on several occasions to the Flower Hospital, asked her to remain briefly in the waiting room, and returned, full of apologies, an hour or so later, announcing with a modest smile that he had just completed a vital, life-saving emergency operation?

Proud as she was of him, and of the fact that New York's most prestigious hospitals had recognised and appreciated her clever husband's talents, Clara could not help feeling a bit lonely. Arthur seemed to have so little time for her. Of course, she told herself (and others), he's busy. He has his profession and his tennis. I mustn't be selfish. She was more than understanding about his long and frequent absences. He had to be out many evenings visiting his patients. Sometimes he was so hard pressed that he did not return until the early hours of the morning. Sometimes she thought he was too good, sacrificed too much of his life for others.

Had poor Clara, the deluded, devoted wife, known what her noble husband was really up to during those long stretches away from Riverside Drive, she would have been a *mariée* far less complacent. The reprehensible truth is that when he was not, for sinister reasons, tinkering with his test tubes and Petri dishes of plagues and pestilences, his agar plates and bouillon bowls of cultivated pathogens, he was tinkering with a young woman homophonously named Horton. *Mrs* Horton.

The bold Arthur had first encountered the beautiful Mrs Horton when, far from the life-and-death dreams and the brave blaze of the operating theatre arcs, he had been prosaically taking a voice culture course at the YMCA and learning French and German the method way with Berlitz.

A variant version has Waite seeing Mrs Horton performing at the Strand Theatre in December 1915, and at the Academy of

Music the following January. Smitten, he had managed to get himself introduced to her, then, turning on all the old wistful Waite smiling charm, induced her to join him in French and German lessons at the Berlitz School, hinting that there might well be a sequel of extensive foreign travel.

Margaret Weaver, born in Cincinnati in 1894, the twenty-years-younger wife of forty-one-year-old Henry Mack Horton, variously described as distinguished aeronautical engineer, broker, and dealer in war supplies, of 56 West Eleventh Street, was, after some small success as an actress and chanteuse, ambitious to become an opera singer – disquieting echoes of Kunigunde Mackamotski, *vulgo* Belle Elmore, who tied the knot with, and the rope's noose for, little Dr Crippen. Bowled over by the beauteous, raven-haired Mrs Horton, 'Dr' Waite was to install her at the elite Plaza Hotel, facing the southern end of Central Park – an exceedingly plushy trysting place. Of this, more anon.

Arthur Warren Waite was not so much bad seed as, to coin an appropriate diagnostic phrase, 'psycho seed'. Like all self-respecting psychopaths, he was subject to the world-owes-me-a-living syndrome. He has been described, and very perspicaciously, as 'the man who would be happy'. So he would – like any psychopath – at any cost – to anyone else. He presents a remarkable case of a totally amoral man, a case unsuitable for treatment. He had decided to play family fortunes, which meant he had to knock out his in-laws.

So be it.

The stakes were high.

*

Aunt Catherine had been unwise enough to play a gentle game of her own: the will game. Indiscreetly, she had discreetly let it be known that upon her demise, at some far distant date of course, her favourite nephew would find himself in receipt of a very substantial *aide-mémoire* of his departed aunt.

Within the family, it was common knowledge that Mr Peck's will left half his fortune to his daughter.

So, if Mr and Mrs Peck died, and Aunt Catherine followed suit, and, perhaps. later on, Clara were to die, that would leave Arthur Warren Waite a very rich and very eligible widower. This now progressed beyond the realm of mere wishful thinking, to become a matter for the ways-and-means committee in Waite's divided skull. And this was, too, where he could at last draw the interest on his long-time investment in a slightly more than dilettantish dedication to the healing art of the bacteriologist.

Mortui vivos docent: what can heal can also destroy.

Almost within hours of his arrival with his still-blushing bride in New York, Waite had started to mount his carefully planned and homicidally orientated assault upon the metropolitan citadel of orthodox medicine. Practising one of those small deceptions which came so easily to him, he let it be generally understood, and, indeed, it came to be widely believed, that he was a fully qualified medical doctor. He was, of course, nothing of the sort, and had no right to the title 'doctor'.

He further fostered the belief, seemingly ratified by the exclusivity and rich appointments of his Riverside Drive apartment, that he was a man of wealth, taste and culture, benevolently interested in scientific research, and most particularly in the study of the microbic causes of disease. For, as we shall presently come to recognise, fell purposes of his own he proceeded to cultivate those who would be able to provide him with an entrée to the somewhat arcane world of bacteriology.

On 17 September 1915, eight days after his wedding, Waite began his close-focus scrutiny of the sub-visible death-dealers, working under the guidance of Dr Louis Heitzman at his laboratory on 78th Street.

The following month, a bacteriological practitioner named Moos, was invited to the flat in Riverside Drive, where Waite had fixed up a small home laboratory, and was anxious to discuss with this expert the comparative efficacies of the various techniques for growing culture of bacteria. He was, Waite volunteered, engaged in research at Fordham Hospital and had been supplied with cultures of diphtheria and typhoid bacilli.

'Dr' Waite had also succeeded in getting himself introduced to Dr Percival L. de Nyce, associate pathologist, and skilled bacteriologist and virologist at New York's highly respected Flower Hospital. Dr Nyce was impressed by Waite's obvious keenness and dedication, but could not help noticing that it was only in the most deadly germs and viruses that he appeared to be really interested, and was slightly puzzled when he complained that the bacteria with which he was currently engaged were not sufficiently virulent for the experiment he had in mind.

It is time now to drop the pretence that Waite's interest was nice-guy humanitarianism, that he cherished the dream of becoming another Pasteur or Koch, saviour of suffering mankind. The experiment he had in mind, had had in mind from the start, was the unlawful killing of his in-laws. With quite extraordinary alacrity, within, literally, weeks of their moving into No. 435, Clara's devoted young husband had issued an affectionate invitation to 'Dad' and 'Mother', as he had taken to calling his Peck in-laws, to pay the still billing and cooing newly-weds a visit at their golden nest; he extended a portentous offer to come stay with them for a while.

Flattered and touched that 'the children' wanted them, Mr and Mrs Peck were delighted to accept. They did not, however, remain for very long on that first visit. The air of New York did not seem to agree with Mr Peck. From practically the moment he arrived, he began to feel off-colour, run down, very different from his usual bouncy self.

Arthur, sympathy personified, had diagnosed a coming cold, made up a special mixture for him, and had even taken the solicitous trouble to spray his father-in-law's throat each evening. All to no avail. Still feeling very seedy, Mr Peck dolefully returned to Grand Rapids and the therapeutic bosom of his own family physician, who, after thoroughly overhauling him and finding nothing wrong, expressed total bafflement. Once back home, however, the indisposition, whatever it was, miraculously soon vanished, and the old drugs magnate was rapidly humming away as healthily and cost effectively as ever.

That had been, as it were, the dummy run. If at first you don't succeed ...

Wreathed in toothsome smiles, the good 'Dr' Waite turned his thoughts to a profitable future.

*

Now Arthur Warren Waite's dream scenario unfolds.

It was Christmas – season of goodwill – ice on the ornamental waters of Central Park and in the cold heart of 'Dr' Waite. It was in no spirit of Dickensian cordiality that he invited the old couple from the Middle West to come and spend a jolly Yuletide in New York. His motive was wholly ulterior.

Unfortunately, or, depending upon the observer's stance in the 'Pecking order', fortunately Mr Peck had perforce to remain for business reasons in Grand Rapids; so, instead, the Waites joined Dad and Mother at the Peck mansion. Arthur, however, was not able to stay for more than a few festive days. Oh, so regretfully, he had to return to New York to perform a delicate eye operation.

Clara, who had remained behind at Grand Rapids, returned home on 10 January 1916, bringing her mother with her. Mrs Peck was permitted but a short spell of enjoyment of the excitements of the big city before being suddenly stricken by a mysterious illness which taxed even the diagnostic genius of her brilliant son-in-law. A local physician, Dr William N. Porter, was called in. His diagnostic ability, it turned out, proved no better than that of the unqualified Waite. Kidney disease, he decided at length, and prescribed accordingly. He took an optimistic view, saying that in his opinion there was no real cause for anxiety.

'Dr' Waite most strongly disagreed. Endowed with that strange instinct with which the merest handful of truly outstanding, born doctors seem to be naturally gifted, he felt the gloomiest forebodings. Mother was, he pronounced with great distress a throb in his voice, very seriously ill. How sadly right he was. How markedly, as he predicted, she failed to respond to the treatment. Clara would afterwards gratefully recall the exemplary way in which Arthur had tended her ailing mother. He brought her flowers and foot-warmers, and, for all the pressures of his demanding professional life, found time to spend long hours playing her favourite gramophone records and crooning to her at her bedside. Later, Clara would remember, too, the strange incident of the gas in the night. It occurred about a week before her mother's death. Arthur was out at the time, ostensibly visiting his patients, and Clara had, as was so often her custom nowadays, gone off alone and lonely to her bed. She had not retired long, was just drifting, relaxed, into a hypnogogic state, when, suddenly, she was wide awake, a strong smell of gas in her nostrils. She promptly got up in some alarm, investigated, and found that the smell was coming from her mother's room. The tap of the unlit gas-fire had been left turned on. Had it not been that one of the windows was inconspicuously partly open – for she noticed, too, that by some malevolent mischance a rag had somehow positioned itself suffocatingly up against the bedroom door – her mother would undoubtedly have been asphyxiated.

Arthur and Clara took it in turns to nurse Mrs Peck. He chose particularly to watch over the patient at night. That was typical of him. Kind and thoughtful as ever, he obviously wanted his wife to get her proper quota of sleep. But, despite all the loving care and attention lavished upon her by the devoted 'children', the patient, fulfilling 'Dr' Waite's prophecy, continued to deteriorate. Poor Mrs Peck passed away in the small hours of Sunday, 30 January 1916. Dr Porter, who had suspected nothing seriously wrong, had opined that there was 'no real cause for anxiety', perhaps slightly shamefacedly, but at any rate readily enough, gave his certificate of death as a result of kidney disease. Mrs Peck had been precisely twenty-eight days in the dying.

The lamentations of none were louder than those of the grief-stricken son-in-law. Herculean, he pulled himself together. A great comfort to his grieving wife, he took all the manifold burdens of death's mandatory practicalities on behalf of the bereaved upon his shoulders. He was a tower of strength. He sorted out certificates and permits, and attended to all the irksome formality requirements for the return of the septuagenarian Mrs Peck's body to Grand Rapids. He hustled and bustled and rounded up Clara and Aunt Catherine, efficiently conveyed them to the railway station and got them safely and punctually aboard the train to Michigan. And, on arrival there, he busied himself further, making all the necessary arrangements for the cremation. Cremation? Oh, yes, didn't they know? ... Hadn't he told them? To be cremated, that was Mother's last wish, whispered to him just before she died.

Among the eyebrows that shot up were those of the Reverend Wishart, that same pastoral gentleman who, it will be remembered, had performed, only a few short months before, the joyous ceremony of Arthur and Clara's wedding, and must now conduct the burial service of the bride's mother. He could not help thinking it odd that Mrs Peck should have decided to be cremated, *to have thus inexplicably changed her mind*, for she had specifically told him, and not all that long ago, that she wanted to be buried in the family vault. Her widower, seventy-two years old, numbed by the shock of sudden bereavement, couldn't remember what his wife had ever said about burial or cremation, but was happy to accept the caring Arthur's word as to Mother's wishes. In a sort of compromise, her ashes were buried in the family vault.

Waite felt, as indeed he might, well pleased with himself. Not only had he seen to it that Mrs Peck's dying wish was honoured, but he had also ensured that all chance – or mischance – of anyone's discovering the true cause of the old lady's decease had been licked away by the red flames, gone up in the grey smoke, of the crematorium.

Two days after Mother's death, the loving son-in-law sat down and wrote a letter to Archibald B. Morrison, the Peck family attorney. In it he asked, 'What will become of Mr Peck's money now that Mrs Peck is dead? Will Mr Peck make a new will?' Then added, sowing seeds, 'He is old and in poor health.' This was wishful, rather than truthful, thinking. It is, in point of fact, flatly contradicted by a statement in a letter which, not long before he died, John Peck wrote to a druggist friend of his – 'I am quite well, and not only that, I am taking good care of my physical body.'

That letter was written in February, 1916, from New York, whither, a week or two after his wife's cremation, he had gone. The great house in Grand Rapids had grown lonely, and old John, overwhelmed by the loss of his lifelong companion, finding the empty, echoing rooms of his grand mansion the domain of unbearable memories, had been really glad to take advantage of his fond son-in-law's warm invitation. He and his daughter had dearly loved Mrs Peck, and it was only natural that they should be eager to be together in this sad season, to console one another in their shared sorrow. How should he know that things had been so ordered that he had come east to go west!

All blissfully unaware, how pleasant it was to sit back in an easy-chair beside the wide, commanding window in the apartment on Riverside Drive, basking in the warmth and radiance of the children's love, watching the sky's reflection over the Hudson, of the sun 'going down in crimson suds', and then, as 'came still evening on, and twilight grey', and the first yellow pinheads of night lights pierced and swayed and shimmered on the dark river's water, there would be to look forward to all the earthy delights of his favourite dishes, religiously served to him at dinner. For, in all this sorry tale, one thing is not to be disputed: old John E. Peck loved his victuals. He was a great trencherman. He always seemed to feel peckish! That, indeed, was the trouble – according to Dr A. A. Moore, the medical man summoned when, a matter of days after the beginning of his visit, Peck fell ill. Nasty digestive disturbances, said the doctor, scribbling a palliative prescription, something soothing for diarrhoea. Nothing lethal. Nothing to worry about. Where have we heard that last phrase before? Has it not a disturbingly familiar ring about it?

Again, as in the case of Mrs Peck, 'Dr' Waite was in prognostic disagreement. With solemn shake of head, he declared, 'He hasn't a very strong constitution. I should not be surprised if he did not live for long.' And again, Waite's prophecy was to prove superior to the proper doctor's diagnosis. But then, as will presently appear, in this case as previously, Waite's accuracy resulted from a bit of insider knowledge!

During the days that followed, Mr Peck's son-in-law was most attentive. The sick man did not like his medicine. 'Dr' Waite soon found a way round that little difficulty. One evening he came into the kitchen and, quite openly, poured some of the medicine into Dad's soup. He came into the kitchen again later, when a pot of tea was being prepared for Mr Peck, and poured some more medicine into the tea-pot.

'Mr Peck didn't like his soup, Dora,' he told the servant, 'so I must put some more medicine in his tea.'

Dr Moore's first visit had been on 5 March. He paid further visits throughout the next week. On the occasion of one of these, 'Dr' Waite drove Dr Moore to his next domiciliary and, en route, asked him: 'If Mr Peck doesn't get well, do you think you ought to tell Clara?' To which Moore replied: 'Well, Dr Waite, don't let's be so pessimistic. I think Mr Peck will be all right.'

Mr Peck, like Mrs Peck, died on a Sunday – 12 March 1916 – six weeks to the day after his wife. That morning, when Dr Moore called he was met at the door by Waite. 'I'm afraid something has happened to Mr Peck,' he said. 'It seems to me he has died.' That was one diagnosis in which they surely concurred.

Once more, there was no suspicion of wrongdoing. No difficulty about the issuing of a death certificate. 'Acute indigestion complicated by heart failure,' was the given cause.

Clara Waite had become a rich orphan.

Events clicked into a familiar pattern. It was like the replay of an old B movie. Clockwork precision. Clockwork efficiency. Clockwork emotion. Arthur again taking over all the arrangements – registrars, undertakers, embalmers, transportation. Arthur again escorting Clara and Aunt Catherine, the survivors, to the station, seating them safely in the five o'clock Grand Rapids train. Beside them, Arthur sank back in well-earned self-satisfaction into the comfortable, first class cushioning. Before them, riding westward in the baggage car ahead, Mr Peck, in his coffin, heading towards the all-consuming, all-truth-burning flames of the crematorium.

And it was still only Monday, 13 March.

The little family party – and the corpse – arrived. Waiting on the platform at Grand Rapids station to meet them were Clara's only and older brother, Percy, Dr Perry Schurtz, the Peck family physician and the ubiquitous Reverend Wishart.

Encore, Waite wept dutifully upon the shoulders of the various members of the Peck pack, delivered up a mournful threnody on the passing of a great and greatly loved man, and quietly, diffidently almost, announced his late father-in-law's last pathetic wish: that he, like his wife, should be cremated, and his ashes mingled with hers.

Then the clockwork spring broke.

This time there was to be no easy acquiescence, no obedient

bending of the family will to the alleged burning desire of the dear departed.

'Everything's fixed,' said Waite in businesslike tones. 'I've arranged for poor Dad's body to go right on to Detroit to be cremated. I'll go with it and see this sad business finished. Would any of you folks like to come with me?'

Percy, prickly, exuding hostility, turned on him. 'Just a minute,' he said. 'I guess we aren't in all that hurry to see the last of Father. I'll see to the coffin.'

Lip-line tightening, face paling, Waite listened in astonishment. He could hardly believe what he was hearing. The ingratitude of it. But he was careful enough, clever enough, not to raise any objections, not to argue.

Percival Peck was demanding the baggage checks for the casket. Standing there, hand outstretched for them.

A very slight, very awkward pause, during which everything seemed to stand stock-still, suspended. Then, as though released from petrification by an enchanter's wand, wordlessly Waite handed them over. Percy ordered his father's remains to be taken to the Grand Rapids undertakers, Sprattler's.

Later, a worried Waite called at Sprattler's. He asked to see the body, said he wanted to put a rose in the casket. His request was refused. He was denied admission.

What had gone wrong?

Of course he knew nothing about the telegram.

*

The telegram in question had arrived from New York shortly before Waite and his party. Addressed to Percival Peck, its message had been brief, disquieting, and to the point.

> Suspicions aroused. Demand autopsy. Keep telegram secret.
>
> K. Adams.

Neither Percy nor anyone else had the faintest idea who K. Adams might be, but Percival Peck was not the sort of man to be deterred by a trifle like that. Besides, he had never liked Arthur, never been very friendly with him. The others might gush and goo over him, fall for his charm, be taken in by that perpetual crocodile smile of his. Let them. He, Mr Percival Peck, did not trust the fellow. Hadn't from the start. Suspected all along he'd only married Clara Louise for her money. He was sure that if there had been foul play of any kind, the odious charmer would be behind it.

Prodded by the telegram, Percy had begun to see certain events in a new light. Arthur's urging the cremation of his mother, the suddenness of both his parents' deaths, how little he really knew about his brother-in-law. In the sudden perplexity of his situation, Percy decided to consult with the two men of the greatest unquestionable probity that he knew. Men of common sense. Wise in human experience, men upon whose unbiased, disinterested advice he knew that he could soundly rely – his family doctor and his pastor. And they had confirmed him in his instinct to take seriously, and act upon, the mysterious telegram.

Dr Schurtz admitted that he had never been entirely satisfied about Mrs Peck's death. He didn't know her wishes about being cremated, but he *did* know about her kidneys. They were, he could testify, as sound as a ten-year-old's when she left for New York. Wryly, he had wondered whatever she could have been drinking in that eastern metropolis.

The Reverend Wishart, who had preached the funeral service over Mr Peck, after Percy had countermanded the onward transmission of the body to Detroit, said that he had noticed Waite, sitting nearby, staring weirdly all through the service at the face in the open casket. After watching Waite's reactions throughout, Mr Wishart found himself convinced by the close of the funeral service that Waite was responsible for the death of the aged man. Call it Divine Inspiration – the Reverend Wishart certainly would – or what you like, but it was 'that certain feeling' which beset Mr Wishart and made him feel intuitively positive that Waite did it.

In order to discover the genesis of that all-important telegram, it is necessary to go back to the Sunday when John Peck died. That morning, Dr Jacob Cornell, of Somerville, New Jersey, a Peck relative who had several times brought his sister, Mrs Henry Hardwicke, and other members of the family over the Hudson to visit 'Uncle John' during his sojourn at Riverside Drive, and knew that the old man had been latterly ailing and complaining, had received the news that he was dead.

Dr Cornell, taking his nephew, Arthur Swinton, with him, had gone at once to No. 435. These important callers were met at the door by Waite, who was up to his shifty eyes in the making of arrangements for the disposal of the body – embalmment and shipment to Detroit via Grand Rapids.

'What did you come for?' Waite asked rudely. 'I thought my wife had called you up and asked you not to come,' he added coldly, speaking through the held half-open front-door.

Dr Cornell, gentlemanly, embarrassed, murmured something about feeling, under the circumstances, it was his duty to call. Sullenly, very grudgingly, Waite let in the visitors, who had come to pay their last respects. They both noticed that he seemed curiously nervous and distrait, that he had lost his usual urbanity and cordiality. Irritable, off-hand, he was completely different from his normal charming, helpful self. Not only did he comport himself oddly before the visitors, but he would not permit them to view the body.

The mask of the smiler had slipped.

It was this inexplicable conduct towards his callers, in conjunction with the unwonted celerity Waite was displaying in getting his dead father-in-law's body embalmed and shipped off to Michigan, that set certain thumbs pricking. Although Dr Cornell himself refused to see anything sinister in Waite's behaviour, a nice-minded, charitable man, he thought that it was either that Waite was just dreadfully upset by the death, or that there was some perfectly sound, but private, reason for the way he had gone on. Not so his sister, Elizabeth C. Hardwicke, listening that evening to the doctor's account of his ill-starred visit of condolence.

Mrs Hardwicke was frankly suspicious. She was one of those who thought the haste with which the old man was being packed off back to Michigan, almost before he was cold, was, to say the very least of it, indecent. What was more, she'd never heard Uncle John complain of his heart, or that there was anything wrong with it. There was something else, and this was what really set her antennae humming. Just about the time that Mr Peck was taken seriously ill, she had happened to be having dinner at the Hotel Plaza with her daughter, Elizabeth, and Arthur Swinton, on 22 February 1916, when 'Dr' Waite, in company with a striking dark-haired woman, had come into the restaurant, He had spotted her even as she spotted him. He promptly strode over to Mrs Hardwicke's table, and greeting her with, of course, a charming smile and easy confidence, told her that he had just completed an important operation at the Bellevue Hospital. Then glibly added, with the bred-in-the-bone psychopath's snake-forked tongue, 'I have brought my own special nurse here with me for dinner, as I felt that she deserved something out of the ordinary for her skill and devotion to my work.' He said that after the meal they were to go on to another hospital, where he was to do another operation.

But Mrs Hardwicke was a shrewd and hard-nosed lady. She had watched Waite and his female companion and, putting one and one together, was perfectly certain that theirs was a deeper relationship than that of doctor and nurse. She had held her suspicions though, until, learning of Mr Peck's death in such quick succession to that of Mrs Peck, impelled by the strength of an almost psychic force, and in defiance of her brother's strict edict against interference, she had caused the mysterious telegram to be sent. One says 'caused' advisedly, because it was not she, but her daughter, Elizabeth, who did the actual sending, for the very sensible reason that her mother could not be sure that Arthur Warren Waite had worked lethal mischief on old Uncle John, and if it all ended up in court with sueings for libel, Elizabeth, not yet twenty-one and a schoolteacher, with no money or property of her own to speak of, could not be taken to the proverbial cleaners.

Clara, who had become ill within six weeks and a day of the double shock of losing both her mother and father, decided to stay behind to recuperate in Grand Rapids. Her husband, thwarted of his cremation, but with no clue as to the edifice of suspicion which was now building against him, fully satisfied that he had successfully bluffed everyone, hurried back to his mythical medical responsibilities – in reality to the wine, women and gaieties of the juicy Big Apple.

While, in all innocence (although that is hardly the right word to describe the good 'doctor's' activities) Waite went about his affairs (that is a much better word!), things which, had he been alert to them, would have occasioned him considerable unease, were afoot in Grand Rapids.

After the Reverend Wishart had concluded the funeral service, Mr Peck's body was not sent to the crematorium. Careful to drop no hint to Arthur of what was going on, Percy asked Dr Schurtz to arrange the carrying out of a secret autopsy. Its result showed that there had been no trace of mortal disease, and absolutely nothing wrong with the old man's heart. What the post-mortem did reveal were a number of suspicious gastro-intestinal lesions, in view of which Dr Schurtz, suspecting poisoning, sent the viscera to Professor Victor Vaughan, Dean of the Medical School at the University of Michigan, for analysis. A Reinsch test rapidly established the presence of arsenic. Since a man's life, as well as the determination of the mode of a man's death, depended upon its probative accuracy, the much lengthier and more complicated

Marsh test was then set up in triplicate, to determine whether or not sufficient arsenic had been absorbed to cause death.

Actually, before Arthur had started back for New York, Percy and Dr Schurtz and the Reverend Wishart, the self-appointed avenging trinity, had held a council of war and, as a first move in their campaign, had hired a New York private eye, Raymond Schindler. While the Waites were out to tea, he had finagled his way into their flat and discovered a small wall safe. In it were bank books and a key. The latter proved to be that of a bank lockbox. Opened, it was found to be brimful of dollars. They were the residue of the $40,000 entrusted to Waite by blandishment-blinded Aunt Catherine Peck for investment. Waite had sent $10,000 of this to his brother, Frank, with a note: 'There's more where this came from.'

From the second he stepped off the train in New York, Waite was shadowed, and Ray Schindler, nipping smartly into an adjoining telephone booth at the station, overheard a call made to Mrs Horton. He was telling her to pay the bill and check out of the Hotel Plaza at once.

The forces of private eye Schindler and his operatives were presently augmented by the additional detective presence of the Reverend Wishart. Convinced that the real truth about the terrible thing which had befallen the late member of his flock was to be learnt only among the sinful purlieus of the wicked city, the Peck family pastor, transformed into a rather Chestertonian figure, a kind of Baptist Father Brown, felt it his pastoral duty to quit his own bailiwick for a few whirlwind weeks of sleuthing in and about the aforesaid wicked city. He came to New York in what he called a disguise – a piquant and touchingly naive concept of such – clad still in his customary blacks and greys, but with a light-grey fedora, worn 'at a jaunty angle'. It was a role which nonetheless pricked his reverence's conscience. He was later to deliver himself of such breast-beating meae culpae as: 'May the Lord forgive me for the lies and deceit I practised. ... I have done more lying since I have been here (in New York) than in all the rest of my life. I have lied and deceived, and, I expect, I have broken your laws. The Lord forgive me. I did it for what I believed to be the right. I have gone down on my knees and prayed for forgiveness for those sins.'

Whatever, between them – that is, Schindler and his operatives, and Wishart and his divine inspiration – their multiple investigations had soon amassed a sufficiency of damning facts to alert and engage the professional curiosity of Assistant District Attorney Francis X. Mausco. And he, in turn, brought more investigators to dig yet deeper.

By now, with investigators amateur, private and public zeroing in on him, Waite and his movements were as closely under the microscope as one of his beloved bacilli. A fourth, and very formidable, investigative group, the voracious hordes of newspaper reporters, was about to join the others, and all four would henceforth be united in the common effort to uncover and piece together the unwholesome *disjecta membra* of 'Dr' Arthur Warren Waite's shady life.

There followed a week of ringing disclosures.

The newspapers, those valiant crusaders, those staunch watchdogs of public interest, tireless seekers after the evil that men do, were busy conducting a thorough raking into Waite's murky past. They were despatching their minions to quarter the city for information about him; their reporters were hounding him in every – and even most innocent – movement. The stringers and legmen scoured not only New York and Michigan, but Glasgow and South Africa also, to bring in titbits for the winnowing. Some highly prejudicial Waite home truths resulted.

For several days, the rumour that the suave young doctor had been in love with an exceptionally pretty woman frequently seen at the Hotel Plaza, where she had a studio, had been doing the rounds. On the morning of 25 March, the New York dailies came out with full, circumstantial accounts of Waite's philanderings. The 'debonair doctor', who had early discovered himself to be a man with power over women, had been seldom loathed to exercise that peculiar influence. In silken dalliance, he had distributed his favours both widely and generously, no lavish expense spared. But there was one lady who had eclipsed all others. They named names, and published pictures. She was Mrs Margaret Horton.

Mrs Henry Hardwicke recognised the young woman in the picture. Arthur and Margaret had registered at the Plaza Hotel as Dr W. Walters (a wily matching of initials with those already marked upon his possessions) and wife, of New Rochelle, Westchester County. Married less than six months, the 'doctor' was revealed as having been carrying on a passionate affair with a married singer – that is how the tabloids lip-smackingly put it.

Mrs Horton, affecting surprise at the conclusions dirty-minded folk drew from the simple desire of two people to be alone to test their language skills without the embarrassment of strangers hearing their slips, subsequently protested, 'We were never there at night. There was no bed in the room. It was fitted up as any artistic studio in a hotel would be. It was just a room to study and practise between classes.'

Although it was revealed that Waite had given Margaret Horton jewellery, valuable items which had been entrusted to him by Aunt Catherine Peck, she continued to insist that she and Waite had merely shared a common interest in art, music, and foreign languages. Mrs Horton's husband was at first very angry when he found out about the association between his wife and 'Dr' Waite, but, calming down, he went on record saying that he considered the relationship an innocent one. Margaret had, he said, made the kind of mistake of which any young woman might be guilty. That she had absolutely nothing to do with the crimes imputed to Waite, he was certain, and he declared that he personally was quite ready to forgive her.

Delving back into the dubious dentist's earlier life imported bad auspices, tidings of peccadillos past, a maculated career of theft, deceits and petty crimes, which did not auger well for Waite's present credibility or future destiny. As a boy, he had been in trouble on a number of occasions over thefts from his parents, relatives, schoolmates, employers, and others. At Dental College at Ann Arbor, he had been expelled from his fraternity for an act of dishonesty – but was later reinstated. The temptation to steal money whenever the opportunity presented was one he simply could never resist. That he had not long ago been arrested or jailed was solely due to the fact that he had always been shielded by his parents and always been in a position to make restitution. At Glasgow University, there had been some chicanery. He had either used false papers to help him to get a quick degree, or imposed on the university authorities by some other form of misrepresentation. In South Africa, he had tried to marry a young heiress of American parentage, but had been foiled when reports of his unsavoury reputation reached the ears of the girl's father.

Well, 'If at first you don't succeed ...' Waite *had* tried again, in Grand Rapids ... and had succeeded!

It was very soon after his rebuff by the American heiress' father that Waite's contract with Messrs Wellman and Bridgeman was cut short. Suspected reason for requested resignation: those old light fingers. No way, the papers pointed out, could Waite have honestly saved $20,000 out of the sort of salary that he was being paid.

Revelations were coming in thick and fast, too, from those other – amateur, private, official – branches of the multiple investigation. From all sides the forces of retribution were amassing and converging upon the, albeit deservedly, misfortunate Waite.

It was discovered that 'Dr' Waite had never taken the State Board Examination to practise dentistry in New York; that he was not known at any of the hospitals to which he had claimed to be a consultant in surgery; that he had obtained from William Weber, an attendant at the Cornell Medical School, cultures of typhoid, diphtheria, and pneumonia germs, and influenza virus.

Waite had for a long while been spending too freely. Under his father-in-law's will, the depleted coffers would, through Clara, have been refurbished. 'Dad' had left more than a million dollars – including a bequest of $2,000 to Waite's father 'out of regard for his son'. He would have had no cause to worry about money for quite a time to come. And when, eventually, he had, there was still Aunt Catherine's legacy, and ... well ... that could be arranged.

But now, in this blaze of publicity, this trial by the media, Waite suddenly knew that he had lost the devious game he had been so callously playing; just how unbelievably callously will in due course become clear. And it was now that he did something extremely peculiar. He telephoned Aunt Catherine and, in a voice crackling with strain and tension, he asked her straight out, point-blank, just like that, 'What is the best thing for a man to do who has been cornered? Do you think suicide would be the right thing?' A thoroughly flustered Aunt Catherine counselled most strongly against it.

It was at this precise psychological moment that the news broke that, after several days of tests, the toxicology laboratory at the University of Michigan had reported the discovery of arsenic somewhat in excess of 5 grains in Mr Peck's remains, and Waite decided to ignore Aunt Catherine's advice.

The police, coming somehow to hear of Waite's *felo de se* intent, arrived at Riverside Drive in time to scotch it. They found him in the room adjoining that in which Mr and Mrs Peck had died, suffering from the effects of an overdose of the sleeping drug, sulphonal. He was still alive. The Master Venenator had failed to turn proficiently his veneficious art upon himself. Rushed to Bellevue Hospital, placed in the care of proper doctors, and dosed with powerful emetics, he was restored, revivified – in preparation for the ritual death to come.

Removed then to the detention ward at Bellevue, he was surrounded there by those who, in police pay, watched and listened. They caught him sending an order for $1,000 to his servant, Dora. He was trying to buy her false testimony. He wanted her to deny ever having seen him slip 'medicine' into his father-in-law's food and drink.

Waite was arrested for murder. He had a smile for the police. He also had a laugh at them. 'Why, the thing is too absurdly amusing even to discuss it,' he chortled. District Attorney Edward H. Swann sat by his hospital cot side. He had taken personal charge of the official investigation.

At first, Waite denied everything. He was coldly informed that a purchase of arsenic had been found and would be proved against him. They knew that, on 9 March, he had asked Dr Richard W. Muller, of 10 East 58th Street, to recommend him to a pharmacist, as he wanted, he said, to purchase some arsenic to destroy a cat. Dr Muller had very kindly telephoned to Timmerman's drug store, at 802 Lexington Avenue, explained that Waite was a dentist, and that it would be all right to let him have the arsenic. The assistant at Timmerman's, after an unsuccessful attempt to persuade Waite that strychnine was more efficacious for the destruction of animals, had sold him 90 grains of white arsenic and made Waite sign the record book. Thus did Arthur acquire his supply of what the French in their cynicism call *poudre de succession* – inheritance powder.

Faced with this alarming piece of evidence, the whilom bold Arthur blustered a little, then came forth with the pathetically futile yarn that he had done what he had done out of kindly consideration for his father-in-law. The old man had been grieving terribly over the loss of his wife. Life had no longer any meaning for him and he had repeatedly said that all he wanted was to die and join her. After a long resistance, out of sheer pity he had finally given in to his father-in-law's insistence, bought the package of arsenic, and given it to him. He had not administered any of the poison. He had not seen Mr Peck take it. All that he had done that was wrong – if it was wrong – was to give, out of mercy, a desperately sad old man the means to end his sadness.

'Of course, you don't believe me,' said Waite to DA Swann. 'I suppose I shall go to the electric chair.'

Yet once more, he proved an accurate prophet.

The DA had another nasty surprise up his sleeve. He knew all about Mr Eugene Oliver Kane. To appreciate the devastating importance of this piece of police knowledge, it is necessary to know that, soon after his last return from Grand Rapids, Waite had had a caller at Riverside Drive. Nervously twiddling his hat in his hand, John Potter, the respectful, black-suited undertaker who had duly undertaken the preparation of Mr Peck for his last earthly journey, was ushered by Dora, the maid, into 'Dr' Waite's somewhat surprised presence. Apologetically, suppliantly, Mr Potter – surely well-named for his avocation in life, he sounds an appropriate member of a pack of Unhappy Family cards, Mr Potter the Undertaker, from the potter's field – politely requested that his bill should be paid.

'What's the hurry? You know the money's safe, don't you?' snapped a, for once, unsmiling Waite.

'It's really Mr Kane, sir, the embalmer. He thinks he might not get his money.'

'Not get his money! Why ever not?'

'Well, sir, there's talk. Some idea that arsenic may have been used.'

Waite knew that it was against the law for arsenic to be put into any preservative mixtures employed upon human bodies. He also knew that arsenic would be found in Mr Peck's body if it were examined.

'I think I'd better see Mr Kane,' he said.

And he had done just that. Gone round to see him. Made

no bones about the unusual undertaking he required from the undertaker. He was, he explained, in a bit of a hole. He was being jobbed [framed], made the victim of circumstance, falsely accused. Kane was able to help him. Would he? He wanted a kind of miracle – to change the water of embalming fluid into the wine of embalming fluid. He wanted Kane to testify that there was arsenic in the embalming fluid with which Mr Peck's body had been treated. Favours don't come cheap in New York. He knew that. Kane would be looked after, well rewarded. The embalmer named his price. There was a brief haggle. $9,000 was agreed. The bargain struck. A further meeting arranged.

Waite, who by now suspected that his movements were being watched, suggested a casual encounter the next day in a cigar store. There, Waite had stepped into a 'phone booth and pushed a fat roll of bills into Kane's pocket, instructing him to prepare a sample of the fluid, stuffed full of arsenic, and send it down to the DA as soon as possible'.

Waite's suspicions were correct. He *was* being followed.

Taken into custody, grilled, the cowardly little embalmer quivered and quailed, broke down immediately, blubbering and blurting. 'Waite told me the DA was going to ask me for a specimen of my embalming fluid. Asked me to send him it doctored with arsenic.' Yes, yes, he had taken the money. 'He gave me a big roll of bills. I was so scared I could hardly tell where I was. I stood there with the money in my hand. Waite told me, "For God's sake get that stuff out of sight." I put it back in my pocket. Then I went right home. I was so nervous about the money that my wife noticed it. She got to worrying me, and at last made me go to a doctor, to find out if I was sick. I knew all right, but I didn't tell her. I shook like a leaf every now and then when I got to thinking about the money in the bureau drawer. Then I took it to Long Island and buried it.' He had not, he insisted, put anything into the sample of the embalming fluid of the kind injected into Mr Peck's corpse. 'I made it up just the same as I always make it – of formaldehyde, glycerine and sodium phosphate.'

The sum of $7,800 was dug up from the place on Long Island indicated by the chastened Mr Kane. What had become of the other $1,200 is a minor mystery never officially solved. It should perhaps be added that Mr Kane's own record was less than immaculate. On more than one occasion he had been suspected of extending a (self) helping hand to well-heeled clients 'in a bit of a hole'.

Awakening from his sulphonal slumbers, as well as his dream of making himself a millionaire, Arthur Warren Waite, fully aware now of his predicament, and the overwhelming evidence against him, dreamt up a new scenario. He would go nap on schizophrenia.

He would call into evidence the Man from Egypt.

*

Arthur Warren Waite was brought to trial in the middle of May, 1916. He pleaded not guilty. A somewhat delicate decision, you might think, in view of the circumstance that, faced by the DA with the discovery of his purchase of arsenic and his bribing of Kane, he had, as we have already seen, cracked and 'coughed'. Moreover, he had then written to a New York newspaper, making public confession of his guilt of the deaths of his in-laws, expressing contrition, and his entire willingness to pay the supreme penalty. He had finally completed the confessional hat-trick by going on to provide the prosecutor with further and better particulars.

He would live – but not for long – to regret the hastiness of his impulsive catharsis. What, in his own interest, he would have been better advised to do, was to have held his tongue and embarked upon the usual plea bargaining trade-off of a life for a death – a State time-and-cash-saving plea of guilty of felonious death-dealing in return for a life-sparing life sentence. Now, though, the social and moral atrocity of his merciless despatch of the amiable old couple having, quite understandably, switched on a savage retaliatory instinct in the breasts of the just, the wretched Waite would not in truth have been permitted to bargain plead guilty, would have been afforded no chance to short circuit the electric chair, so that perhaps that 'delicate decision' to make a not guilty plea was not his decision at all, but a necessary law enforcement. And thus deprived of his best defence – guilt – he adopted the second best; that of contriving a guilty, but by reason of obvious insanity, verdict. This would iron out many puzzles in his conduct and deportment.

A man being tried for double murder might reasonably be expected to exhibit some small signs of perturbation, a slight hint of strain here, a visible shaft of anxiety there. Not so, relaxed, urbane, quizzically amused 'Dr' Waite. His perpetual smile seemed always poised on the lip's edge of laughter. His inappropriate gaiety had first bubbled over way back at the time when they were picking a jury. There had been one prospective juryman who, on challenge, had been asked if he was opposed to capital punishment. 'Not in *this* case,' he had replied emphatically, and the laughter of no one in the courtroom rang louder than Waite's. He was to laugh again, and heartily, many, many times during the presentation of the prosecution's case.

On the day Waite took the stand the courtroom was packed wall-to-wall. All eyes became cameras, zooming in on the good-looking 'film star' young man, with the small, almost feminine (as they were so described) features, as he rose from his seat at the table beside his counsel, Walter R. Duell. He had groomed himself with especial care for the occasion. He moved swiftly forward across the floor. He appeared eager to reach the witness chair.

It was pantomime time!

He was to play the court jester – the not-so-mad Fool.

And make no mistake, for all its integral beastliness, there is a certain amount of comedy – black comedy – in the case. Waite, 'with the air of a man relating a diverting story at a cocktail party', was, as it were, button-holing the jury. A nod, nod, wink, wink, performance worthy of a Hollywood Great.

First of all, Counsellor Duell took his client step by embarrassing step over the buried terrain of his earlier life. How he had cheated at examinations at Ann Arbor, by stealing the laboratory work of a more gifted student and passing it off as his own. How he had stolen $1,000 from a fellow student's trunk, and only saved his bacon by a shamefaced recompense. He confessed, too, his subsequent small thefts and expulsion from his fraternity at the University of Michigan, and his hefty appropriations from his employers in South Africa, so that he might have a worthwhile, easy-come-easy-go fortune to bring home to Grand Rapids with him. He admitted also to snivelling little petty thefts by the 'great surgeon' from the purse of his trusting mother-in-law. To all these shaming, blush-making thefts and wrongdoings, Waite confessed without let or hindrance; no dimunition in the brightness of that smile, not the smallest falter in his amiable, punctilious manner. In short, he did it all with the true psychopath's lack of what the psychiatrists call affect, that is to say, without any token of the existence of embarrassment, guilt, or remorse.

Having thus painlessly submitted to the laying surgically bare of these unhealthy infrastructures of his life history, Waite was now about to be led on to tell of infinitely greater and graver obliquities and iniquities. The more terrible his story, the more coolly he would tell it, and the greater, hopefully, would be the chance that the jury would think him a madman. To this end he refuted none of the testimony given against him. Rather, aided and abetted by his attorney, he strove conscientiously to do all in his power to support and embellish it, to blacken himself still further.

Yes ... yes, everything the prosecution said about him was true. He was an even more outrageous and contradictory character than they had made out.

Yes ... he had married Clara Louise Peck in order to become rich and independent. Life without money was torture, and not worth living. To get the Peck fortune, or at least a large slice of it, into his hands, he would have to dispose of his wife's parents, her aunt – perhaps his wife herself.

When he had first made these admissions to the police, his stunned interrogator had asked him, 'Are you crazy?' That was before Waite had decided to play-act just that. 'I think not,' he had replied, 'unless it's crazy to want money.' Given time, he added, he would almost certainly have murdered Clara. 'She was not my equal in anything. When I had got rid of her, I meant to find a more beautiful wife.'

The motive was clear. Arthur Warren Waite had been poisoning off the Pecks for cash, and, as my father, a learned attorney, was wont to observe, money is the purest of all motives.

Counsel decided to hammer the point home. Make sure. 'Why do you say you wanted to kill them?' Waite came right up to proof. Hit it bang on the head. 'For their money. I've always needed lots of money, and it has never worried me how I get hold of it.' The perfect, textbook 'split personality' answer. Surely there, laconically, spoke two people.

The honest man: 'For their money.'

The psychopath: 'Never worried me how I got hold of it.'

There was the dapper, debonair dentist, far from down in the mouth, up there 'singing' like a man carried away. Possessed, standing up, moved to testify to a breast-beating Moody and Sankey revivalist meeting – or a classic clinical exemplar of Dr William Sargant's dissociation phenomenon.

The delivery of his testimony was, like the performances of Elizabethan actors, punctuated by stage-front asides – further incontrovertible pointers to his quintessential psychopathy. Asides about himself and the world (revolving) around him, such confidences as that he had always considered himself to be 'attractive and charming'. And, spoken in accents disarming, 'Everyone liked me'.

The extraordinary narration began. It was like nothing a jury had ever listened to before. Brutal, if not brutish, honesty. Devastating directness. As befitted one who sought refuge in a defence of complete moral imbecility, Waite began with cheery admissions of various attempts to murder Aunt Catherine Peck. To this end, he had gone to the Cornell University Medical School and there persuaded William Weber, an attendant, who had no authority to pass out such merchandise of death, to give him test tube cultures of various pathogenic micro-organisms. For 'persuaded', read 'bribed'. For 'give', read 'sell'.

'I gave her repeated doses of germs. Then some arsenic. And after that I put some ground glass in her marmalade, but she thought it was sand and returned it to the grocer. I also injected live germs into a can of fish before presenting it to her.'

He had, however, temporarily abandoned his attempt to wipe out Aunt Catherine when Mrs Peck came to stay. He could not see the point of murdering the aunt when there were much richer pickings – or should it be 'peckings'? – to be obtained by murdering his mother-in-law.

As Auden and MacNeice reflect in their Icelandic correspondence:

> Adventurers, though, must take things as they find them,
> And look for pickings where the pickings are.
> The drives of love and hunger are behind them,
> They can't afford to be particular.

'Dr' Waite proceeded now to tell of the murder of Mrs Peck. She had been easy to kill.'I started poisoning her from the very first meal after she arrived. I gave her six assorted tubes of pneumonia and diphtheria germs and influenza virus in her food. She then became ill and took to her bed.'

After Mrs Peck had been ill for some days, Waite had volunteered to sit up with her one night, and when the time came to give her a dose of the medicine prescribed for her by Dr Porter, 'I ground up twelve five-grain veronal tablets and gave that to her in solution in her medicine.'

'And then what did you do after you had given your mother-in-law the fatal dose of poison?' asked Counsel.

'Why, I guess I went back to sleep, of course. I woke up in the small hours and went along to my mother-in-law's room. She was dead. I came quietly out of the room and went back to bed again so that it would be my wife who would discover the body.' He darted a sweet, boyish smile at the jurors. It was slaughter most suave.

The jurors aforesaid, who had patently regarded Waite with some horror at the start of is evidence, had, as it progressed, become infected by his charm. That unwavering smile, that unwearying politeness, those faultless manners, had all been quietly and insidiously achieving their intended effect.

Now Waite was speaking again, using that soothing, melodiously British-accented voice of his like a musical instrument. In the same suave, emotionless way, he was gently describing his weeks-long struggle to kill his father-in-law. Old Mr Peck had been a much tougher proposition than his wife. 'I gave him large doses of about everything I had. I used to insert tubes of typhoid, diphtheria and pneumonia germs and influenza virus in his soup and rice-puddings, but,' said Waite ruefully, 'they didn't seem to affect him. Then I tried tubercular sputum. I procured a nasal spray into which I put it, and induced him to use that, but it didn't work. I also gave him a throat spray, laced with germs. Nothing seemed to have the slightest effect on him. When that didn't work either, I got a lot of calomel and fed him that, in order to weaken his system, so that he could not resist the germs, but it failed. He recovered every time.'

But Arthur, as we have already noted, was a try, try, try again man.

'I tried many other things in the hope that he would succumb. I would get him to go out and expose himself to draughts. I would open his bedroom window in the hope that it would give him pneumonia, or at least that he would catch a cold. For the same reason I dampened his bed sheets, put water in his rubbers [gumboots], and wet the seat of the automobile before taking him out for a drive. None of these things worked either.'

Waite had toyed with the idea of faking a car accident.

'I tried to get him out in an automobile with me. My idea was to stall at the top of a hill with him in the back seat, I planned to jump and let him go over a cliff in the car. I couldn't do that either. Once, I got some hydrochloric acid and put it in the radiator in his room, expecting the fumes would affect him. They didn't. One night I turned on the gas in his room, but the superintendent came up and told me about the leak. I had to shut it off.'

Other interim attempts included letting off the occasional modest-sized canister or two of chlorine gas in the bedroom – 'I hoped the gas would weaken his resistance like it did with the soldiers at the front. I used to put some stuff on the electric heater so that if he noticed a funny smell I could say it was something burning' – and feeding him a mixture of burnt fly-papers and veronal.

Finally, Waite had given his stubbornly surviving victim arsenic.

'I gave him a lot in his food.'

Indeed he did. He spiked Mr Peck's eggnog with it. He sprinkled the shiny white powder liberally in soup, oatmeal, rice-pudding, milk and tea, in piecemeal poisonings until he had used up the whole of his 90 grain purchase on – or in – his misfortunate father-in-law. Yet even after a single helping of 18 grains, at least six times the normally fatal dose and enough to knock a team of draught-horses clean off their hooves, the formidable old gentleman was still alive, albeit in a bad way.

'On the night of 12 March, he was in great pain and groaning. I had been left to watch by his bedside while my wife got some rest. He was, as I said, groaning with pain and begging for something that would relieve it.'

How this relief was provided – it was lip-twitchingly, rib-ticklingly funny – Waite went on to recount to his captivated audience of jurors with the same smiling sangfroid: 'Clara kept various drugs and medicaments about the house. In her medicine chest there was a small bottle of chloroform. I saturated a cloth with some of it and went over to him and said, "Dad, here's some ether and ammonia which will relieve your pain."'

Instead of the usual professional 'open wide', Waite crooned soothingly 'breathe deep'. Mr Peck breathed deep. Soon he would breathe his last. He felt relieved. The agony receded. His pain and weakness were such that he continued to inhale the numbing vapour until he became unconscious – unconsciously embracing death's ultimate anodyne.

Then, swift as a rattlesnake but without the serpent's warning, Waite struck. Poured more chloroform on the cloth, repositioned it, pressed it, moulded it, around the limp man's nose and mouth. He fetched a pillow then and with its feather-down touch administered the *coup de dis-grace*, holding it with steel vice grip over the sick man's face. He did not release it until old John E. Peck was dead.

Incredibly, the sheer bonhomie of the narrator began to communicate itself to his listeners, as he sat hour after hour in the witness-chair, head erect, motionless, reciting in incongruously affectless tone and smiling manner a hideous account of horrendous deeds. The man oozed charm. The charm seemed to spread over and defuse the explosive cruelty of the words of his blood-curdling tale of viciously calculated murder. Almost without realising it, members of the jury found themselves nodding in understanding, swapping smiles in sympathy with him, at the irksome difficulties he was encountering in destroying 'Dad'. The odd juror even gave vent to the occasional muffled giggle. Undoubtedly, there was in it an element of the hysterical laughter at a funeral, the curious acquiescence of Stockholm syndrome; but what was being unmistakably demonstrated was that Waite was a very, very dangerous man.

At the time when, after his suicide attempt or gesture – who can be sure which? – Waite had been questioned by the DA in hospital, and had at once admitted that he had given his father-in-law arsenic, the DA had asked, 'Had you any accomplices?'

'Only this other fellow', the self-accused man had replied. A throwaway line, delivered with elaborate carelessness.

'What other fellow?'

'The Man from Egypt.'

Encouraged, Waite carefully elaborated. 'He's always been inside me ever since I can remember. He has made me do things against my will. He made me take up the study of germs, as if I used them I wouldn't be detected. I was compelled against my will to put them in my father-in-law's food. Try as I would, I couldn't get rid of my murderous other self. Often I've gone for long walks and fought against the evil one, and tried to run away from him, but he was so fleet of foot he always caught me up.'

Me, I'm from Missouri, as American doubting Thomases say, about the Man from Egypt, but so earnestly did Waite tell his story that it was partly believed. On the witness stand he made no attempt to hide the appallingly evil personality of the Man from Egypt. On the contrary, only too eagerly did he call into evidence the alter ego, who, he stoutly maintained, had compelled him to contemplate and to commit crimes which shocked even case-hardened New York.

'Did this Egyptian make you kill Mr Peck?'

'When my father-in-law came to stay with us I wanted to help him all I could. Then the Man from Egypt said Mr Peck was too old to live, that he ought to die, and if he did die I wouldn't have to worry about money. He brushed aside all my arguments. When Mr Peck had first visited us, the Man from Egypt made me spray his throat with germs, but though they made him ill, they didn't kill him. I was ordered on his second visit to use arsenic, as it was quicker. I was to put it in his soup and tea and eggnog. I did my best, but the Man from Egypt was in control. Try as I would, I found it impossible to get rid of him.'

Then, solemnly, Waite told the court: 'But now that he has forced me to do these things he has left me, and for the first time I feel that my soul is free. He seemed to leave me last night and he hasn't returned again today to torture me with his evil suggestions.' The prisoner looked around with shining eyes, imploring the court's sympathy.

A nice piece of foundation laying – or lying – for future psychotherapeutic miracles, which would return him, cured, to live a full, rich and happy life back once more in the world of the normal. For the nonce, however, Waite declared that he was a 'split personality', and that the half of him that drove him to murder was an Ancient Egyptian. Reincarnation was a topic to which he referred frequently – although he does seem to have got his wires somewhat crossed, reincarnation, metempsychosis, 'split personality', and multiple personality. 'I believe,' he asserted, 'that, although my body lives in America, my soul lives in Ancient Egypt. It is the Man from Egypt who has committed these foul crimes.'

All this preternaturally serious talk of the Man from Egypt had exactly the effect that Waite foresaw. It was so wild that it seemed as though only a madman could so present it. The laboured psychological alibi – 'the *real me* was somewhere else at the material time' – falls echoing tediously upon the modern ear. More than ninety years on, one is reminded of the similar claims of so many others, such as that of Ken Bianchi, one of the Californian Hillside Strangler's hands (the other Strangler's hand was Bianchi's cousin, Angelo Buono), and his multiple personality act, seeking to offload the blame on to his co-corporeal inhabitant, 'Steve Walker', the vicious, unprincipled 'Violent Man', uninvited co-tenant of his body!

When the prosecution pressed Waite for details of his other life by the banks of the Nile, he was remarkably unforthcoming. He mentioned Caesar and Cleopatra and the palm trees and the pyramids, which latter he characterised with the highly un-Ancient Egyptian descriptive 'voluptuous'.

The whole purpose of this charade was to implant in the minds of the jury the idea that a man as intelligent, as civilised, as the delightful doctor had clearly established himself to be, could by no stretch of the imagination have carried out the heinous crimes to which he had so freely admitted, and at the same time be sane. And just to help them along, Waite would suddenly interject out of the crazy blue some such observation as, 'Whatever they may say of me, I pride myself on being kind and always giving water to flowers so they will not die.'

The wiseacres, cynical newspapers, and seasoned lawyers, could see the plea of insanity plainly approaching over the horizon. As in the Gary Heidnik case (1988) – murders committed in Philadelphia; trial in Pittsburgh following change of *venire* motion – when the enormity, the sheer bizarre horror, of the crime demands it, the best defence is admission of guilt with an insanity plea in mitigation tacked on to it.

'Any person who puts dog food and human remains in a food processor and calls it a gourmet meal and feeds it to others is out to lunch.' – Counsellor A. Charles Peruto, Jr Defence Counsel for Gary Heidnik.

Waite's attorney then produced psychiatrists, alienists as they were then known, to provide expert testimony that a man who could do, and afterwards talk about, such deeds in cold blood, could not be held to be sane within the meaning of the law. The

State called alienists of its own, who said that Waite, having displayed normal responses to diagnostic tests to which they had subjected him, must be adjudged sane. One psychiatrist told the court that Waite had informed him, 'Miss Catherine Peck said that she remembered how beautifully I had sung hymns in church while my wife's relations were visiting us, she could not believe that I committed the crimes. It was my *real* self that appeared then.'

Dr Jeliffe, the leading alienist for the prosecution, said, 'In my opinion, the prisoner was sane and knew the nature and quality of his act. He was fully aware of all the phases of his crimes. In my opinion, he is an average man, somewhat superficial, inclined to be snobbish, and of no great intellectual attainments.'

The judge finally ruled in favour of the prosecution alienist's findings. (He had, it has been scandalously asserted, been 'in part, swayed by his irritation over Waite's constant smile.') There was one man who heartily agreed with His Honour, who had never for one single moment believed that Waite was insane. That man was Percival Peck.

The trial moved on.

Very much the man of the world, 'Dr' Waite cocked an amused ear as witness after witness unfolded a black tale against him. Occasionally he emitted a good-humoured chuckle. He heard unperturbed of the discovery at his apartment of books concerning the usage and effects of arsenic, with pages tell-tale marked and turned down at the corner. Poisoners seem to be constitutionally careless in such matters – *videlicet*: the Donellan, Bartlett, and Fullam-Clark, Agra, cases. He heard the court being told of his two attempts to bribe witnesses: Dora, the maid, and Eugene Kane.

The appearance on the witness-stand of the little, bespectacled embalmer, twitching and peeking like some small disturbed pest animal, seemed to tickle Waite, who burst out into frank laughter several times during Kane's testificatory twitterings.

To be honest, Kane did not cut too impressive a figure under examination. The nuclear shiftiness of the man peeped through the swaddling layers of timidity. He had just explained how Waite had come out of a telephone booth and 'pushed a roll of notes in my pocket':

> Prosecutor: 'Did you know what it was for?'
> Kane: 'No, I thought it must be for something I had done.'
> Prosecutor: 'He told you, though, didn't he?'
> Kane: 'He said: 'Put some arsenic into that fluid and send it down to the District Attorney.'
> Prosecutor: 'Were you nervous?'
> Kane: 'I certainly was.'
> Prosecutor: 'Did you count the money when you got home?'
> Kane: 'No. I tried to, but I was too nervous. I saw some fifties and some hundreds, that's all.'
> Prosecutor: 'Any large bills?'
> Kane: 'Yes, sir. Two five-hundred-dollar bills. I hid the money in a closet. I tried to count it two or three times. Finally, I went to Long Island and buried it. I went to Greenport, way to the east of the island.'

Clara Waite, called to the stand, told the court of her surprise when, after her mother's unexpected death, her husband had said that it had been Mrs Peck's last wish to be cremated; 'It was the first I'd heard of it,'she remarked. On the last night of her mother's life, Clara had heard her heavy breathing; Arthur had said Mother had a very bad cold. In the morning she had found her dead. On the night of 12 March, she had heard Arthur, who had been sitting up with her father, ring the doctor. Later, he came into the bedroom in his robe, looking disturbed, and said, 'I don't think Dad's too good.' She had rushed to her father's room, but he was already dead. Once again, she was surprised when Arthur told her,

'It was Dad's wish to be cremated.' Nevertheless, she had accepted his word.

The surprise of the trial was on the third day, when the Hardwickes, mother and daughter, gave evidence. The daughter, Elizabeth, tall, attractive, composed, a teacher by profession, testified that it was she who sent the cryptic telegram signed 'K. Adams' (the name of a friend) at her mother's behest. The mother, Mrs Henry Hardwicke, said that after being told by her brother, Dr Cornell, of the chilly reception given to him when he called to offer the Waites his condolences, she fell to thinking. She remembered meeting the 'doctor' and his 'nurse' in the dining room at the Hotel Plaza. She realised that Arthur would now be in control of a very large sum of money. She became somehow convinced that he was responsible for the two deaths, and she had asked her daughter to send the pseudonymous telegram. Had it not been for that telegram, Mr Peck's body would have been cremated and there would have been no evidence of his having been poisoned.

It was the disclosure of Margaret Horton when she went on to the witness-stand which effectively put an end to any thin remaining chance Waite might have had of bypassing Death Row. And this is what did it. Mrs Horton recalled that at the time when rumours and insinuendos were thick as midges in the air, Arthur had invited her to his laboratory, where he had shown her 'tiny germs wriggling under a microscope'. That was when she had brought everything out into the open by asking him point-blank, 'You didn't really do it, did you, Arthur?' And he had answered, 'Yes. It's true. I did.'

Then, after his arrest, he had sent her a letter which, on counsel's advice, she subsequently destroyed. Under pressure she was able to remember the following words from it: 'If they prove it, I suppose it will mean *la chaise*, but I hope and expect to spend a while in detention as an imbecile, and then I'll be free again to join you.' It was this, perhaps more than anything else, which led Judge Shearn to rule that Waite was not 'an imbecile'.

Since Margaret Horton had been identified as the woman who had accompanied Waite on the occasion when he bought germs at Cornell Medical School, it had for a while seemed advisable for her to retain her own attorney, with the equivalent of an English watching brief, but she was never seriously considered as being involved in the murders.

One entire day towards the end of the trial was taken up with a series of witnesses paying cordial tribute to the gentle heart and genteel manners of the immaculate Arthur. Indeed, literally dozens of people who thought they knew the good doctor really well, were truly flabbergasted. He was so nice, so kind. What's more, he had a strong streak of piety in him. All through the time that he was alleged to be in the process of poisoning his relatives, he had been attending church regularly. He was such a pleasant person. There wasn't an ounce of malice in him. All he ever wanted was to be happy, and have those around him happy, too. If all that was being said against him was true ... why then, he really must be a Jekyll and Hyde.

After his arrest, his wife had declared, 'I was so shocked and amazed that I could not believe all those stories about his various affairs to be true. It seems impossible that a man who has been so uniformly kind and gentle to me, and apparently so loyal, could be guilty of the crime with which he is charged.'

Testified Margaret Horton: 'Dr Waite had an extraordinarily kind heart. He loved all the fine sentiments and the beautiful things of life. He used to say to me, "Margaret, when you sing you make me weep, because you make me think of beautiful things". He loved music. It was love of music that drew us together.'

Now the 'doctor' was facing the music alone.

A modicum less rosy was the testimonial proffered by Mr Percival Peck. 'I know that Arthur is guilty. The electric chair will be too good for him. Even if he were tortured, his death would never bring back my beloved parents or pay for his horrible deeds. I will do all in my power to see that he is found guilty and executed. He is surely entitled to no consideration whatever. I am convinced that he married my sister with but one idea, and that was to get her money. Even before her mother died, he predicted an untimely death for us all. We believed him to be a surgeon, and when Mother died we suspected nothing. Even when the news of Father's death came, we did not suspect – until we got that telegram. I am sure if it had not been for that, my sister and my aunt would have died next.'

Percy Peck remained adamantine to the end. He approached the prosecution just before the trial and told them, 'I have only one favour to ask, and that is that I have a seat through every minute of the trial near that man, so that I can see the last gleam of hope gradually fade from his face.'

The trial of Arthur Warren Waite was, as a matter of fact, much shorter than are the majority of sensational American murder trials. It lasted only five days.

Counsel for the defence's final speech was powerful and persuasive. 'Waite has told you the truth. There is no part of his story that is not true. He has no moral sense whatever. What are we going to do with such a man as this? You would not send to the electric chair an idiot, a lunatic or a child. On the other hand, we cannot permit such a man as Waite to be at large. We must remove him from society by placing him in an institution.'

This brought the judge down on Counsel like a ton of bricks.

'You are not,' Judge Shearn told the jury, 'concerned at all with the question of the punishment of this man. The question raised by the defendant's counsel of what to do with such a man is not the question at all. The law determines what shall be done. Your function is to determine the facts, so that the law may operate. Do not get it into your heads that you are called upon to determine anything but the facts. Juries have no right to set up standards of what constitutes right and wrong, and no right to discuss how the law shall deal with a man like this. You must not attempt to usurp the functions of the Legislature. In this case no claim is made that the defendant did it in the heat of passion. On the contrary, he himself admits premeditation, intent and a motive. No matter what the defendant has confessed, you must remember the burden still rests upon the prosecution to establish his guilt beyond a reasonable doubt. The defendant is entitled to have the case determined on the facts and not on what he says.'

The judge's direction in regard to the issue of legal insanity is a model of clarity and sound judicial sense. 'You might infer from arguments of counsel and some of the evidence that you are here to hold a medical clinic. That is not so at all. It would be absurd to ask twelve laymen to determine whether from the medical point of view a man is sane or insane, especially as men learned in the profession do not agree on the matter. The question is not whether he is sane, but whether he was responsible under the tests prescribed by law. That is not a test for experts, but for men of common sense. Moral indifference is not insanity. The claim that the defendant was weak in willpower, and that he was unable to resist suggestions like those from the 'Man from Egypt' has also been passed on by the higher courts, who have held that, no matter what medical authority there may be for such a claim, it cannot be assented to by the courts. Indulgence in evil passion weakens the willpower and at the same time the sense of responsibility.'

For all the jokes and smiles, when it came to the nitty and gritty, decision time, the jury proved to be not so impressionable. The thistledown of charm wore thin against the spikier teazels of reality. It took them just twenty minutes and one ballot to reach a verdict of guilty.

An oddball to the end, Waite greeted his conviction and sentence to death with a sigh, and said: 'What a relief!'

He was quickly taken off to Sing Sing by train, and was reported as being, on both the New York and Sing Sing railroad station platforms, 'almost playful, saying that he was going to a nice quiet place, where, later, he would have a nice long rest'.

From the end of May 1916, until the following April, Waite waited in his nice quiet place upriver.

'He was,' wrote Edward H. Smith in a memorable passage in his *Famous American Poison Mysteries* (1926), 'pleasant and condescending to the rough men in the prison house with him. He let them know that though they were in death the same, in life there were gulfs and chasms between them – even in that dim half-life in the shadow of the chair. And the undermen of the death house, used to humility and obsequiousness, accepted the snobbery with pathetic submission.'

On 3 April 1917, the Court of Appeal having found nothing to say on the question of guilt, affirmed the conviction without opinion stated, and decided that Waite's sentence must stand. Thereupon, the trial judge, wishing not to appear overhasty, delayed a month before setting the new date of execution for the week beginning Monday 21 May.

Meanwhile, Waite's attorney made application to Governor Whitman to have a panel of doctors examine Waite to determine the issue of his sanity. This Commission in Lunacy in due course reported its finding that he was perfectly sane. Governor Whitman washed his hands of the matter, and the news was conveyed to the prisoner in Sing Sing that he must die. When told, Waite merely smiled, hummed a tune, and said, 'Is that so?' The condemned man then pulled out of the hat a gesture well matching his court performance of a year earlier. He sat down in the death cell and penned the following note to Warden Moyer:

Dear Sir,

In one of the newspapers today is the statement: 'A. W. Waite to die next week.' On inquiry I learn that you have power to name the day. I am sure you would not be averse to obliging me if you found it possible and reasonable to do so and I wondered if we could not arrange for Monday of next week. There really is a reason for asking this, although I will not trouble you with explanations. I would be very grateful indeed for this favour.

Yours respectfully,
Arthur Warren Waite

Tidings of this latest piece of 'nerve' reaching the public beyond the Sing Sing fences evoked gasps of surprise, edged with grudging admiration.

Now that's what they called macho – or would have done if the term had been invented then.

Warden Moyer did not oblige. He fixed the night of Thursday 24 May for Waite's electrocution.

During that last waiting year of his curtailed life, Waite had only two regular visitors, his brother, Frank, and his attorney, Walter Duell. Iron-nerved, iron-willed, keeping himself to himself, he had killed the lonely hours reading the prose of Poe, Ibsen, Maeterlinck, and the Bible, the poetry of Keats and Browning. He was writing poetry, too. He dedicated a long poem to himself, an address to his body by his soul after death.

And thou art dead, dear comrade,
In whom I dwelt a time,
With whom I strolled through star-kissed bowers
Of fragrant jessamine,
And thou wert weak, O comrade,
Thyself in self did fail,
And now the stars are turned to tears
And sobs the nightingale.
And though I now must leave you,
The same old songs I'll sing,

And o'er yon hill the same soft dew
Will spread its silver wing.
Across the fields, among the stars,
I now must go alone,
Your spirit now will roam afar,
And leave you, friend, alone.

He never wearied of talking about himself. Another good psychopathic trait.

'My life consisted of lying, cheating, stealing and killing, but my personality was that of a gentleman, and I went for music, art and poetry ... I was looking over the ten Commandments, and I found I had broken all but one. The one about profanity. I have never been profane.'

He continued to display right up to the fall of the curtain that curious double personality.

When the hour struck, he said his farewells unmoved by the grief of his brother, unconcerned about the illness of his distraught mother. That old psychopathy had him in its spell. *Noli me tangere. Nemo me lacessit.*

His last evening on earth he sat reading – the Bible, Keats, Browning. He also wrote to Dr Amos O. Squire, the Sing Sing prison doctor, carefully sealing the folded sheet of paper in a double envelope. In full, tight control of himself, he was fleetingly annoyed when guards arrived to escort him to the death chamber. They had interrupted his last reading of Robert Browning:

Life's a little thing!
Such as it is, then,
Pass life pleasantly ...

It was shortly after 11 p.m. Composed and unafraid, Waite walked down the corridor to the execution chamber. His calmness intact, he waved as he passed to the other inhabitants of death row, a temporarily chastened tenantry, and called out to them, 'Goodbye, boys!', and sauntered on, that boyish smile of old still playing about his somewhat effeminate lips, to keep his appointment in a Samarra called Sing Sing with Marksman Death.

A second's split he hesitated upon the threshold of the grim place of the chair, registering the uninviting aspect of its harsh and comfortless embrace. Wrote one who was present, 'I saw him step into the room. I saw him advance the few steps to the chair. Waite blinked at the glare of the lights. He waved his hand. There were twenty people in the room. He was strapped to the chair. While he was being pinioned Dr Squire approached, asked him if he had any last word he wished conveyed to anyone. "No thank you, doctor, there is no one to whom I care to leave a farewell message."'

The psychopath's typical lonely exit.

As the electrodes were being fixed about his body and clamped to his shaven-patched scalp, he looked around and spoke his last ever words. 'Is this all there is to it?' he asked.

Within seconds, a double shock of 2,000 volts had crashed through his body – a taut jerking against the straps – a stray will-o'-the-wisp of smoke from the burnt flesh – and he was dead. He was twenty-nine years old.

American law requires that an autopsy must be carried out on an executed person at once, and this is usually done in a small chamber situated directly behind the room in which the execution has taken place. In Waite's case the post-mortem revealed evidence of an old meningitis on the right cerebellum, probably due to a fall or a blow on the head in childhood. The doctors did not think that it could in any way have affected his sanity. He was found, too, to have an abnormally large heart; enlarged perhaps as a result of his athletic activities. He was otherwise normal, no disease, and said to have been exceptionally well developed physically.

When, the autopsy over, Dr Squire opened his double-sealed

letter from Waite, he found a curious content. Upon a single sheet of paper, a sort of visiting-card of his stay on earth, Waite had written:

> Call us with morning faces,
> Eager to labour, eager to be happy ...

That was all.

Two weeks after the execution, Waite's widow filed suit to recover the $7,800 remaining of the $9,000 that her husband had paid to Kane. Three years later, Clara remarried in Pasadena.

Margaret Horton was offered, and accepted, a ten-weeks' contract to sing and play the piano at Loew's 175th Street Theatre, an engagement which, so speculated the cynical, had at least as much to do with her connection with the sensational Waite affair as the artistic attraction of her reportedly 'militant contralto' voice.

There was, it turns out, even in the central figure of this criminous drama, less than meets the eye. Waite is something of a disappointment. He was not, it transpires upon conscientious investigation, the innovative genius, the only begetter of the method, the genie of the germ. Back in 1912, Henri Girard, a Frenchman and 'flashy insurance tout', had pressed *Bacillus typhosus* – the typhoid germ – into homicidal service. And in Germany, in 1913, there was another active pioneer of bacteriological homicide, the germ slayer, Karl Hopf.

Quite possibly, though, the role model for Waite was Dr Bennett Clark Hyde, of Kansas City. Well-named Hyde, this ferociously avaricious medico had married one of millionaire Thomas Swope's nieces. Having first put down old Colonel Swope – a Papa Peck figure – Dr Hyde proceeded to decimate the ranks of relatives standing between him and the Swope millions, with the help of tubes of typhoid bacilli. Caught out and put on trial in 1910, Hyde had, by a series of extraordinary pieces of luck, contrived to escape his deserts.

For days before his execution, Waite was in communication with a woman spiritualist to whom he faithfully promised that, after he was dead, he would return and give her some message to prove the existence of a world beyond the electric chair. But after the last crackle, sizzle, stop, the rest was silence. Predictably, this psychopath let her down. *Plus ça change ...*

10

THE ICE CREAM GANG COMETH

A balmy West Coast June day. After a fifty-four-day trial – Scotland's longest in a criminal cause – on charges involving drug-dealing and its orbital satellites murder, attempted murder, and kneecapping, the twenty-eight-year-old Glasgow hardman stands, surrounded by an immobilised phalanx of bemused 'polis' men, on the Justiciary Court House steps. Arms outstretched, like a missionary about to emit a benediction, his shrewd eyes survey the scene of his freshly laundered triumph. Look, he has come through the judicial cleansing machine; he emerged clean as a whistle, Sanforised by fifteen men good and true. The cameras click like rapid-fire false teeth in a film-star burst of flashes. Vindicated, jury-certified upright citizen of no mean city, Paul Ferris 'smiled twice', as they have it in Glaswegian parlance – once like everyone else, then an involuntary encore presented by the 'chiv' memorial scar snaking from the right side of an ungenerously lipped mouth to the shadow below a firm-set jawline. A final significant gesture … then it was off, that fine June day in 1952, to a champagne-sipping celebration.

No corks popping, though, for the almost biblically nicknamed Blind Jonah; only thirty-six, his face described variously as 'a hot cross bun of knife-work', and 'a sort of flesh map of the gang battles of Glasgow', Mr Jonah Mackenzie was a walking object lesson in survival. Not that he walked too well after the knife attack that severed the leg muscles. Reputedly one of Young Arthur's Team aka the Thompson Gang – the opposition to Mr Ferris' Barlanark Team – he is said, by Mr Ferris, to have brought a great many of his troubles on himself, by lending a hand in the murder of Arthur Thompson Jnr, and kneecapping William Gillen, a Barlanark aide. Blind Jonah was made the (head)butt of unfeeling hard man humour:

> What kind of weapon does Blind Jonah use?
> Answer: A Braille gun.

No fizzy either at Mr Ferris' festal free-for-all for Limpy Willie Gillen, aforesaid, a turncoat Barlanarkian barnacle who had the temerity to nominate his whilom boss as his kneecapper. Not so, said Mr Ferris' jury. And there was no celebrating at locally dubbed 'Southfork' – two stone-cladded-into-one council houses, garnished with Spanish patio, satellite dish and refined ornatures of that fashion, Provanmill Road, home of the man they called the Godfather of Glasgow, Arthur Thompson Snr. Of whose issue the thirty-one-year-old son, 'Young Arthur' aka 'Fat Boy', was into wholesale heroin as a dealer, before being dealt out himself by a blow-away job – fatally shot while enjoying an innocuous weekend furlough from an eleven stretch in jail. The jury had likewise pronounced seven-times-libelled Mr Ferris unconnected with this sad event.

Who wiped out Fat Boy? Melted him down? Echo answers who. But, deservedly or undeservedly, two hard men of Mr Ferris' Barlanark Team, Joe 'Bananas' Hanlon and Bobby Glover, were scythed down by the Grim Reaper on the very morning of Young Arthur's funeral. Bananas and Bobby stood not upon the order of their attendance. In point of fact, they lay, cherubic, side by side; death did not divide them, in their car, parked outside the earthly Valhalla of a favourite pub, twin bullet holes in the nape of their necks, and, for good measure and as a reminder (to others) of the importance of rectitude, even in a life of crime, a carefully aimed bullet apiece up the rectum.

Both the Thompsons and the Ferrises hail from Blackhill, an abysmally drear scheme (écossais for Council Estate) to the north-east of city centre. Thompson Snr is a man with a chequered past – convictions for assault, housebreaking, robbery, safe-blowing and extortion – which he does not deny. But for nearly a quarter of a century since his last malfeasance Mr Thompson had contrived to steer well clear of those little lapses such as he had permitted himself to indulge in the sixties. Standing, of recent times, below the security camera limpeted upon the stucco of his fortress home, he rubbished the notion of his being the Glasgow Godfather. 'I would have to start talking like Don Corleone,' he chaffed merrily, adding, with less twinkle, 'It's pure nonsense.'

As the 1980s mounted, so did the spiral of violence. The tensions of the participating factions escalated way out of control. It was in 1985 that Young Arthur had been sentenced to eleven years for trafficking in heroin. While he was inside, a battle had to be joined for the preservation of his trading territory back outside. A first major indication of the flaring of the drug war was when, in 1986, old Arthur was wounded in the groin while innocently tinkering with his motor. (For the record, in 1989 Young Arthur's sister, Margaret, died with a heroin needle in her own groin: a cruel irony which brings no moralising gratification in its wake.)

Drug rivalries came bursting, literally, into the open in 1990, when a hand grenade was rolled into the pub where Ferris' Barlanarks did their drinking. Hard on the heels of that, Arthur

Thompson Snr was put into hospital, after being the victim of a most determined hit-and-run car accident.

Repercussively, Paul Ferris' father, Willie, a cripple already, who walked with the aid of two sticks, came in for some pretty rough handling with hammer, baseball bat, and razor. Following one such attack, he had to have more than 100 stitches. His tyres were slashed, and his car, with its 'Disabled' label, subsequently torched. Torched, too, was Joe 'Bananas' Hanlon's ice cream van, sales point also for heroin. And later, his XR2 was blown up, and he was shot in the penis.

Then, in August, 1990, came the rubbing out of Young Arthur and the consequent erasure – the execution – of Joe and Bobby.

Hard line humour:

> What is the favourite song on Glasgow's karaoke machines?
> Answer: Yes, we have Joe Bananas.

It took three bullets to fell Arthur Thompson Jnr. No. 1 nicked his cheek. No. 2 chipped his ribs. No. 3 hit, bang smack home, in his heart.

Famous last words to his sister: 'I've been shot, hen. I'm going to collapse.'

The whisper rustling on the dead air was that a £30,000 contract was out on Ferris.

Hard folk joke:

> What's the difference between Paul Ferris and Elvis Presley?
> Answer: Paul Ferris is definitely dead.

Mr Ferris himself treated this maleficent ribaldry with all the indignation an innocent man naturally feels for such manipulative fat-chewing.

And yet, Glasgow is no kingdom of empty threats. Dark promises are kept, bloody vendettas retained. The plain truth is that this roaring Runyonland north of the border preserves the ancient order – or, rather, *dis*order – hymned by that thirties prose bard of the Gorbals, A. McArthur, and his *No Mean City* accomplice, H. Kingsley Long. Who today knows anything of McArthur, the little Gorbals grocer who set himself the task of immortalising the blood-frothed spilth and sport of the razor gangs of his local streets, and succeeded in it so magnificently? Not great literature, but he produced a wondrously powerful manuscript; no mean feat considering his tenuous literacy, which, after being shorn of sundry stylistic quiddities and licked into grammatical shape by the co-author, very likely a relative of his London publisher, John Long, *No Mean City*, published in 1936, became a bestseller. It has to date sold upwards of 17 million copies. McArthur set to, with a co-author again, hoping to repeat his success with a sequel, *No Bad Money*. Sadly, there was to be no second small miracle. What modest confidence McArthur had built up in his writing ability pitifully and swiftly drained away. Depressed, he pitifully and swiftly drained away the contents of far too many bottles. They found him dead on the banks of the Clyde, brimful of methylated spirits.

But the gangs of Glasgow had come into being a good half-century before McArthur began his basically accurate but, even so, highly coloured, chronicles. The first named collection of organised Glaswegian hooligans to take shape out of the fogs and rain-mists of the remoter reaches of the past was the Penny Mob, who were brawling around the Townhead district in the 1880s. This earliest recorded as such gang numbered about 300 and took its name from the fact that every member had to chip in a penny a week to a kitty which provided money for the payment of fines imposed on members of the mob by the courts. The leaders of the Penny Mob packs were known, rather oddly, as 'Chairmen', the title bestowed upon them actually in court reports of the time. The Penny Mobsmen would be encountered lolling on street corners, prowling among the sprawling East End tenements looking for mischief, and making nuisances of themselves in and around city pubs. Quite a sizable proportion of Penny Mob violence was, it seems, the Dead Sea fruit of religious intolerance.

The next collection of unworthies to figure with any prominence on the Glasgow roll of dishonour were those young turn-of-the-century tearaways, aged mainly between sixteen and twenty, who banded themselves together in gangs of 100 or more under such bizarre banners as the Hi Hi, operating in the Northern Police Division area; the Ping Pong, in the Eastern Division; and the San Toy, the Tim Malloy, the South Side Stickers, and the Village Boys in the Southern District. These gangs attached great importance to territoriality, identifying themselves with specific tracts and sections of the city which they regarded as their exclusive preserves. The San Toy Boys, particular rivals of the Penny Mob, came from Calton, rather nearer to the city centre. Extremely belligerent, their war cry as they charged into street battle was, 'We are the young Santoys and we can fight the Tim Malloys!'

None of the early twentieth-century gang members carried razors, knives, or bicycle chains. They were armed with knuckledusters, heavy old-fashioned bolts, shaped like small, lethal dumb-bells, a brass rod with a hefty doorknob at the end, and, a great favourite this, a small poker, carried hidden up the sleeve. The young gangsters would waylay folk coming out of places of entertainment and demand money with menaces, go into shops for cigarettes and public houses for drinks – all to be handed over, of course, without payment. Whatever, with ego-boosting grandiloquence, they called themselves, the hooligans were originally known to everyone else in Glasgow as 'Keelies' – a keelie is defined in the Scots dictionary as 'a street-arab, a pickpocket' – but for many years now the name has been changed to 'neds'. No one seems to remember how or when the term originated. The dictionary definition is 'a donkey, a simpleton'.

In the years leading up to the First World War the Glasgow gangs proliferated. The Redskins was an exceptionally vicious gang numbering among its members several young girls, one of whom was the legendary and truly formidable Aggie Reid, who lived in a women's hostel in Trongate. Her record of arrests for assault was both long and alarming. It took at least four policemen to get her into a van. Boasting an organised membership of a thousand, the Redskins took over the East End, vanquishing the Hi Hi and the Calton Black Hand, and seeing off also the Hazel Bells from Mile End and Bridgeton, the Baltic Fleet from Baltic Street, and the Kelly Boys from Govan. Fisticuff fighting was despised. Battle was waged preferably with meat cleavers, or, failing that, with hammers. Protection money was extracted from shopkeepers and other tradesmen, and the gangs did not think twice about openly attacking and robbing people in the street in broad daylight. Leaders were no longer 'Chairmen' but 'Kings', and there were also 'Queens', invariably the prettiest, and not uncommonly the wildest, under twenty-one. If any Redskin found him or herself in trouble, a special loud, quick, tuneless whistle would bring rapid relief reinforcements.

Throughout the duration of the First World War (1914–18) gangland activity subsided. There was fighting of a different kind to be done, a new arena for the channelling of brute energies. For those keeping the home fires burning, peak production demands at the shipyards and in the munitions factories reduced that endemic unemployment out of which street violence and villainy had arisen and been recruited.

With the war's end, however, all the old spectres – unrequited slumland hunger and thirst, dizzy new heights of unemployment – stalked the streets, where the surviving heroes who had fought to make Scotland a land fit for heroes to live in now sold matches and bootlaces. So, ill-shod feet came marching back to the sounding of drumbeats calling up the old troops of Redskins and Calton Black

Banders, and conscripting willing new 'soldiers' to old gangs to replace those which, through loss of leadership and attrition of the passage of time and war, had simply dwindled away. Gradually the hoodlum body was revitalised. In his memoirs, *Life Begins at Midnight*, the late Detective Chief Superintendent Robert Colquhoun remembered 1923 as a vintage year for Glasgow's gangs. The Cheeky Forty and the Black Diamonds were his very particular bêtes noires in his bailiwick, St Rollox. Elsewhere in the town, he said the Redskins, the Norman Conks, and the Billy Boys were entrenched, and a new outfit, the Beehives, was just beginning to buzz.

Three more names to conjure with.

The hostility between the Norman Conks – an unexpectedly erudite corruption of William the Norman Conqueror, in conjunction with the fact that the gang's headquarters was in Norman Street, explains the nomenclature – and the Billy Boys, more prosaically doffing their nominal caps to that other King William of Orange, aka King Billy, both stomping the East End, was a matter more than territorial. Glasgow and many things Glaswegian, it must be understood, are shot through with the steel thread of religion. It goes back to the impact upon the native Protestant Scots of Irish Catholic immigrant workers, brought over at the time of the Industrial Revolution. The old rivalry survives, even though the initial cause of that rivalry has diminished as religion withers nationally. It was former Chief Constable of Glasgow, Sir David McNee, who said that one of his senior officers described the football matches between green-shirted Catholic Celtic, and blue-shirted Protestant Rangers, as 'the biggest outdoor religious festival held anywhere in the world'.

The Norman Conks were led by a ferocious character named 'Bull' Bowman, under whose sanguineous command they ported their favourite arms, 42-inch-long pickshafts, weighing close on three pounds, backed up by a variegated armoury of swords, hatchets, and lovingly sharpened bicycle chains, worn like a rosary around the necks of their 'Queens', because they knew that the police hesitated to search girls for fear of accusations of improper assault. For hand-to-hand infighting, beer bottles were the first choice. Favourite targets of these cherished weapons were, of course, the Billy Boys.

The Billy Boys' boss was William (Billy) Fullerton, who used to work in Gilmour's Club in Olympia Street, Bridgeton. The gang, 800 strong, had kept up the Penny Mob tradition of exacting a weekly payment and, allowing no doubt for inflation, a tuppence per week contribution was marked up on all membership cards. The resultant nest egg, tucked safely away in the local bank, provided funds for fines and also for the bringing of small comforts to wives whose men were, for reasons not unconnected with the courts, temporarily out of circulation. At one stage, the nest egg, to which, incidentally, local shopkeepers were also 'invited' to donate, topped well in excess of £1,200, and Fullerton lifted about half of this sum to kit out a flute and drum band, Rabid Orangemen. The Billy Boys were henceforth able to taunt the Catholic arch-enemy by marching down Norman Street on Saints' and Holy Days, fluting and drumming lusty Orange airs. The Conks' religious response was a hail of pickshafts, bricks, bottles, and bucketfuls of ordure. The tale is still told of how on one such occasion, when things had really got out of hand and attracted a full-scale charge of mounted police, a quick-thinking Billy Boy, Elijah Cooper, took a smart header into the big drum he had been beating and rolled off hidden therein to avoid the drumming hooves of the police steeds.

The Beehive Corner Boys, so christened originally after their meeting place, but subsequently abbreviated to the Beehive Gang, developed along different lines from most of the other gangs, whose main objects were to display ego-building machismo to their Queens, to maintain a firm hold on their territory, and to bash, slash and generally mutilate a respectable quota of the enemy. To them, heavy crime was incidental, happenstance, peripheral. But to the misbehaving Beehives, serious crime was very much an integral part of their agenda. Thieving, housebreaking, shopbreaking, safe-blowing, hold-up jobs, and intimidation were all on the menu; the Beehive was evidently posing a greater threat to the respectable citizenry.

Beehive organisation was, moreover, formidable – almost militant – with young recruits enlisting in the cadet branch, earning promotion to auxiliary membership, and final enrolment to the hard inner core, attained only after success in various tests and trials.

Weaponry: Razors, hatchets, chains and bottles.

Footwear: Fighting boots with carpenters' nails projecting wickedly from the toecaps.

Headgear: Cap with razorblade stitched in the peak.

King of the hive was Peter Williamson, powerfully built, in his early twenties, a legend in his own lifetime, as the cliché has it, for his prowess with his fists. Second in command was his friend, Harry McMenemy. The real mastermind was said to b a character named Howie. The Beehive did not survive the Second World War. Peter Williamson did. He went into the army and was soon made up to sergeant. Demobbed, he returned to Glasgow – and safe-blowing – and Peterhead!

The Beehive territory was especially the Cumberland Street area of the Gorbals, and, by 1931, when following his gang-busting success in Sheffield, my good friend Sir Percy Sillitoe was appointed Chief Constable of Glasgow, the Beehives were the undoubted rulers of their chosen domain.

Over the preceding decade the gangland scene had undergone inevitable changes. The Billy Boys were still in there battling away against the Norman Conks. Also in the East End were the Romeo Boys, the San Toy, and its Gallowgate subsidiary the Bridgegate

Boys, the Stickit Boys, and the Derry Boys from Bridgeton, and the Antique Mob from Shettleston. The legions from the South Side numbered among them the Black Diamond Boys, the Hammer Boys, and the Dirty Dozen. Govan contributed the Kelly-bow. A state of open warfare was disastrously ongoing between the South Side Stickers and the San Toy Boys.

The Parlour Boys – so called because their headquarters was the Bedford Parlour Dance Hall in Celtic Street – was another of the smaller, though perilous to ignore, gangs. Their leader, twenty-six-year-old James 'Razzle-Dazzle' Dalziel, was so self-consciously macho that he sneered at dancing with girls as effeminate and would only take the floor with another burly male member of the gang.

In the Glasgow of the 1930s it was a case of one thing laughing at another; for, while civic pride was in full swell, 'Glesca toon' busy boasting and boosting itself as the Second City of the British Empire, life for the painful majority was no picnic in the grim valley of the Clyde. One man in three was out of work. Times were rough and things got rougher.

It was the Gorbals that in these depressed years introduced a new weapon to the skirmish scene – the open razor. The phrase 'razor slashing' started to appear in the public prints. The regular pitched battles for transient supremacy raged. Pathetic, cloth-capped young men, the losers, were carted off, bloodstained bundles, to lock-up or casualty. Older, more cunning men, veteran survivors of the war to end wars, began first to infiltrate and then to take command of the war to end want, their personal want, on the crustless streets. The gang battles, the internecine warrings, escalated to pretty terrifying proportions. Ghurka knives and bayonets were added to the inventory, souvenirs in some cases, no doubt, of previous combat engagements overseas.

Sillitoe countered with an even tougher offensive. Using without compunction the toughest men in his force, on the poacher-turned-gamekeeper principle, he had them conveyed under cover, in furniture vans and suchlike inconspicuous transports, to the site of the hasslings, and there unleashed them with wink-as-good-as-a-nod permission to bring to play whatever exercise of strength they liked to sanitise the streets. And Sillitoe was winning when, in 1939, the Second World War interrupted his street-gang sweeping campaign. He relinquished his Chief Constableship in 1943.

The 1935–45 war that coffined and buried so many of the old ways, good and bad, brought in its wake to Glasgow changes of catastrophic dimension. Socialist City Fathers occupying the chambers of civic power decreed a new order for auld Glasgie. The noisome, festering, massively overcrowded, old sandstone tenements – of the Glasgow ghettos, McArthur's Land – were to be razed. Bulldozers should do what the Blitz did not. New schemes 'amid the green hills far away' on the virgin fringes of the city. Bright new dormitories for the deserving. But the idealists should have listened and been warned – did not their own national poet caution, 'The best laid schemes ... Gang aft a-gley'? And these, it has with hindsight to be admitted, were surely not the best. Oh, the houses, acres and acres of vast, lookalike, balconied grey battleships, breasting the green wave-crests of the circumjacent hills, were fine. Nothing a-gley there; the baths and indoor toilets were all present and correct, the paint was bright, the wallpaper cheery, roofs watertight. But – and it was a very big but – the enthusiastic, well-intentioned planners forgot to graft a heart into the place. Essentials, basic and more, had been remembered and supplied, but amenities had been forgotten. No places of sport or entertainment had been laid on. There was a dearth of shops. Bus services to the city centre were poor. Boredom and depression became the next-door neighbours of the inhabitants of the new, cut-off townships. Easterhouse, Drumchapel, Castlemilk and Pollok ... the names droop off the tongue like a litany of despair.

Here, in this concrete and chrome heaven turned to hell, was a splendid new breeding ground for the fresh gangs.

Meanwhile, those left behind – those not yet included in, and encompassed by, the urban drift – found idle hands' solutions to relieve the novel boredom and frustration. The inner city infrastructure might be crumbling but, despite decimated territories and depopulated streets, it was still hardy enough to support a thinning scatter of gangs, whose members, in their bewilderment at the disintegration of their former environment, sought, by stepping up their desolated rage against what remaining enemies they could contrive to find, the comforting solace of violence.

So it was that, in the late 1950s, the old, if not venerable, Glasgow tradition of street gangs and territorial violence came back with a terrible new celerity. Even more disturbing was the revelation that the use of the considerably more lethal knife had replaced the – horribly mutilating but far less life-threatening – razor, as the new weapon wielded with ruthless disregard for fatal consequence.

The new gang names started to appear. Alongside the Tongs from Townhead, the Cumbie from the Gorbals, the Fleet from Maryhill, and the Govan Team, there came the Buck and the Drummie from Drumchapel, the Toi and the Young Team from Castlemilk, the Bal Toi, the Torran Toi and the Bar L (named after Barlinnie Prison) from Easterhouse, as well as the Shamrock from Blackhill – that same Blackhill which formerly spawned the Thompsons and the Ferrises.

The wings of the new breed of hoodlums were well clipped by the late Lord Cameron and his fellow judges at the High Court, who handed out hefty exemplary sentences. But the containment of the mayhem and the ferocity was destined to be scuppered by the emergence in the early sixties of the drug problem. This was to become so grievous and far-reaching in its consequences, especially among the young, that the concomitant increase of other crimes, such as the opening of local shebeens, illegal money-lending at extortionate interest rates, as well as the traditional bread-and-butter villainies, theft and protection racketeering, paled.

The 1970s and 1980s witnessed a dramatic upsurge in the incidences of murder and serious assaults committed by gang members.

The first half of the 1980s will always be remembered for the ferocious Glasgow Ice Cream Wars, and their terrible culmination in what has been frequently described as Scotland's most horrific mass murder. Despite the long and strongly suggested rumour that drugs were at the back of it all, the best authority – and I am including in this assay the statement of the campaigning journalists Douglas Skelton and Lisa Brownlie, the authors of *Frightener*, a close-focus study of the ice cream scene – denied this. At the root of the trouble was the good, old-fashioned profit motive, gone obscenely wrong.

In order to understand, which is not to say to sympathise with, the market pressures leading to inevitable commercial battlings, all one needs to comprehend is the central struggle for control of the 'runs' or 'sales' pitches of the numerous ice cream vans operating on the various council estates. These sales of ice cream, sweeties, soft drinks, crisps, and cigarettes did not amount to peanuts. Without over-exerting yourself you could rake in profits ranging between £800 and £2,300 a week – the higher figure if you were prepared to reset stolen wares.

Theoretically, anybody could enter into this free enterprise. There were two routes: you could buy your own van and pay to garage it at the premises of such cash and carry firms as Fifti Ices, who would also sell you stock; or you could lease a van by the week. If you chose the latter course you had a choice of three hire firms – the Marchetti Brothers, Capaldi & Sons, and the Viking Ice Cream Company. You would pay £50 to £60 a week for the vehicle, the hire company being responsible for all the costs, other than petrol, of keeping the van on the road, that is to say maintenance, insurance, tax, and so on.

As realisation of the rich pickings to be had from this nice little earner dawned, insalubrious interests were raised, insalubrious characters muscled in, and feuding over the best runs broke out. Each side was, according to the police, backed by well-known criminals. Out came the balaclava clad strongmen, wielding baseball bats and shotguns; fifty-seven varieties of scare tactics were put into force, including discretionary torchings.

The ultimate torching was the setting on fire, in the small hours of Monday, 16 April 1984, of the top-floor flat, No. 29 Bankend Street, in the district of Ruchazie, where Andrew Doyle, eighteen-year-old driver of an ice cream van put on the disputed Garthamlock run by Marchetti Brothers, lived. Six people perished, including Andrew and an eighteen-month-old baby.

The gangland boss identified as responsible by the police was thirty-one-year-old Thomas Campbell, a hard man's hard man known with a shudder-inducing laconism throughout the underworld as 'T. C.' His lieutenant in the matter was said to be Joseph Steele, hitherto qualifying as nothing more nefarious than a petty thief. Tried in September 1984, these two received life sentences. But there are those who believe that Campbell and Steele were the victims of a miscarriage of justice. This does not *necessarily* imply innocence – indeed, the word in the street at the time was that they were guilty – but what it *does* suggest is that, innocent or guilty of the act impugned, the verdict was legally unacceptable if false evidence was used to secure the convictions. In March 2004, Campbell and Steele had their convictions quashed and walked free from the Court of Appeal. They had succeeded in clearing their names.

What, one cannot help wondering, does the future hold for Glasgow, erstwhile City of European Culture, city with a drink problem three times as grievous as anywhere else in Britain, and frequently hailed as the alcoholic capital of Western Europe?

Cornets and wafers, reefers and coke, choc-bars and heroin, sniffers and needlers. There will always be inlets and outlets for merchants of greed and gangs to chalk up unhealthy profits. There's only one way out: raise a cup of Glasgow's favourite drink, kneecappucino, and gang up on the gangs.

11

SHE-DEVIL WITH A PERAMBULATOR

The love of Mrs Mary Eleanor Pearcey for Frank Samuel Hogg may not have been pure, but it was cruelly true. And it was in the name of love – that tender force which should beget and cherish life – that she perpetrated a savagery so severe that it set the nape of Victorian London tingling with the fear that Jack the Ripper was back at work.

A russet woman – compelling russet-coloured hair, thick and soft as antler velvet, parted in the middle, tumbling in mossy loops above her ears, an overflowing russet stream which seemed somehow to drown out the imperfections of a nose too large, a mouth too wide, teeth too prominent, a chin too weak and receding; hair to lasciviously complement the fine blue eyes, bold against russet and sallow skin. The face is long. So is the neck; very long and very thin. The figure is full and tall for her time – 5 feet 6 inches – powerful to the verge of masculinity. Hands, feminine, small and shapely.

But this is no ordinary woman. She is only twenty-four now, but she has been different from all others from the beginning. Born at Ightham in Kent, in March 1866, she had since birth been reported subject to epileptic fits. Her family moving to Stepney soon after her birth, she was to spend her youth in London's Ripperine East End. Her father died in 1882, when she was rising sixteen. Her grief was extreme. She was found in the garden, suspended by a rope about that long, thin neck. She had stood upon a basket and kicked it away. She was black in the face, but alive.

After the loss of her husband, the widowed Mrs Wheeler, mother to Mary, moved to Kentish Town, where her daughter found work in a sealskin factory.

Her mother finds her an enigma. Flesh of – and not of – her flesh. She has siblings, a brother, a sister, apparently of the coinage of normalcy.

She has early perceived the red alert of sexuality and attended it. But has never married, although pretended it, having borne both the title and status of marriage. There was one Pearcey, John Charles Pearcey, a young carpenter, with whom, in 1885, she had shared pseudo-marital domesticity, shedding for him her given name of Mary Eleanor Wheeler. After a year or two the loose partnership grew looser. Pearcey, it has been said, left her, becoming tired of her infidelities. For whatever reason, the relationship palled, and ended in pseudo-divorce. With pride, and, as it transpired, cunning purpose, she continued however to bear the label of her whilom illicit connubiality, Mrs Pearcey.

Pearcey flown, others came and went, attracted by the moth lamp of sexual magic that burnt in her bedroom window. Of different ilk, less nectar-sipping flighty, was the more mature visiting fireman from Northfleet, Gravesend, Mr Charles Creighton. He was a businessman, well-heeled and well-satisfied enough to pay his key money – the rent of Mrs Pearcey's North London premises, the ground floor flat at No. 2 Priory Street, Kentish Town, and the upkeep, partial, anyway, of its mistress. From the time of his advent, September, 1888, he called punctiliously once a week to inspect both pieces of his property. Instalments kept up, her body and all but her heart belonged to the (sugar) daddy.

But *she* and her *cor cordis* were reserved for another, who, seen through the distorting lens of her own lonely need, she held more precious than life itself.

This other, doing absolutely nothing to deserve it, but accepting the irrational, obsessional, unearned devotion which he inspired as his woman-given right, the unworthy object of all this misbegotten, misshapen love, was middle-aged, bearded, amoral, self-centred, self-pitying, lachrymose Frank Samuel Hogg. Hogg by name and nature, he was a feckless fellow, but dowered with that syrup of sentimentality which so often does bastard service for genuine sympathy. He was selfish, conceited, opinionated, and unapologetically arrogant, these qualities being compounded within him in just the right quantity and combination to produce the standard irresistible psychopath.

His marriage to Phoebe Styles, in November, 1888, was the early fruit of his psychopathy. Having impregnated her, he was induced, but not without the weight of her hefty brothers' muscular logic, to see the social desirability of matrimony as premium to parenthood. The ensuant fell, not perhaps surprisingly, somewhat short of idyllic. Even the arrival, six months later, of bouncing baby Phoebe, to be known as Tiggie, failed to inject a rejuvenescence, if that is the correct word to apply to something which does not seem to have been joyfully juvenescent in the first place. In fact, Hogg greeted the nativity of Phoebe Hanslope with outbursts of hot male tears upon Mary Eleanor's shoulder and hysterical threats of suicide. Nor was it only verbal comfort which, undoubtedly encouraged by his sister, Clara, he sought of Mary Eleanor. Such, indeed, is the intricacy of the most peculiar tripartite situation obtaining between the three females in the life of this odious caliph of Kentish Town, that it seems necessary at this juncture to submit it to some scrutiny.

First, there was Phoebe, wife and mother of his baby daughter. A large, plain woman of thirty-one. Rather sickly and on the thin side. Redeemed by a head of striking black wavy hair and lovely violet-blue eyes. He had taken her after their exigent marriage to live in rooms at his mother and sister's house, at 141 Prince of Wales Road, Kentish Town.

Secondly, there was Mary Eleanor Pearcey or Wheeler. Hogg had known her, most likely in all the graduated significances of that term, for two or three years before his circumstantially enforced alliance with Phoebe Styles – although he vehemently denied having been, as he so delicately put it, 'criminally intimate' with her before December 1888. However, living with his family thus conveniently, just around the corner from Priory Street, he continued to 'know' her after his marriage several times a week, acquaintance being facilitated by his being supplied with his own latchkey to No. 2.

Thirdly, there was Clara Hogg, his sister. She and Phoebe Styles do not seem to have got along too well. Reportedly, they quarrelled frequently. On the other hand, Clara was friendly with Mary Eleanor and seems to have given tacit encouragement to brother Frank in his dalliance with her.

Oddly, a much less fraught relationship prospered between Phoebe and her husband's mistress than existed between the sisters-in-law. When, in the February of 1890, Phoebe had been taken ill – the result, claimed the Hogg clan, of a miscarriage brought about, countered the aggrieved Styles tribe (Phoebe's sister, Martha, a domestic at Egham, in Surrey, and her niece, Elizabeth, in service in St John's Wood), by undernourishment, neglect and ill-treatment. Mary Eleanor it was who beat a path to the ailing Phoebe's bedside, laden with delicacies, and bearing charity's basket-load of sympathetic understanding.

Actually, Phoebe and Clara had been frequent friendly visitors to Mary Eleanor's home long before Phoebe's ascension into the branches of the Hogg family tree. And, a later twist, there were even to be quarrels between Frank and Phoebe because of secret notes written by Mary Eleanor to *Phoebe.* Notes which Phoebe would not allow Frank to read!

In lugubrious Kentish and Camden Towns, across the mounting months, life inexorably shaped its pattern towards its pre-ordained grand climacteric. Frank, formerly manager of his mother's grocery shop, sometime dealer in furniture, moved lethargically on to work, sporadically, for his brother, who was in a good way of business as a furniture remover. Phoebe attended to the domestic needs and demands of her slovenly spouse. Mary Eleanor receiving in regular clandestine ecstasy the wayward and perfidious Frank in her back-parlour bedroom, arrived at the conclusion that not only was Frank Hogg essential to her happiness, but that the realisation of *his* happiness must henceforth be her sacred duty. Clara, watching, knowing and sharp-eyed, saw her pampered brother join the phalanx of visitors, all of whom paid, in one way or another, for the privilege of passing into Mary Eleanor's ominous parlour.

So tripped by the months for wife, mistress, and sister. Perhaps, ignorance on the one side maintained, and yearning on the other subdued, they might have lengthened into innocent and happy hypocritical years, but it came to pass in the precarious balance of Mary Eleanor's incessantly brooding and epilepsy-tainted thinking that the resolution of her all-consuming emotional dilemma must be the killing of Phoebe.

Assembled now are all the essential ingredients of Greek tragedy come to Kentish Town. Hellenic horror in Hampstead. The Venus of Camden Town has resolved to snap her flytrap.

*

Thursday, 23 October, 1890.

'D' for 'Do it Day.'

The plan goes into operation. Mary Eleanor scribbles one of those little secret notes.

> Dearest,
>
> Come round this afternoon and bring our little darling. Don't fail.

Phoebe did fail. She could not make it. She lived to die another day. Mary Eleanor was standing, spider awaiting fly, at the door of her ugly yellow brick house, when, by the long flexure of the arm of startling coincidence, her ex-lover Pearcey passed. Why, he asked her, were all the blinds drawn? Her fourteen-year-old brother had died, she said, and the funeral was to be on Tuesday. It was not true. Pearcey offered his condolences, and for the second and last time passed out of her life.

No Phoebe.

Teatime came and went.

Operation aborted.

Friday 24 October, 1890.

'A' for 'Achieve it Day.'

The plan succeeds.

Mary Eleanor, frustrated and hungry for blood, was abroad in good time this morning. At about 11 a.m. in the street where the Hoggs lived, she gave a small boy, little Willie Homes, a penny to deliver a note to Mrs Phoebe Hogg at No. 141. And at half-past three that afternoon, Phoebe, watched by her sister-in-law, Clara, left Prince of Wales Road without telling a soul where she was going. She took baby Phoebe, best-dressed in brown pelisse and beaver bonnet tied with spick blue ribbons, with her in her bassinette.

Advantaged with the clear signposting of hindsight, it is possible to trace that last pilgrimage of the lost. Down Kentish Town Road, large hooped, spiky pram, wheels spinning merrily, smartly into

Royal College Street, sharp right, branch off into the drab street – then Priory Street, since renamed Ivor Street – where, by Priory Place, a railway arch spans, dark Titanic, the exit, and then those last few free yards to the unassuming, three-storey, no basement house, where, all unknowing, she and her little child have a rendezvous to keep with all eternity. Pull the bassinette up the step; park it in the narrow, dark entrance hall.

What comes now can only be dreadful conjecture. One living witness alone emerges from the carnage to tell, and she, the assassin, had sealed the compact of blood with silence. But it must have been that the tall, plain woman, her eighteen-month toddler clutched in her arms, blind to all sign or scent of danger, strangers, too, in those comfortably familiar environs to fear, followed the younger, smaller woman, her friend, trustingly into either the front parlour or the poky kitchen at the hall's end. Was there, one wonders, the pretence of some refinement? Did china wink and tea steam upon a neatly laid table, with thin-cut bread and butter and strawberry jam and scones? There is no knowing. There may or may not have been the charade of afternoon tea.

But what happened before the tea-hour had run its disrupted course is written in splashes of blood on kitchen walls and ceiling – the mute and harrowing tale of a terrifying struggle which frothed and spurted back and forth across that tiny claustrophobic area. The broken window panes, the shattered chinaware, the dented, splintered wood, tell plainly: Phoebe Hogg was not easy to kill. Neighbours heard noise. Bangs. Crashes. A child screaming. And, good neighbour-like, ignored them. 'I keep myself to myself. Never interfere.' What the 'banging and hammering' noises heard around 4 p.m. were, was the plying of poker and knife to the fracturing of a skull, and the cutting of a throat, so deep and severe as almost to hack the head clean from the body, leaving it attached there by only a fragile anchorage of torn skin flap and shredded strands of muscle. 'I make it my business to mind my own business.'

Slaughter over. Mopping-up operations. The washing away of blood. The sponging of rugs. The wiping of walls. The packing away of bodies, mother and child, in the bassinette. Neatly covered. A shroud of freshly-laundered, starch-crisp antimacassar. All cleaned clean away. Washed Pilate hands.

Mary Eleanor was not, as we have said, the same as other women. Her crime was literally insane jealousy. This epileptic Venus consummated her passion with a killing – two killings – of the innocent. She moved isolate, alone, in a big wind, on the quivering wing of madness.

Still, motionless, crouched at web's centre like a poised black widow spider, corpses trussed secure as spider's larder flies, Mary Eleanor, a murderess now, awaits the friendly passport of darkness before putting on her bonnet and starting forth with her perambulator's load of carcasses.

Bump the weighty pram down the front door step. Out into dark and chill October twilight. Did the moon perhaps ride high in the North London sky that night? Did Selene set the animals howling in Regent's Park Zoo? Did Artemis set up an echoing howling through the bone mazes of Mary Eleanor's skull and soul?

The doleful odyssey is well begun. The bassinette wheels whirr and blurr – faster, faster, spokes invisibly revolving, eating up mile after mile of London paving stones. Anonymous streets whisk by. A bent, pale-faced, puffing woman, diminutive, with head drooped right over the pram's high white china handlebar, is to be glimpsed battling in and out of successive gas lamp pools of light, pushing and straining, back braced, up the inclines her overloaded pramful of ... washing.

Screw eyes against the darkness. Peer closer. A little epileptic froth at the corner of Mary Eleanor's mouth. A glazed blue eye deflecting the gaslight's shafts and beams. Up Kentish Town Road she goes – Prince of Wales Road – past the Hoggs' very door – across where Haverstock Hill meets Chalk Farm Road – Adelaide

Road – Eton Avenue – Crossfield Road, where, hard by Adamson Road, on to the pathway beside a building plot, straddled by its starkly roofless part-built house, her dark voices tell her: tip Phoebe out – the mother, not the child.

On then, on a further mile, to dump the wasted body of plump baby Phoebe in the place of the nettles, a wasteland by the Cock and Hoop on Finchley Road. And on, a third mile, to St John's Wood, Hamilton Terrace. There to jettison the blood-sticky baby carriage made hearse. To kick herself free from the perilous basket on wheels. Then home ... home ... home.

But the epic journey is not quite at its end. Disembarrassed of the bassinette and its temporary tenantry, driven by God alone knows what weird buffetings of relief, Mary Eleanor's lightened footsteps pointed her out of the Hampstead darkness to the bright spaces of Great Portland Street. There, at eight o'clock, she was seen and recognised by a girl who worked in a West End drapery house and knew her well. Mrs Pearcey was standing, in the girl's own – innocently symbolic – words, 'on a dark flagstone'. The girl did not approach her. She did not like what she saw. For Mrs Pearcey, whom she knew as normally nice and neat and tidy and ladylike, stood now hat awry, hair rough, gloveless, and with what seemed like dark stained hands. Untidy and dejected, she was looking rapidly from one side to the other in a very peculiar and disinhibited sort of way. She might, the girl thought, have had too much to drink, and she decided to give her a wide berth.

When at last she reached home, a note awaited Mary Eleanor. It was from Frank Hogg. Arriving back from work late that Friday evening, he found neither wife nor baby at Prince of Wales Road, simply a scribbled line on a scrap of paper, 'Look in the saucepan', meaning that his dinner awaited him there. Typically seizing his chance, that slug-pale, hirsute Lothario had slipped round into No. 2 with his latchkey. But he was out of luck there, too. Mary Eleanor was not at home. He took an envelope from the mantelshelf in the bedroom and wrote upon it, 'Twenty past ten. Cannot stay'. Then he slipped quietly out again. Obviously, he did not go into the kitchen. Why should he?

No sign still of the two Phoebes when, soon after 6 a.m. the following morning, Frank Hogg left his home for work. He was not seriously worried. He assumed that they must have gone to visit Phoebe's sick father at Chorleywood. Frank was back at Prince of Wales Road for breakfast at 8 a.m. After swilling down a last cup of tea, the lethargic Frank bestirred himself and lumbered off to Chorleywood to fetch the missus home. He was flummoxed to find that she was not – had not been – there. Meanwhile, sister Clara was reading with rapidly mounting unease an account in that morning's paper of the discovery of the body of a murdered woman in a street in a part of Hampstead close to the route which Phoebe would have taken had she been travelling to Chorleywood from Swiss Cottage station. Moreover, the description of the clothes which the murdered woman was wearing seemed to tally with Phoebe's.

When Frank returned from his fruitless journey, alarmed now and heedful of his sister's suspicions, he asked her to go round to Priory Street and ask Mary Eleanor if she had seen or heard anything of Phoebe. At first she denied all knowledge; but there must have been something in the way that she answered, perhaps some subtlety in her tone of voice, which left shrewd Clara unconvinced. Choosing her words carefully, phrasing her question differently, she put it to Mary Eleanor again. 'Well,' came the reply, 'as you press me, I'll tell you. Phoebe did come at about five o'clock and asked me if I would mind the baby for a little while. I refused, and she then asked me if I would lend her some money. I said I couldn't as I had only a shilling and three halfpence in my purse, but I said she could have the shilling if she liked. I didn't tell you before because Phoebe asked me not to let anybody know she'd been here. That's why I said "No."' Mary Eleanor added that Phoebe had then left the house. The obvious implication was that Phoebe would not want Frank to learn that she had been obliged to try to borrow, as he would almost certainly think that it reflected badly on him.

This conversation puzzled Clara. It did not ring true. For if there was one thing she knew about Phoebe it was that she was absolutely fanatical about not getting into debt. It amounted to a positive phobia. No way would she ask for a loan – even the most trifling one. No, it just went against everything that she knew of her sister-in-law. But Clara was too streetwise and wily a bird to give anything away. She held her whisht, said nothing, although the wick of a tiny light of suspicion had just been ignited in her mind.

'I'm going,' said Clara, 'to ask to see the body of that woman they've found murdered. Just in case. It might be Phoebe. It'll set my mind at rest. Will you come with me?' Pouring scorn on this fancifully premature identification, incredibly Mary Eleanor agreed to go with Clara Hogg to Hampstead police station. They were taken to Hampstead Mortuary. Shrinking together, they peered at the blood-caked mask on the slab. Mary Eleanor, the strong vein cords on either side of her long, thin neck, raised and pulsing like prodded white worms under the stress, grew hysterical. 'That's not her. It's not her. It's not her. Let's go. Let's get out of this place,' she kept repeating, plucking like a crazed harpist at Clara's sleeve and torso.

Clara was not so sure. 'They're her clothes,' she said, eyeing the black cashmere dress, the unmistakable imitation astrakhan-trimmed black jacket, the underclothes, with their neatly embroidered initials, 'P. H.', in red cotton, and, the clincher, the metal brooch with a true lovers' knot.

Their chaperone, Detective Inspector Thomas Bannister, who happened to be in attendance at the mortuary at the time, sponged the crusted blood and matted hair from the face of the thing on the slab, made it more stark and whitely presentable. Bannister brought the women back. They looked again. 'It's Phoebe,' said Clara. She stretched her hand out, fingering the corpse's clothing. 'Oh, don't touch her,' Mary Eleanor screamed, trying to pull Clara away. 'Don't drag me,' said Clara sharply.

Bannister had been watching all this closely. He spoke up. 'Don't drag her about. She can bear it, if you leave her alone.' In his mind the die was cast. He did not, could not, as yet, distil the why and wherefore of it, but the good detective's third eye had snapped open to focus irreversibly on the ruffled russet woman. His poker player's face betraying nothing, he sent the women on with Detective Constable Murray to Portland Town (now called St John's Wood) police station to see the bassinette. It had been standing abandoned by some railings on the pavement of Hamilton Terrace, St John's Wood, before being discovered by Elizabeth Andrews, a cook. That was at 8 p.m. on Friday 24 October – just about an hour after a young clerk named Macdonald, homeward bound at workday's end for Belsize Park, stumbled upon Phoebe's body. Elizabeth Andrews reported her discovery to PC John Rosser, the local beat policeman. The pram was still wet with blood and in it lay a pathetic, half-eaten piece of butterscotch, bearing the marks of a child's teeth. Clara duly identified the pram as having belonged to her sister-in-law.

Under a police sergeant's solicitous escort, the women were taken back to 141 Prince of Wales Road, where an interrogation of them and of Frank Hogg began, and where was revealed, Frank's far from impressive façade rapidly disintegrating, nestling in his pocket the key to No. 2, with all its implications, with which his ever-loving, ever-ready Mary Eleanor had equipped him. The cat had been sprung from the bag. Suspicion's crystals were precipitated into a recognisable form. The protagonists were courteously requested to accompany the officers to Hampstead police station to assist them in their inquiries.

And there Mary Eleanor gradually emerged as the most significant figure. Would she, asked Detective Inspector Bannister, object to one or two of his men inspecting her apartments? 'Not at all,' she said, 'but I would like to go with them.' So, at about three o'clock that Saturday afternoon, while Bannister, accompanied by Superintendent Beard and Mr Melville Macnaghten, went to the Hoggs' home to make a search, off she went in a cab with Sergeant Nursey and Detective Constable Edward Parsons to Priory Street.

Their arrival was discreet. Mary Eleanor had always done her best to maintain high level discretion on her home ground. The persona which she had laboured to project there was one of refinement and respectability. Sheltering behind the deliberately retained style and status of *Mrs* Pearcey, she had contrived for herself a wholesome bunch of bogus relatives, giving it out that the elderly gentleman – Mr Crichton – who visited her every Monday was her father, that Frank Hogg was her brother, Phoebe Hogg her sister-in-law, and one of her other regular gentlemen callers was made known as her husband. Thus did she endeavour to hide the secrets of her professional life from Mr Walter Butler and his wife, Sarah, to whom she sub-let the two upper storeys of her rented house.

Opening as quietly as possible the front door with her latchkey, Mary Eleanor ushered her latest couple of very out-of-the-ordinary gentlemen visitors into her abode. The rooms were small but attractively furnished. On your left as you came into the entrance hall was the front parlour, its window facing on to Priory Street. In it, much prized, stood an upright piano. A folding door opened to a bedroom overlooking a yard at the rear. There was also at the back a bijou kitchen. Tight-lipped, the policemen took in other, less favourable features of the housescape, and Nursey, excusing himself, departed to dispatch an urgent telegram to Bannister. Parsons stayed with Mary Eleanor in the parlour, doing his best to engage her in conversation. She spoke, misty-eyed, of her 'poor, dear, dead Phoebe', whom she had loved so much, and rambled on in maudlin fashion about the 'dear baby', who was just beginning to prattle 'oh, so prettily', and of whom there was still no sign. Then, suddenly bored, she crossed to the cottage piano and began to play on it and sing. This could well have been a classic display of *la belle indifference* of the hysteric, had she been an hysteric; but, weighing all the diagnostic symptoms, the scales seem to come very decidedly down in the territory of true psychosis.

On receipt of Nursey's telegram, Detective Inspector Bannister came hurrying over to Priory Street. Guided by his sergeant, he raked through the blood-spattered kitchen, finding there, in a table drawer, two fearsome carving knives, their handles stained darkly with blood, a recently washed apron and skirt, and a vermilion-smeared rug, reeking strongly of paraffin. There was also a poker – long, heavy, ring-handled – encrusted with blood and matted hair. The curtains were missing; the window panes broken. The curtains he found, incarnadined, in an outhouse, stowed away with a blood-stiffened tablecloth. And in the dustbin, secreted away, but awaiting discovery, like the single vital clue in a classic detective story, a button. Distinctively embossed with a Grecian figure playing the lyre, it matched those on Phoebe's jacket, one of which was missing from the sleeve. Face set into the expression of grim severity elicited by the less pleasing bonuses of his office, he made his way to the parlour, where the notes of music splashed merrily around, like jolly goldfish darting in a bowl.

Mary Eleanor was seated at the piano, fixed and wooden as a fairground automaton; a painted-on smile, an epileptic jerking of hands, head, and neck; an alternating whistling and slightly off-key crooning. There was something eerie and chilling about the set scene. She seemed smilingly distraught, her speech a chuckling incoherence. Like a pianola possessed, the piano went on automatically chipping out chunks of meaningless melody, as in answer to his solemn questioning about the gratuitous blood-splotchings in the kitchen she chanted, reminiscent of the nursery rhyme's knife-wielding farmer's wife, 'Killing mice. Killing mice. Killing mice'.

She struck Bannister as being patently mad as a March hare, but he had, of course, no alternative but to arrest her. 'Mrs Pearcey, I am going to arrest you for the wilful murder of Mrs Hogg last night, and also on suspicion for the wilful murder of the female child of Mrs Hogg.'

Mary Eleanor jumped up from the piano stool. 'You can arrest me if you like. I'm quite willing to go with you. But I think you've made a great mistake.' He led her quietly away to Kentish Town police station. On the way she told him, 'I wouldn't do such a thing. I wouldn't hurt anyone.'

Is it not, as Miss Tennyson Jesse has so astutely descried, a Zola-esque tale? Its whole atmosphere is of sordidness and domestic intrigue, its milieu of lower-working-class struggle against poverty and failing onslaughts upon the bastions of self-betterment. Is not Mary Eleanor the veritable Thérèse Raquin *britannique*? A woman 'remorseless, eaten up with her own desires, and with all the persistence of an animal with its nose on the trail'. She was rightly to be feared, and if the word of Phoebe's sister, Martha Styles, is to be relied upon, and there is every reason to believe that it may be, likewise the confirmatory word of her niece, Elizabeth, then Phoebe did in fact experience the warning pricklings of that self-preservatory fear. Some three weeks before her successful dispatchment, Phoebe had received one of Mary Eleanor's mystery notes, this one inviting a rendezvous at a public house. Phoebe went there to receive a further invitation to accompany Mary Eleanor on an excursion to Southend that very day, in order to look over an empty house which she said she was thinking of taking. Atrophied, dim out of somewhere in our human primeval past, some premonitory instinct pealed its caution. Phoebe declined. Afterwards she told Martha, 'If I'd gone to Southend no one would have thought of looking out for me there in an empty house.' An odd remark. Was Phoebe, one wonders, perhaps inclined to be psychic?

It was early on the morning of Sunday 6 October that the body of baby Phoebe was found face down in the place of the nettles – where Oliver Smith, the tinker, grazed his ponies. She was fully clothed, except for a missing shoe and stocking. There were no signs of violence on the little body. Certain marks visible on the child's neck were due to the pressure of its clothing, which was tight on its plump, well-nourished body. Phoebe Hanslope was conveyed to Hampstead Mortuary, where she was formally identified by a very distressed Frank Hogg. The precise cause of the child's death has never been decided. Dr Augustus Joseph Pepper, that same specialist, who, exactly twenty years later, would give evidence for the prosecution at the trial of Dr Crippen, testified that the cause of Baby Phoebe's death was either smothering, suffocation, or exposure to the cold. He did not think that the child could have been carried in the pram at the same time as its mother because 'the perambulator was not covered with blood and the child's clothes were not so covered, as they must have been, had it been in the vehicle'. This does not present an especially persuasive argument, for it surely only required that the child's body be separately wrapped for bloodstaining to be entirely avoided. The baby could have been suffocated under her mother's corpse in the pram. She could have been smothered beneath a cushion at Priory Street. Or, just possibly, she could have been tossed out alive to die of exposure on the Finchley Road waste ground. There is no way of knowing. Let us pray that, whichever way, it was swift and merciful.

At Kentish Town policed station Mary Eleanor was charged and searched. When she removed her gloves her hands were seen to have cuts and scratches on them. She was wearing two rings. One was of brass. The other, a broad, gold wedding ring, was at first thought to be the one that had been dragged from Phoebe Hogg's finger. But, although Mrs Hogg's ring was in fact missing, there was sound evidence to show that the rings on Mary Eleanor's fingers were both her own. Her underclothes, apparently unchanged for twenty-four hours, bore quite considerable bloodstaining. They, together with the rest of her clothes, were taken away, and she was supplied with workhouse garments in their place. Sarah Sawhill, who searched female prisoners at Kentish Town police station, subsequently told of a conversation with Mary Eleanor. She stated that the prisoner had remarked to her that she had been affronted by Mrs Hogg, who had apparently cut her in the street, but who had, in response to a note, come round to tea between four and a quarter past. As they were having tea, Mrs Hogg made a remark that Mary Eleanor did not like, and 'one word brought up another. Perhaps I had better not say any more.'

Mary Eleanor Pearcey, still wearing her dark workhouse clothes and a green straw hat with matching ribbon, was arraigned before the magistrates at Marylebone police court on 27 October, and after the usual adjournments and series of remands to Holloway Gaol, was committed, on 18 November to the Central Criminal Court. Her trial was set down for Monday 1 December 1890, before Mr Justice Denman, sitting at the Old Bailey. She was defended by Mr Arthur Hutton, instructed by Mr F. Freke Palmer. Mr Forrest Fulton represented the Crown.

Mary Eleanor took her place in the dock, wearing now a black dress, over which was a brown buttoned cloak. She looked, with her hair brushed attractively back and her shining blue eyes, pleasing and intelligent, yet she seemed curiously indifferent to everything. The stoic way in which she conducted herself throughout mirrored the correctness of her solicitor's judgement that she had 'as much resolution as twenty ordinary women'. She sat between the wardresses, calm, remote, dignified and enigmatic. Mostly she stared straight in front of her, hands folded in lap, only an occasional slight twitching of her mouth or jumping of the orbicular muscle beneath her lower eyelid betraying the overwhelming feeling of terror she was masking. Her demeanour was in marked contrast to that of the sobbing hulk, Hogg, in the witness box. He may, as he let it be known, have been a regular church worshipper, she may have been flighty and immoral – amoral is possibly a better word – but there could be no argument as to which was the more sterling character. Her spineless lover cut a shoddy and unpopular figure in, and out of, court. There was something ineluctably antipathetic about him. Judge and jury seeming to disregard his tragic and bereaved situation, continually referred to him as 'the man Hogg'. Public sympathy with him ran low, too. His was surely the uniquely unwelcome distinction of being hissed, booed and hooted at as, drenched by pouring rain, he attended the burial of his wife and child in St Pancras Cemetery. There were, of course, those who were convinced that Hogg had had a podgy hand in the slaying of Phoebe. Physically, he absolutely did not. He had an alibi of police-tested platinum. Throughout the crucial time he had removed himself on a removal job far, far away from the heady purlieus of Camden and Kentish Towns. What is more, Mary Eleanor herself left behind a letter, addressed to Clara Hogg, in which she categorically absolved the faithless Frank of all knowledge of, never mind participation in, the elimination of Phoebe.

That some other hypnotised male might have rendered assistance in one way or another has always been bruited. There is not the smallest evidence for it, but many have felt that another should have sat beside Mary Eleanor in the dock, and possibly stood beside her on the scaffold.

The trial ended on the fourth day. The judge delivered himself of a two-and-three-quarter-hour summing-up. It did not lean conspicuously to the prisoner's favour, but neither was it unfair. The jury retired at 1.20 p.m. They were out fifty-two minutes.

Their verdict went unanimously against Mary Eleanor. The chaplain, whose face at such times became the face of doom, the face of death itself, shuffled forward, servile to secular authority, to do his Christian duty with the black cap – to place it ritually atop the judge's bewigged head. Mary Eleanor heard the old, callously worded formula of judicial death passed upon her with that identical impassivity, a lack of affect, which she had most bizarrely displayed the entire trial through. Then she disappeared into the black maw of the prison house, there to see out her three clear Sundays.

During that ultimate trinity of weeks, as she lay condemned in Newgate, she requested repeatedly to be permitted to see Frank Hogg. At last, as she entered the very shadow of the noose, all hopes of appeal and clemency drained away, a written order was forthcoming granting permission for him to visit her between two and four o'clock of the last afternoon the law had sanctioned her on earth. Her mother and her sister, Charlotte Amy, came to take their final farewell. They left. She waited, flushed and excited as a bride. No Frank. Time passed. He did not appear. Overcome, crumpling for the first and only time, she slumped upon her bed in the condemned cell, her hands over her face, and wept and wept and wept.

At a few minutes before eight o'clock on the bitterly cold and foggy morning of Tuesday 23 December 1890, the prisoner's 'passing bell' sounding its heavy tolling upon the frost-steeped air, the knot of death's invigilators came soft-footed to Mary Eleanor's cell door. She met them, as she had all the tragedies of her short, brave life, face on, with the courtesy of fortitude. Upright, unflinching, she took the place prescribed for her by protocol, following in procession behind the sheriff and the whey-faced chaplain, moving with dignity to her chalk-marked spot.

Mr Hangman Berry received her in his shed with great politeness. 'Good morning, Madam,' he said, shaking her hand. Then, with compassionate celerity, pinioned and hooded her, and, ere the last note's echo had shivered from St Sepulchre's clock, Mary Eleanor had flown and the black flag had struck, flapping, from its mast. Later, the heavy-booted warders would hustle her empty shell away beneath those other black flags, that paved Dead Man's Walk.

Mary Eleanor herself is said to have commented to the chaplain, the Reverend Mr Duffield, before they broke her neck, 'The sentence is just, but the evidence was false.'

But *was* it? Was she not, if there ever was one, a suitable case for treatment in Broadmoor? Albeit, the defence of epilepsy has since become a forensic cliché, but the Pearcey case gives one pause. It is an undisputed fact that Mary Eleanor had actually been subject to severe attacks of epilepsy since birth. Her mother had also suffered from fits before her daughter was born. On three or four occasions, while in a state of epileptic trance, Mary Eleanor had attempted to commit suicide. Once, as we have already seen, by hanging; twice by taking poison. After these epileptic seizures, manifestations of violence invariably ensued, but when the paroxysm had passed she could remember nothing of what had taken place.

On the Sunday preceding the murders –19 October – she had complained very much of headaches, and said that she felt she was going out of her mind. It was the opinion of the eminent alienist, Dr L. Forbes Winslow, that the brutality of the murders, together with the violence and strength exhibited, indicated the probability of the crimes having been committed while in a condition of acute, violent epileptic trance. This accorded well with the widely felt doubt that a normal woman could have brought to bear the sheer physical force and fury of the attack. Mary Eleanor Pearcey was not a big, powerful woman; from what *normal* source could she have recruited the demonic strength required to wield poker and knife with such devastating savagery, to lift and crush the bigger, heavier woman's dead weight body into the bassinette – even allowing for the fact that 'folding' it in would be made easier because the head could be doubled back on its broken stalk of loose hanging skin – and then, on top of all that, to wheel the heavy burden of death at least 3 miles, much of it uphill?

Mary Eleanor's persistent denials of all knowledge of the crimes would, if true, support a diagnosis of epileptic fury. At the very end, on the eve of her execution, all further need of play-acting and pretence evaporated, a day so cold and dark that her last meeting with her mother and sister at Newgate was permitted in the warmth and comfort of the Chief Warden's room. Beseeched by her mother to tell her the truth, she said, 'Mother, I knew nothing about it. Oh, Mother, as I expect to meet my Maker in a few hours, I cannot tell a lie. I know nothing whatever about the murder. If I knew, I would willingly say so for my own sake now.'

In this context it is worth recalling the evidence of Mary Eleanor's Priory Street tenants, the Butlers. They said that they remembered stumbling against a perambulator which was partially blocking the passage of the entrance hall of No. 2. That was at about six o'clock on the evening of Friday 24 October. The hall was in darkness, although a light was generally kept burning there. Mrs Pearcey called out 'Mind!', and Sarah Butler had answered 'All right.' When Walter Butler, a labourer, returned home from work a little later, Mrs Pearcey had immediately appeared in the hall saying, 'Let me lead you Mr Butler, as there is a perambulator here,' and she took him by the hand and guided him past it. Both the Butlers thought that their landlady was behaving oddly. 'She talked very funny and looked boozed,' said Walter Butler. And that is consistent with a person in an epileptic episode.

It must be said that, by order of the Home Secretary, she was, in fact, on 19 December, medically examined. These medical gentlemen, attached to the Home Office, who 'possibly had not the same interest in the case that I had,' writes Dr Forbes Winslow, 'and were not so cognisant of the actual facts, and who had not been visited by her relations and friends, or knew the history of her case, or perused any documents bearing on it ... were simply sent to form an opinion as to the objective, not the subjective, condition of the prisoner.' They found, after spending one hour with her, no medical reason to interfere with the law's taking its course. Mrs Pearcey's solicitor said, 'I felt very much disappointed with the Home Secretary's decision because of the extraordinary mass of reliable information which I had collected to show that the prisoner was insane.'

All her life Mary Eleanor had a dream.

'Ever since I can remember I've been haunted by a queer dream ... It comes and goes again, but I'm never without it very long. In that dream I see a great archway, and through it I go to darkness, dreadful darkness, that seems to hide something more terrible beyond. I've never seen that arch yet so far as I know, but some day I shall come to it, and then my dream will come true.'

Was it that grand railway arch spanning the end of Prior Street through which she trundled her terrible pram? Or was it the great frowning arch of Newgate, through which she walked to the gallows? There is no saying for sure. But one thing is certain. Mary Eleanor had found her archway.

*

A curious codicil.

When, on the eve of her execution, her solicitor came to bid her goodbye, she asked him to insert for her a small notice in a Madrid newspaper'

M.E.C.P. – Last wish of
M.E.W. Have not betrayed.

Asked by him if this message was relevant to the case, she answered, 'Never mind.' Mr Freke Palmer was afterwards to say that he understood it to refer to a marriage which had taken place between Mary Eleanor Wheeler and one E.C.P., whose name she had taken an oath never to divulge, and who was to remain for all time the faint enigma around which was wrapped the enduring mystery of Mary Eleanor Pearcey. The keeper of the archway, one might almost say ...

12

THE BROUGHTY FERRY AFFAIR

Sealed of the tribe of the eccentric, old Miss Jean Milne, living her singular eremitical life in the big, neglected mansion, in its two acres of circumambient grounds, was the theoretical victimologist's delight. There she sat, like a fly at the centre of its vacuum, begging a spider to throw its lethal web about her. And one October day in 1912, the anonymous spider obliged.

The case began with a sharp postman's observation that the letter box of Elmgrove House, Broughty Ferry, Dundee, which for a fortnight he had been conscientiously feeding, had, on Saturday 2 November 1912, reached a state of satiety. This circumstance he decided it to be his bounden duty to convey to the local constabulary.

Legend required that the reclusive Miss Milne, despite the fact that she was a mere sixty-five years of age, must be 'Old' Miss Milne, as it also requires that, despite a lack of true evidence, she must likewise be labelled 'eccentric'. 'Uncommon' might be a more apt appellative.

She was the only sister and heiress of a wealthy tobacco manufacturer of Dundee, who had died nine years before. Though well provided with money, she chose the simple life, occupying the merest fraction of the fourteen rooms in her late brother's rambling mansion, employing no servants, using only candles for illumination, living alone and isolate behind the screen of trees and shrubbery.

What small idiosyncratic foibles – if that be not too strong a word – marked her out as individual were a love for gay and girlish clothes and a positive passion for magazines and devotional literature. It was her harmless, but perilous, practice to sit reading late at night in her religious library, blinds up, curtains undrawn, a tempting bait for any ill-intentioned trespasser a-prowl in the thickets of her shrubbery.

When, on the morning of the Sabbath, the police forced an entry to brooding Elmgrove House, they found Miss Milne silently awaiting them in the hall. She lay, fully dressed, her ankles bound tightly together with a curtain cord, at the foot of the stairs, partly covered with a sheet. There were wounds upon her head, from which blood had flowed freely.

Beside her body lay the sitting-room poker, bloodstained. The wires of the nearby telephone had been cut, obviously with the pair of garden shears lying next to it. The curtains of the glass door in the hall had been carefully tied together in such a way as to prevent anyone outside from seeing through into the interior of the house. All around was the evidence of a savage struggle. Miss Milne had not yielded up her life easily. It was estimated that she had been dead for at least three weeks. She had last been seen alive on 15 October.

On the evening of Wednesday 16 October, Mr David Kinnear, an elder of St Andrew's United Free Church, of which Miss Milne was a member, called at Elmgrove with her communion card. He found the place in darkness and his repeated knockings and ringings went unanswered.

From this, and other pieces of evidence, the police thought that it was most probable that the crime had been committed on the night of 15 October. But presently there appeared one Alexander Troup, a former gardener at Elmgrove, who stated that, calling at the house in his capacity of collector for the Broughty Benevolent Trust on the morning of 21 October, he had seen, partly hidden by the curtain, a woman at an upper window whom he took to be Miss Milne. He rang the doorbell twice. There was no reply. He had returned again that same afternoon. He then noticed that the cover on the front-door lock which had been down in the morning was now up. That meant, he thought, that a key must have been inserted in the front-door lock in the intervening time between his calls.

The motive for the murder was obscure. Certainly it was not robbery. No fewer than seven diamond rings cluttered the fingers of the dead woman. Other valuable rings, together with her gold watch and chain, lay open and unmolested upon her bedroom dressing table. In a drawer there was a purse containing £17 in gold. No item of silver, nor any other object of worth, was missing from the house. The theory of invasive tramp or peripatetic chance-seizing burglar held no water – or blood.

A clue which only added to overwhelming official bafflement was the recovery from the ashes of the dining-room grate of the remains of a half-smoked cigar. Also, although Miss Milne was of notoriously inhospitable habits, the table was laid for high tea for two persons, the centrepiece of which rare feast was a twopenny meat pie. Ergo, clanked out the mechanism of police reasoning, the lady 'expected, and received, company, and her visitor was of the male persuasion'.

Then came the discovery that, shortly before her death, Miss Milne had ordered a supply of whisky and wine from a local dealer, explaining that she was expecting 'a gentleman friend to dinner'.

The keen eye of Detective Lieutenant John Thomson Trench, of the Glasgow City Police, who had been called in by the mazed locals, spotted that the blouse and undergarments of the deceased had been perforated by some sharp instrument, which he thought was probably a two-pronged fork. Such an instrument, a carving fork from the household set in the sitting-room sideboard, had been found on the hall floor, half-hidden beneath a trunk.

The picture was to be further complicated by the revelation of the periodic 'globe-trotting' proclivities of the staid châtelaine of Elmgrove. Apparenly, every so often she would be seized with a lust for life, with a capital L – the capital being London – and off, unobserved, to the flesh pots would slip, in girlish lamb's finery, the retiring spinster of Broughty Ferry. She was known to take up temporary residence at such metropolitan haunts of splendour as the Bonnington Hotel, in Southampton Row, and the Strand Palace Hotel.

She had been at the Strand Palace in April, May and June 1912, and had expressed her intention of returning to town for Christmas. She had also, in September 1912, gone on a cruise aboard the *Chevalier*, from Glasgow round the coast to Inverness.

There was some evidence, too, albeit of the hearsay brand, that Miss Jean, turning kittenish, had confided a gigglish account of an affair of the heart, or sweetheart, indicating that she was very likely to be getting a 'companion – for life'.

Had the dream, born perhaps at some *thé dansant*, turned into a nightmare? Was her prospective late bridegroom Death?

These riddles Trench sagely pondered, casting about, always casting about, for wisps and shreds of clues.

To begin with, there was no sign of any break-in at Elmgrove House. The windows were all – had been for years – hermetically sealed. Doors and locks were left untampered. Like Miss Gilchrist in the Oscar Slater case – another in which Lieutenant Trench was deeply involved – the victim had with her own hand unbarred the door to death and had herself admitted her assassin. The probability, too, is that in neither case was the visitor a stranger.

Trench noted the garden shears beside the violated telephone, the rake and hoe nearby. Had she perhaps been gardening before the visitation? Miss Milne was known to have had a taste for gardening.

There was surely a clue in the cutting of the telephone wires. The instrument was serviced by a party line, which meant that it was impossible to disconnect it by simply removing the receiver. The only way was to cut the wires. That the murderer did so suggested that he knew the instrument.

Trench's opinion was that Miss Milne's assailant had not intended to kill her. He must have thought her merely stunned. Otherwise, why tie her up and immobilise the telephone? Corpses do not walk or make telephone calls.

The piled-up contents of the letter box proved to consist mainly of begging letters, but it was rumoured – the police never pronounced officially on this – that the correspondence did reveal the identity of Miss Milne's London 'gentleman friend', a certain dashing American. This never, however, came to anything.

A local housemaid, Margaret Campbell, and a scavenger in the employment of the burgh, James Don, both came forward, tempted perhaps by the offer of £100 reward, to state that they had seen a strange man in, and emerging from, the grounds of Miss Milne's house. A notice was issued bearing the descriptions supplied by these witnesses.

Another who claimed to have had a privileged peep at the mysterious stranger was John Wood, a jobbing gardener who had worked occasionally for Miss Milne during the last six years of her life. She had, he said, spoken to him of a gentleman; he thought she had said that he was a German tea-planter, whom she had met in the Strand Palace, and Wood said that he had met this man at Elmgrove on 19 September, the day before Miss Milne left for her cruise, when the gentleman called upon her there.

It was now that something very strange happened – an event which might easily have had fatal consequences for an innocent party. A copy of the reward bill already referred to was routinely delivered to the prison authorities at Maidstone, in Kent. Casting custodial eyes over their current guests, they alighted upon a 'mystery' Colonial, giving the name of Charles Warner, and the address of 210 Wilton Avenue, Toronto. The occasion of this gentleman's lodging with them was his deliberate avoidance of payment for his lodging elsewhere, to wit, the Rose and Crown at Tonbridge, the landlord of which he had attempted to bilk of his seven shillings due bed-and-board money. This crafty Canadian they perceived to fit peculiarly aptly the descriptive bill. They photographed him and despatched his likeness to Scotland. As a result, a trainload of five witnesses was sent down to Maidstone to attend an identification parade. All five unhesitatingly fingered him, as the Americans say.

Taken thereafter to London, Warner was confronted by six more witnesses who had seen the 'dashing American' in company with Miss Milne at the Bonnington and Strand Palace hotels. His persuasive Canadian accent notwithstanding, not one of them identified him as the man. Nevertheless, Warner was conveyed to Dundee.

But Trench was not satisfied. He felt intuitively that Warner was innocent. He listened intently to the tale that gentleman told of having come over to 'do' Europe. He had visited Paris, Amsterdam, Brussels and Antwerp. Where had he been around 16 October last? In Antwerp. Could he prove it? Well ... then Warner remembered. Yes, at the very time of the murder, having run clean out of money, he had pawned his waistcoat for one franc.

Trench left immediately for Antwerp, found the pawnshop, handed over one franc-plus, and returned to Dundee, under his arm a brown paper parcel containing the perfect alibi. Charles Warren was off the hook. Never, it must be said, was anyone found to take his place in that uncomfortable situation. The Broughty Ferry mystery remains just that.

13

THE MIDNIGHT GARDENER

Like everything else about the neat suburban villa in Erith Road, Belvedere, on the London lip of north-west Kent, the garden was immaculate. House and garden reflected the obsessional personality of their owner, Charles Frederick Lewis, aged sixty, educational officer of Erith, who lived there with his wife, Maude, two years younger, and twenty-year-old Freda, whom they had adopted after her father perished in the *Titanic* disaster.

But to the uncompromisingly critical eye of Charles Lewis, that perfect garden lacked one vital feature – a lily pond; for, like Monet, Mr Lewis found in the vision of their still, shining surfaces and curling green delight a most soothing prospect.

So it was that for nearly a month now he had been hard at work in his spare time, helped by Maude and Freda, preparing the foundations for the kidney-shaped lily pond of his dreams, which this Whit weekend of 1931 should see completed.

The stone nymphs lay prone in waiting on the lawn. All that was needed now was a final thick layer of cement.

Whit Monday came – and went.

Of Mr Lewis, upon whose creative activities the neighbours

were inclined to keep an interested – not to say envious – eye, there was no sign. What should have been the great celebratory day of the pool passed dully. The fact of the matter was that Mr Lewis, whose neurotic energy permitted him no single moment's luxury of idleness, had already embarked upon the next job-in-waiting on his do-it-yourself list, re-papering the dining room.

Had, however, his inquisitive neighbours extended their curtain-peeping vigil into the dark hours of Monday night, their persistence would have been rewarded. For it was then, when all was still, and only the blank and empty windows of the music school on the one side, and those of the adjoining villa on the other, stared blindly, that the furtive, burdened figure of the midnight gardener appeared, shambling along the 50 yards leading from the house to the half-finished lily pond.

The following morning – Tuesday 2 June – a Mr John Davidson walked into a shipping office in Cannon Street and booked a passage to Leith aboard the London & Edinburgh Shipping Company's steamer the *Royal Scot*, sailing from Wapping on 5 June. That Tuesday morning also, Mr Lewis telephoned the principal of the college at Stockwell, where Freda was training to become a teacher.

'Freda will not return tonight,' he told her curtly. 'I will write to you about it.' And abruptly rang off. The letter which arrived next day said that Freda had met with an accident and might not be back for some time.

Letters from Charles Lewis began to arrive, too, at the homes of various relatives. They said that both Maude and Freda had had accidents and that he would be sending details later.

Then ... nothing. Absolute silence.

On Friday 5 June, one worried relative arrived from Wales to find the house in Erith Road locked and deserted. Thoroughly uneasy, he went to Blackheath Road police station. The police telephoned Erith Education Authority. Mr Lewis had not, they said, been back to his office since the holiday. He had rung up saying that his wife was dead.

Hearing this, the police went round to Erith Road. They forced a window and entered the house. There was no sign of any mischief. The furniture piled in the centre of the dining room and the stripped walls indicated that the energetic Mr Lewis had already set about his next DIY task. The three beds in the house had been slept in, but were unmade. Also, and it was something that alerted suspicion, one sheet from each bed was missing. A thorough search of the whole place revealed no soiled sheets anywhere. Police minds turned to ready-made shrouds.

Neighbours were questioned. No one had seen Mr Lewis, Mrs Lewis, Freda nor, come to think of it, their little terrier, for days. Glancing out of the window, Superintendent Brown's eye was caught by the flapping of tarpaulin half-covering the unfinished lily pond.

> When I look into the fish ponds in my garden,
> Methinks I see a thing arm'd with a rake
> That seems to strike at me.
>
> — Webster, *The Duchess of Malfi*

With pickaxes, the police it was who struck, and raked aside the hard-set concrete ... and there the 'things' were: two women, the dog, and the three missing sheets.

Sir Bernard Spilsbury's post-mortem attributed all three deaths to cyanide. A chemist in Eardley Road, Belvedere, reported selling, six weeks before, two and a half ounces of cyanide – for use as an insecticide – to Mr Lewis, who had duly signed the poisons book.

Lewis's description was circulated. Height: Six feet. Slim build. Hair: Grizzled grey. Eyes: Grey. Gold-rimmed spectacles. Walks with a limp, suggestive of a withered leg.

The *Royal Scot* was 14 miles north of Whitby when one of his six fellow passengers asked Mr Davidson sympathetically about his injured leg. Davidson reacted oddly; he rose without a word and limped out of the smoking room.

A steward, who happened to be just passing by Mr Davidson's cabin, heard a splash. He caught a glimpse of the man in the water. Mr Davidson had jumped overboard.

The ship stopped. Boats were lowered. They searched in vain.

Mr Davidson was, of course, Charles Frederick Lewis.

When the dead man's affairs were looked into it was revealed that, a few years before, there had been a discrepancy of some hundreds of pounds in the Erith Education Committee's accounts, of which he had charge. Colleagues recalled an angry discussion between Lewis and his chief, Mr Flux. Flux had so worked himself up that he had a seizure, lost the power of speech, and died soon afterwards.

Now, an auditor's investigation showed irregularities amounting to between £500 and £600 which, beginning before the death of Mr Flux, continued right up to the time of the disappearance of Mr Lewis.

Haunted by guilt and fear of exposure, and having issued, as it were, an irrefutable Tennysonian invitation to his wife – that to include daughter and dog – Charles Frederick Lewis elected to write with his own hand a Strindbergian end to the affair: to balance the books by total erasure.

14

THE VENENIFEROUS WIDOW OF WINDY NOOK

The very name of the place where the widow had her arachnidan being, Windy Nook, a whilom village embedded now in Felling, a dour suburban stretch on the south bank of the Tyne, just beyond the tentacled embrace of Gateshead, sets pictures flickering through the mind. A monochrome scene, grained and jerky like a 1930s film. The thin, mean wind, the grudging soil, bleak-branched and gale-bent trees, stunted. A miserly terrain that bore and shaped likewise stunted men and women; gnarled in the bud, thin-lipped from long compression, hard-stone-eyed from want. To talk of the greedy, grasping folk of the north-east is out of either ignorance of, or insensitivity to, the keen knife of poverty that sliced life up there down to the tough rind.

It was this chill east side of the industrial North Country that begat that terrible Victorian bogeywoman, Mary Ann Cotton, secret poisoner supreme, Britain's most numerous multicide, until eclipsed by the awful advent of the good Dr Shipman. This is the story of another Mary from County Durham – Mary Elizabeth Wilson.

But, before that, she bore three different surnames, baptismal and married. Marriage, for Mary, was a habit; and a very bad habit – worse for her husbands, four of them, counting in one of the so-called common-law variety. It is the story of a classic poisoning case.

Our harrowing tale begins gently enough, back in the last lingering days of the neo-Georgian twilight, the sadly lamented end of the golden Edwardian afternoon. It is 1914 – *before* 5 August. Mary is twenty-two and newly-wed. Her husband, John Knowles, was the son of the house where she had been employed as a domestic servant. Those were the times when even the moderately well-to-do could afford to keep an underpaid, overworked drudge. She must have seen the match as self-betterment. Not that John Knowles was ever to amount to much. He found work, and his level, as a labourer. He neither aspired nor ascended. The marriage was not, by all accounts, a happy one. A given reason for this – its threadbare provision aside – is because Mary's husband was such a bad-tempered man. Nevertheless, it, and she, endured. It lasted for over forty years – nominally, anyway. As one commentator felicitously put it, 'They remained living under the same roof, although not on the same mattress.'

In fact, a marital escape hatch had opened, and deliverance out of bucolic ennui appeared, in the lucky brush-flaunting shape of a chimney sweep. It is an old north country superstition that to meet a sweep going to or from the church on your wedding day is very lucky. In Mary's case, the meeting with John George Russell, sweep, long after her wedding day certainly seemed lucky to her. He arrived at the Knowles' as innocent lodger, but had soon graduated to guilty bed and bawd – with John *primus* as overlooking *mari complaisant*. 'As long as his meals arrived on the table in good time, and his shirts, socks and other laundry were washed, aired and put away in the old-fashioned chest of drawers, he was apparently content', is how the late Leonard Gribble most neatly summarised the domestic status quo.

In such a state of sexual truce, live and let love, the assisted passage of marriage defied the traps and perils imported by the years. The thunder of the guns of the First World War receded. The holocaust of the Second World War blazed itself out. Mary and her two Johnnies survived unscathed into the blighted landscape of post-war, unfit-for-heroes-to-live-in Blighty.

The year is 1955. Mrs Mary Knowles is still an ordinary – albeit sexually beleaguered – north country housewife. But something extraordinary is about to happen to her – something irreversible. She is about to opt out of the common run of normal, decent humanity, to elect a moral excommunication. From now on she will be different from those with whom she rubs shoulders in shops, on buses, in pubs. She will have abandoned her birthright place in the tidy ranks of humankind, her safe, stolid niche on the working-class shelf, and joined the bizarre, tatterdemalion underworld of Boschian *terata*. As she stands, aged sixty-three, upon the edge of the horrendous, poised for the performance of the act that will transform her into an outcast, let us take a closer look at this woman.

We see a plain, pinkish-cheeked, rather stout and homely body, tight-curlered, gingery-streaked-with-grey hair, bright calculating eyes, parsimonious lips drawn back to show a dental crockery so obviously false that it looks as though it has been put together from flat slabs of porcelain. A guarded and unforgiving face. A self-possessed woman, known to be grasping, earthy in a North Country way, addicted to trashy romantic magazines and paperback novelettes picked up from market bookstalls; even more addicted to the bottle. Hardly a femme fatale, but, as events were to prove, there must have been some quality of magnetism there.

For forty-one years this unprepossessing matron maintained a relatively normal balance. She had her boudoir secrets, but they were neither rare nor exotic. Then something changed ... or broke. She found within herself a dreadful potential, a terrifying and cruel capacity for evil. Are we in the realms of freak physiology, mischievous endocrines – or what religious men call demonic possession? Perhaps selfishness multiplied by itself to the power of infinite insanity? But no one has ever used that word about Mary Elizabeth. They have just called her wicked.

It was in the early summer, with the sullen moorland countryside kissed by sunshine and showers to its loveliest and most misleading, with the *huis clos* of the seedy little house and its tenantry of two spent, equally seedy, little old men reaching a psychologically claustrophobic climacteric of burdensome boredom, that Mary discovered Rodine, the would-be widow's phosphoric friend.

In July, her husband fell sick.

In August, he died.

The flowers on John Knowles' grave had barely withered, before his lightly grieving widow began to confide to the ears of her sympathising neighbours her feeling that it was time she had a change. In fact, she intimated, her late husband had agreed with her about the desirability of making a move. That was just before he died. Now, after what had happened, with the sad memories clinging to what had been their home these many years, she really did want to leave. The neighbours nodded in sage and sympathetic understanding – of course, poor thing.

And so she moved. Not far, but to a new house; a new start. Well … almost. There was still one more change pending. John Russell, her long-time lover-lodger, she took with her. Not, however, without duly warning, 'I may have to put up the rent. But that's only because things are more pricey now. Otherwise, everything will be just the way it was.'

Lies.

The thread which had snapped – been snapped – in the old home had changed the arrangement, the weft and warp and tensions, of the other threads in the Widow Knowles' life. And the thread which had acted for all those cabined years as puppet-string to her compliant sweep was now affected, very noticeably weakened and grown thin in the hands of the puppet-mistress. It. too, was soon to break.

Autumn came. The moors turned brown and gold. Then winter arrived, early, pencilling the land with tracings of frost and snow. The cold winds blew. At Christmas it was John's turn to take to his bed – alone. The unfestive fact is that Mary, having found how easy it was to dispose of the unwanted man in her life, and finding another now not precisely welcome, decided to try again. This, and her subsequent conduct, seemed to set at totally contradictory variance the old adage, which it restated as: 'If at first you *do* succeed, try, try – and try – again.' She had now determined to make, as it were, a clean sweep. Russell's indisposition worsened. Before January 1956 was out, so was he.

It may have struck the good people of Windy Nook that there was something a bit strange, a bit fishy, about two men who had been living under the same roof dying in quick succession like that. But it passed as tragic coincidence. Anyhow, folk up there were used to the good Lord's jolly jokes! And, after all, they were both old men, and the doctor had certified natural causes. Moreover, both men were of humble station in life, and the terrible, frightening, pathetic thing is that once they had been translated into anonymous humps on the smooth sward of the Durham burying ground, the community in which they had been known for upwards of three score years soon forgot that they had ever lived.

With Johns *primus* and *secundus* both dead within five months, the double widow promptly set about the sanitary dusting away of memories. She had her late lover's room, from wainscot to ceiling, refurbished. Fresh paint. Bright new wallpaper. 'It isn't as though he passed away because he had anything contagious, or infectious, is it? But you can't take chances with health, I always say,' she explained to her street acquaintances.

Another winter melted. Spring and the primroses and the

snowdrops arrived. Crocuses thrust green spears up through the coffin-hard frozen ground. Below, the two Johnnies lay sound asleep in their – for the moment – undisturbed earthen beds. Pale sunlight intensified, deepened, and grew warmly stronger. The widow's weeds blossomed into seductive flowers, caressed by a reawakening desire of life. Mary was on the husband hunt again.

Came the summer. It was now that she was introduced to Oliver James Leonard. Estate agent retired, seventy-six years of age. Lodger with the Widow Knowles' friends, Mr and Mrs Connolly, at Hebburn-on-Tyne, about four miles east of Gateshead. Blunt, plain-speaking, crude, Mrs Knowles minced no words. Out with it point-blank. 'Has the old bugger any money?' she asked Mrs Connolly. 'A little, as far as I know', was the reply that sealed Mr Leonard's fate.

The Widow Knowles was a fast worker. That same week, lamb to the slaughter, Leonard was off to lodge with her. He was not all lamb, though. He was of a bossy nature. A few prodromal sparks flew. A row blazed. Three days later Mrs Knowles was knocking on Alice Connolly's door, demanding that she take back her annexed lodger. 'He won't sign any money over to me until he puts a ring on my finger,' she shouted angrily. 'So get the old bugger out.'

After some slightly jagged-edged toing and froing, the storm cones were lowered. Avarice triumphed. Peace was patched up; beggars can't be choosers. On the first day of autumn, 21 September 1956, at Jarrow Register Office, Mary and Oliver were wed. For love or money, Mary does not seem to have been able to make a success of matrimony. It was as if some bad fairy at her cradle-side had nuptially ill-wished her. Before the skin under her new wedding ring had had time to rub shiny, Mr L. was poorly in the doddery aftermath of a shocking cold. And before he had time to recover from that – he was dead.

It was late on Wednesday night, 3 October 1957, just thirteen days after the wedding, that a neighbour, Mrs Ellen Russell, was awakened by the new Mrs Leonard with the tidings that Mr Leonard was ill. Mrs Russell went back to Mrs Leonard's house with her. They found the old man on the floor, white-faced, speechless, breathing heavily and in obvious pain. That universal panacea, a nice strong cup of tea, was brewed in a trice. Offered it, Mr Leonard tasted it, spat it out, and knocked the cup out of Mrs Russell's hand.

'I think he's dying', was that astonished lady's reaction.

'I think so, too', said Mrs Leonard quickly, adding 'I've called you because you'll be handy if he does'.

He did.

The following day the widow reported his death to their GP, Dr John Hubert Laydon. The doctor remembered that the old man had come to see him the previous day for treatment for a bad cold. Obviously it was a case of senility – no need to see the body. With a clear conscience he filled in a death certificate – (1) Myocardiac degeneration. (2) Chronic nephritis.

Leonard was buried in Hebburn Cemetery on 5 October 1956.

His widow collected £75, which was all he had. When Leonard's son, with whom, admittedly, he had been on bad terms, came calling to see his father's will, Mary sent him packing with a flea in his ear.

'Go and see the solicitor,' she told him sharply.

It is extraordinary how, presumably, guilt makes murderers and murderesses tactlessly abrupt with the relatives of their victims – as witness the cases of Seddon and the Vonderahes, the Stauntons and Mrs Butterfield, and George Joseph Smith's gratuitously offensive response to a solicitor acting for the family of one of his balneal victims.

Then it was time for the enacted epicedium, the public keening, the clearly articulated threnody. Time for the laying bare of the broken heart, the exhibition of the life lying in ruins, the lamentations – 'I have been terribly unlucky in love ... it's almost as though I'm blighted.' If you have lachrymals prepare to fill them now. Before, as to the chiming of a Cinderella's clock, it is time to fold away grief with the death certificate in your handbag and trot off back to the *thé dansant* of life.

It was not long before Mary was casting a glittering eye around again for a husband. The black widow was hungry for another mate, a money spider, to devour, suck dry, and spew forth. She looked hard. She looked long. Took her time; a full twelvemonth. Then, she set her rakish widow's cap at another old man ... and pounced.

Ernest George Lawrence Wilson, a seventy-five-year-old retired engineer, had put it around that he was on the look-out for a housekeeper. What, he hinted, was on offer was a tidy little £100 investment in the Co-op, a paid-up insurance policy, and a nice home – to the right applicant. This news item coming to the voracious ear of our Mary, she made haste to investigate. Investment and policy must have passed muster, but the nice home turned out to be a dirty council bungalow, rented for *6s 6d* a week. The closer Mr Wilson came into focus, the less dazzling appeared the benefits and inducements on offer. Notwithstanding, possibly with a short-term policy well in mind, Mary Leonard accepted, sold up her furniture and went to live at the bungalow in Rectory Road, Windy Nook, with Wilson.

On 30 October 1957 they were married at Jarrow.

The wedding was by no stretch of the imagination a lavish do. They held a small reception at which Mr Wilson entertained the guests by playing the piano. The bride, looking trim and triumphant, wore a smart, tailor-made costume. Toasts were drunk. There was no shortage of liquor. And there was tea, coffee, sandwiches, and cakes in abundance – an over-abundance, in fact, calling forth from the bride a joke, which, later, would be held in sinister evidence against her. To a guest's polite observation regarding the overwhelming plenitude of the reception's provisions, the leftover victuals, the new Mrs Wilson cracked, 'We'll just save them for the funeral,' before adding, 'although I might give this one a week's extension.'

Exercising woman's privilege, she changed her mind. Mr Wilson lived, like his marital predecessor, just thirteen days.

Back at the Rectory Road bungalow, the epithalamia well past, poor Ernest was now securely lodged in the hinged clasp of the praying mantis widow. He was to be, like some kinds of male spider, eaten after – in his case, one suspects, without even – the ritual nuptial dance. As she had done in self-protective prelude to the swift demise of the late Oliver Leonard, Mrs Wilson took the sagacious precautionary step of involving a doctor *before* administering the *coup mortel.* With a cunning born of loving practice, she persuaded the unsuspecting Ernest that he had upset his stomach by eating too much liver for supper. She told him to stay in bed and she would get the doctor to look in and give him something that would put him right. When Dr Wallace came, old Ernest told him that he was not ill. The doctor nodded as he scribbled a prescription. But Mrs Wilson's objective had been achieved. She had implanted in the doctor's head the notion that old Mr Wilson was ailing.

Late on the Monday night – 11 November 1957 – Mary called at the nearby house of her friend, Mrs Grace Liddell, also a widow. She told her that her husband had been taken into hospital suddenly and she didn't fancy staying in the bungalow on her own. Mrs Liddell said that she would put her up for the night.

On Tuesday morning, Mrs Liddell saw Mrs Wilson back to her bungalow. As they walked up the garden path, Mary handed her friend the keys to open the front-door.

'You're going to get a shock,' she said.

Mrs Liddell unlocked the door and stepped inside. She had just time to register the fact that the house was in a filthy condition before recoiling from her predicted shock. There was Ernest

– stone-white, marble-cold – laid out on a trestle table, ready for burial.

She turned to Mary. It was an almost automatic reaction. 'Have you done anything to Ernest?' she asked.

'Don't be silly,' said the Black Widow.

Dr Wallace was not too surprised when he was told that old Ernest Wilson was dead. He was as good as gold about issuing a death certificate – cardiomuscular failure and myocardiac degeneration.

If Ernest's death less than a fortnight after his wedding had not aroused suspicion, the Widow Wilson's subsequent behaviour would certainly have done so. To the undertaker who came to measure Ernest for his coffin, she suggested – shades of Seddon and Brides-in-the-Bath Smith – albeit half arch humour, half avid intent, that, as she had given him so much business, he might give her a wholesale price. The old theory that the murderer *wants* to be caught seems well supported by the quite extraordinary conduct and comportment of the bereaved Mary Wilson. And, indeed, official interest had by now become engaged. The pace at which she was losing husbands savoured, as Lady Bracknell might have said, of criminal carelessness. Less elegantly, one of the local detectives put it like this: 'She certainly seemed hell-bent in getting rid of them – as though she was working against the clock.'

But what frankly baffled the police when they first began their inquiries was the question of motive. Surely the paltry gleanings from these deaths could not be an inducement to murder, powerful enough incentive to put your neck in danger of a noose. They were still privately inclined to put the deaths down to coincidence. Such things do happen. But, as the rumours multiplied and stray reports of suspicious behaviour came to their knowledge, the police decided to take such action as would indicate one way or the other what credence they should give to local gossip and feeling. They applied for, and were granted, permission to exhume the Widow Wilson's last two spouses.

Those exhumations were carried out under conditions of great secrecy on 30 November 1957. While the general practitioners who had attended the dead men had had no reason to think that the deaths were anything other than natural, a disquietingly different state of affairs was revealed when the specialists, the pathologists, took over and unpicked the bodies at the seams. Flying scalpel, prying microscope, and bubbling test tube revealed that neither Wilson nor Leonard had died a natural death. The post-mortem showed that Wilson had no serious organic disease, and that Leonard's heart was as sound as a buffalo's, and there was no sign of chronic nephritis. What was found was, in Wilson's case, congestion in the oesophagus and intestines, and that the liver, instead of presenting the normal sort of chocolate-brownish colour, was yellow. What was found in both bodies was elemental phosphorus, a deadly poison, in sufficient quantity to kill.

*

Aware after the examination of the growing climate of suspicion that she had made away with both her husbands, the Widow Wilson is reported to have said, 'I know what people are saying. They think I murdered them. They say I murdered them to get money for drink. That's rubbish. I know I upset some people by that joke at my wedding, but I think that really people are jealous of me because I have always tried to laugh my way through life. I've had plenty of troubles, but I believe in keeping cheerful. My conscience is clear. I have looked after all my men as a good wife should. Who knows? I might marry again if the right man comes along. I refuse to let gossip ruin my life.' Then, after another bit of reckless gallows humour – 'I didn't kill them. They were dead already.' – the incautious Mary sped hastily off to spend the rest of her last day of liberty trying to sell Ernest's gold watch and chain.

Mrs Wilson seemed honestly surprised when the police called on her shortly after the resurrections of Oliver and Ernest, and began asking some extremely deep-digging questions. She did her not very successful best to provide propitiatory answers. The police, unpropitiated, thereupon invited her to accompany them to the station, where, in due course, they charged her with the murders of both men. Her day of judgment had come. Mary Elizabeth Wilson, the much widowed, took her place before her earthly judges.

Leeds Assizes. March, 1958. On the bench: The Red Judge, Mr Justice Hinchcliffe. His first murder trial. Leading for the Crown: Mr Geoffrey Veale, QC. Leading for the defence: Miss Rose Heilbron, QC. A jury constituted of nine men and three women.

The case was unusual in several respects. The prisoner was the first person to be tried simultaneously for two murders since the passing of the new Homicide Act 1957, under which hanging was generally abolished; but the allegation was that she had murdered her last two husbands on different occasions, which, if proved against her, would make her crime a capital one, for which, on conviction, she could only be sentenced to death. Clearly Miss Heilbron would – and did – at the start of the trial, in the absence of the jury, make a submission for separate trials. It was refused. 'I don't think separate trials are desirable in the interests of justice in this case,' ruled the judge. The prosecution's claim that they were entitled to look from the facts of one case to those of the other, for the purpose of considering whether what had happened was an accident or evidenced system, as in the George Joseph Smith Brides-in-the-Bath case, succeeded.

Unusual also was the circumstance that, whereas it was the custom of either the Attorney General or, more rarely, the Solicitor General, to prosecute in person in a poison trial, in this case the practice was not followed. Geoffrey Veale had recently succeeded Hinchcliffe J as Recorder of Leeds.

Mr Veale rose and opened the prosecution case. He described

Mrs Wilson as a wicked woman who had, in succession, married two men and then deliberately poisoned them in order to get the paltry benefits she hoped she might obtain from their deaths. In the examinations which followed the exhumations of Leonard and Wilson, there was exhibited the indisputable presence of elemental phosphorus. There was also found in Wilson's stomach a quantity of wheat bran. Rat poison, beetle, and cockroach poison are made up of a mixture of phosphorus, wheat bran and syrup. 'If,' he asked, 'you get in somebody's stomach, phosphorus and wheat bran, can it lead to any other conclusion but that that person has taken either rat or beetle poison?'

Veale proceeded to outline to the jury the story of the prisoner's meeting with Oliver Leonard, her enquiries as to his financial standing, her seduction of him as a lodger, and subsequent marriage to him. 'It may be you will come to the conclusion that the accused tried at once to get hold of such money as Leonard had. Leonard died two days after he had seen a doctor, who had thought that he was in good health for his age, and had given him a bottle of cough mixture.'

We come now to Mr Wilson. On 11 November 1957, a Dr Wallace visited Wilson. He had been sent for by Mrs Wilson. She told him that her husband had been bad through the night, but Wilson apparently did not complain. Dr Wallace thought there was some degeneration of the heart muscle, and gave him some tablets and a cough mixture, but he did not consider that there was anything alarming about his condition. Next day, the doctor received an urgent telephone call telling him that Wilson was ill or dying. He went at once, and found Wilson dead.

'Another case,' Veale pointed out, 'where no doctor saw the victim shortly before death.'

That night of 11 November, Mrs Wilson went to stay with a Mrs Liddell, and told her that her husband was bad and was always wanting water. 'Notice that observation. You will hear that an intense thirst is one of the symptoms of phosphorus poisoning.'

Veale said that three days after the funeral Mrs Wilson drew sums of £9 4*s* 11*d* and £15 13*s* 4*d* on two insurance policies. There was one piece of evidence which he thought that the jury might feel to be significant. It was the fact that no tin or container of rat or beetle poison was found. If it had been a case in either instance of accident or suicide, the container would have been there.

Mrs Alice Mary Connelly testified that it was while Mr Leonard was a lodger with her and her husband that he had been introduced to Mrs Wilson – or, rather, Mrs Knowles, as she was then. Mrs Knowles had asked if she could speak with him, and was with him for twenty minutes. The next day she announced, 'We're going to get married. He'll be leaving you.'

Cross-examined by Miss Heilbon, Mrs Connelly agreed that because of Mrs Knowles she was losing a good lodger, but denied that she was upset because, she said, she felt that the couple would be happy.

Dr John Hubert Laydon went into the witness box. He stated that he had seen Mr Leonard on Monday 1 October 1956. He was at that time a perfectly healthy man for his age. There was some bronchitis and a degree of arterial trouble, but he was not making much of his ailments. Dr Laydon said that he certainly did not suspect poisoning when he saw Leonard that day. He was not, however, surprised when he heard of his death, and had filled in a death certificate without actually seeing the body.

Miss Heilbron asked how he knew that Leonard was dead.

He replied. 'Some person came in and told me Mr Leonard was dead, and I filled in the death certificate.'

'How,' asked Miss Heilbron, 'did you fill in the blank, the gap between when you saw him and a week later?'

'It wasn't a week. It was two days later. The man's condition is not going to change in two days. My examination on 1 October, warranted his sudden death on the 3 October.' Dr Laydon added that a doctor was permitted to issue a death certificate without seeing the body if he had seen the person within fourteen days of the death. He felt fully justified in giving the death certificate.

Turning now to the case of Ernest Wilson.

Mrs Grace Marion Liddell told how on 11 November 1957, she was in bed when Mrs Wilson called on her and asked if she could stay the night. She had said that she could, and she did. Mrs Liddell recounted how, the next morning, she had gone with Mrs Wilson to the bungalow in Rectory Road. 'She told me I would get a shock when I went in. I went in and I did get a shock.' Mr Wilson's corpse was laid out on a trestle 'with a white thing over his face. I took the white thing off and kissed him'. The witness added that the bungalow was in a dreadful state – 'worse than a dog kennel'.

Dr William Proudfoot Wallace told the court that he had been sent for by Mrs Wilson on 11 November 1957. When he arrived at the bungalow, Mrs Wilson told him that her husband had been ill all night. He found Mr Wilson sitting up in bed. He was quite cheerful. The doctor said that he came to the conclusion that Wilson was suffering from myocardial degeneration. He prescribed a cough mixture and some tablets, in neither of which there was any phosphorus, and decided to call and see Wilson again in three days' time. However, on the morning of 12 November, he had received a call from a telephone box telling him that Wilson was very ill. He went at once and found that he was dead.

And that was the GPs in the case dealt with. Now it was the turn of the pathologists and forensic scientists.

First, Dr William Stewart, who performed the post-mortem on the disinterred body of Ernest Wilson, late of Collingwood Street, Hebburn-on-Tyne.

Dr Stewart did not think that death was due to natural causes. It was the result of poisoning.

Miss Heilbron asked him, the inflection of her voice underlining for the jury's benefit the import of her question, 'These cases of Wilson and Leonard were the first cases of phosphorus poisoning you have done in your life?'

'Yes.'

Dr Ian McKenzie Barclay, of the Forensic Science Laboratory, Gosforth, Newcastle upon Tyne, replying to Miss Heilbron, said that, outside chemical laboratories, the only other source of which he knew where elemental phosphorus, with which Mrs Wilson was alleged to have poisoned her two husbands, could be found, was in rat and beetle poison.

'Do you know it is found in a pill?' asked Miss Heilbron.

'Maybe.'

'Do you know yellow phosphorus pills are on the lists of five well-known manufacturing chemists?'

'No.'

'You never inquired?'

'No.'

'Have you ever heard of Damiana pills being used as an aphrodisiac?'

'I have never heard of that.'

Counsel said that she would be producing a box of these pills bought that morning. Obviously, the defence line was going to be that Messrs Leonard and Wilson had both reacted to the (well) hidden charms of their new bride by dashing forth to fortify their flagging libidos with uplifting Damiana dosages.

In reply to further questions, Dr Barclay agreed that it was usual to keep elemental phosphorus submerged in water because it is unstable, anxious to pick up oxygen and reach a stable or oxidised state.

Miss Heilbron: 'Have you heard of any cases where phosphorus has been found in the body after as long as thirteen months?'

Dr Barclay: 'To the best of my knowledge there is no previously recorded case of phosphorus being recovered after as long as that. I know of no other case longer than six months.'

'Is it not, therefore, surprising, as this is the first recorded case, to find phosphorus in a body so long after?'

'I don't think it is surprising, for the reason that phosphorus can be protected by the fatty material and its free state preserved. It might be described as being sealed up in the fat.'

Counsel leapt in very quick off the mark. 'Yet the organ we know was fatty, the liver, was the one in which you found so little phosphorus you could not quantify it?'

'Yes, but the amounts which eventually arrive in that organ are so small they are of microgram quantity, about one-millionth of a gram per cent of tissue.'

With regard to the amount of elemental phosphorus constituting a fatal dose, Dr Barclay said, 'You must take a fair amount to make sure that a small proportion gets to work.'

One grain is equivalent to 64.5 milligrams. So, a fatal dose of one and a half grains would be about 100 milligrams.

Dr Barclay explained that there were two types of yellow phosphorus poisoning. In the first, where there was an ingestion of an apparently large amount, death ensued fairly rapidly. In the second, where the amount ingested was much smaller, there were mild symptoms for one or two days. For another two or three days the person seemed to be back to normal, before suddenly – on the fifth, sixth or seventh day – death took place. It was in this second type that jaundice became apparent. The cases of both Leonard and Wilson belonged to the first type, death occurring in the first phase, comparatively quickly.

Dr David Ernest Price, a pathologist, also thought that both men died in the first stage of poisoning.

In reply to Miss Heilbron's question as to whether it was right that there was no scientific method of assessing the amount of phosphorus ingested in a body after two weeks because no one knew the rate of oxidisation, he said, 'All I can say is that I recovered yellow phosphorus indicative of the consumption of a relatively large dose.'

Dr Alan Stewart Curry, scientific officer of the Home Office Laboratory, Harrogate, deponed that he had received from Dr Barclay specimens for analysis to see if he could find in them any poison or drug other than phosphorus. He found none. Purely for his own interest, he tested also for elemental phosphorus. That test yielded positive results.

Miss Heilbron asked if he had ever heard of elemental phosphorus being used in pills.

'The French,' he said, 'used it at the beginning of this century. There have been many strange things used in pills. I have never come across elemental phosphorus used in pills, but it did have some use at the beginning of the century. I read the other day that phosphorus has no place in modern clinical medicine.'

Miss Heilbron handed a small bottle to Dr Curry. 'Look at his bottle of Damiana pills.'

'May I break one?' Dr Curry took a pill from the bottle and crushed it with a coin on the ledge of the witness box, then scooped the fragments into the palm of his hand and sniffed them. 'Yes,' he said. 'There is a little phosphorus there – at least the smell of it.'

'Do you know that that pill is used, or can be used, as an aphrodisiac?'

'No, I don't. It is said to be in the *British Pharmacopoeia* of 1934.'

'Yes, but I am producing this bottle in 1958,' said Counsel. She then referred to *The American Illustrated Medical Dictionary* (Dorland), 1951 edition, and quoted it as saying that phosphorus could be used for rickets, nervous and cerebral disease, and as a genital stimulant in sexual exhaustion.

Dr Curry's reaction to this information was, 'That's an amazing assortment. I don't think it would affect these things.' He also said that he doubted that, unless a very large amount of pills had been taken, phosphorus would be found in the body. It was the exception rather than the rule to isolate phosphorus – 'I have isolated it before, but you are very lucky to get it.'

Miss Heilbron called William Dixon, a former Newcastle CID sergeant, now employed as a private detective. He testified that, on the instructions of Mrs Wilson's solicitors, he had made inquiries to see if he could obtain Damiana pills. He visited three wholesalers in Newcastle and each had a stock. The bottle of pills which Counsel had shown to the court was handed to him, and Dixon said that he had bought them from the retail section of a Newcastle chemist. They were sold over the counter and no doctor's prescription was needed.

Mr Veale asked, 'Has the bottle got a label "Poison" on it in red?'

'Yes.'

Next came Mr Angus Fraser McIntosh, Rodine's manager, of Crieff, Perthshire. He spoke of examining pills bought at a Newcastle chemist's. He said that each pill – there were fifty to the bottle – contained one-hundredth of a grain of elemental phosphorus; just short of a milligram. The amount of phosphorus found in Wilson's body was 2.7 milligrams, equal to five of the pills. In the case of Leonard, the 3.8 milligrams found was equal to six or seven pills. Pharmaceutically, the pills were an aphrodisiac for the treatment of sexual debility and to increase sexual desire. He understood that a fatal dose of phosphorus was one and a half grains, so to obtain a fatal dose from the pills it would be necessary to swallow 150 of them.

Veale: 'To get a fatal dose you would have to take three whole bottles full?'

McIntosh: 'That is right.'

Dr Francis Camps was called by the defence. He came into the case in the role of defendant's best friend, but he came as an expert outsider, for he had not himself examined the bodies. His evidence would therefore be based on medical and scientific reports. He had, however, one great advantage over most of the other doctors involved – he had actually seen several cases of phosphorus poisoning. He agreed that treatment was available, and that that treatment was better given in hospital. Mrs Wilson had, of course, made no effort to get treatment for her husband.

Miss Heilbron asked Dr Camps what would be the respective causes of death in the first and second types of phosphorus poisoning. He replied that in the first, it would be heart failure. In the second, it would be liver failure, but there would also be renal failure, and the heart muscle and various other muscles would be affected.

A question of paramount importance to the defence was how, if she were guilty, Mrs Wilson had administered the phosphorus. Dr Camps said that in a previous case of phosphorus poisoning which he had investigated, in order to see how easy it was to take rat poison, various methods of administration were tested – such as in beer, cider and spirits, in tea, and on bread and blackcurrant jam. The latter, it was found, would hide the taste and appearance, but, he added, he would expect to find evidence of the jam.

Miss Heilbron: 'Can you administer Rodine as it is?'

Dr Camps: 'A person would have to be blind and without taste or smell. There is a cloud of vapour as soon as you open the tin. A strong odour. The taste is horrible.'

He further said that if Rodine was taken in jam, a great deal depended on the jam and the type of vehicle used with it. In a case of this sort it was essential to examine the contents of the stomach, to find any foreign bodies and to see what kind of food had been taken. If the phosphorus had not been given in tea, there was a strong possibility that it was disguised in cough mixture. Both men had similar bottles of it, and one of the bottles contained a teaspoonful of Rodine.

Asked if he was prepared to give a cause of death, Dr Camps replied, 'The findings of the cause of death are pathologically contradictory. In view of the contradictory findings, and in the absence of microscopic evidence, I would not be prepared to say.' But when asked to *suggest* a cause of death, he would say that Wilson died from heart failure and Leonard from cerebral thrombosis. These were, however, only suggestions. 'If I were asked to put a cause of death, I would put "unascertainable".'

Further pressed, Dr Camps would not commit himself with regard to the cause of death in the case of Wilson, but he did not think that it must necessarily have been phosphorus poisoning. 'I think it would be dangerous to say that, because other causes of death have not been excluded.'

Miss Heilbron inquired: 'What other causes could there have been in an old man of seventy-six on the findings here?'

'The commonest cause of death at that age is undoubtedly heart condition.'

'Is diabetes a possibility?'

'No, I don't think it is a possible cause of death, but it is a possible cause of fatty changes in the liver. But there are lots of other things which might be a cause of change.'

In cross-examination Mr Veale handed Camps a bottle. Camps sniffed it and said that it smelled like cough mixture.

'Would you,' asked Veale, 'be surprised that there is more than a teaspoonful of Rodine rat poison in that bottle?'

Camps' reply was, 'Yes, that is, I believe, exactly what I said about disguise. This,' and he held the bottle up to his nose again, 'is a very good disguise.'

Answering further questions, Camps stated that he had been professionally involved in a number of phosphorus poisoning cases. He described what he called first and second stage cases. In the first stage, death occurred usually between six and ten hours, after sickness, pain, intense thirst and prostration. In second stage cases, death took longer, causing changes in the liver. He thought that if Leonard and Wilson had died of phosphorus poisoning, they were second stage cases, because of the fatty changes that had taken place in their livers. He had seen the liver sections from both bodies. This was in direct contradiction of the opinion expressed by Dr Barclay.

Commenting on the evidence given by Dr William Stewart, who examined the bodies after the exhumations, Camps pointed out that Dr Stewart had said that he did not take sections of other parts of the bodies. He had thought they were unnecessary. Said Camps, 'No autopsy in any case of poison can be complete without full pathological examination of the adjoining organs.'

Veale asked Camps whether it was some form of coincidence that they were investigating the deaths of not one, but two men who had something in the gullet, intestines and liver, and also had phosphorus in the stomach.

Camps: 'I don't think the gullet and liver have any significance. The only thing I would think of any significance, which could be interpreted, is phosphorus.'

'What about symptoms?' demanded Veale. 'We have a pallor, pain, restlessness and mental change in Leonard's case.'

Camps: 'If that was put to a student in examination he would not mention phosphorus poisoning in his diagnosis. It is only a picture of anyone dying.'

Veale: 'You said Wilson died of heart failure, something that stopped his heart. What was it?'

Camps: 'I don't know.'

Veale: 'But might not phosphorus poisoning have stopped Wilson's heart?'

Camps: 'It could have done. The only thing that worries me is that there are, in my view, too many things missing.'

Veale: 'You have not had the advantage of being present at the post-mortems.'

Camps: 'No.'

Veale: 'Of seeing the actual livers.'

Camps: 'I saw what remained of them.'

Dr Camps was cautious when his attention was called to the opinion expressed by Dr Price that the deaths were due to phosphorus poisoning.

Veale suggested that Dr Price and Dr Stewart were right, and Dr Camps was wrong.

Camps rejoined, 'I don't think Dr Price materially differs from me, from what I have heard. I have read the transcripts.'

Veale: 'He says the cause of death was phosphorus poisoning. Do you agree?'

Camps: 'I would not go as far as to say that.'

In her final address to the jury, Miss Heilbron explained why Mrs Wilson had not gone into the witness box to give evidence. 'She has given a very full and frank statement to the police. She has said the deaths are a mystery, and she certainly cannot assist you on the scientific side. Don't hold it against her, because she has accepted my advice.'

This brought instant and sharp rebuke from the judge. 'The jury do not want to know what advice you gave to the prisoner. You know you should not have said it.'

Counsel, having made her point, made her apologies. 'I am sorry, my lord.'

Referring to the evidence given by the prosecution's scientific witnesses, Miss Heilbron said, 'They are all human, all fallible, and all can make mistakes.' She said that one invariable symptom of phosphorus poisoning was vomiting. In neither case had the prosecution produced any evidence that vomiting had occurred.

Dealing with Dr Stewart's testimony that in each case there was fatty degeneration of the liver as a result of phosphorus poisoning, she suggested that the post-mortem examinations left much to be desired. Dr Stewart had said that the heart muscle was perfectly healthy, and that he did not make a microscopic examination because he could see that much with the naked eye. 'Is this tremendous artifice of science, the microscope, not to be used to discover all the facts?' she demanded.

Counsel made great play with the fact that in neither instance had the death certificate given the true cause of death, and that neither of the bodies had been seen after death by the family doctor – although this was actually quite a common practice where nothing other than natural causes was suspected.

As regards the Damiana pills, Counsel said that she had introduced them in order to show an alternative method of obtaining phosphorus 'What more natural than that these old men, finding a wife in the evening of their lives, should purchase these pills for the purpose for which they are apparently known? Is it not another coincidence in this woman's favour? Bear in mind the agony of this old woman and the phrase she used when one of her husbands died – "I'm lonely now he's gone." There is no evidence that Mrs Wilson had possessed phosphorus. This woman has gone through a heavy ordeal and a terrible agony. Do you think the evidence proves she is the diabolical poisoner she is said to be? I ask you to say she is not guilty.'

No one could have been defended more ably.

Addressing the jury on behalf of the Crown, Mr Veale said that the issues were not complicated, but as simple and plain as a pikestaff. Phosphorus was not something to be taken by accident. What, he asked, was the relevance of the pills introduced by the defence – pills containing microscopic quantities of phosphorus? A fatal dose was about 150 pills. They were supplied in shops in small bottles. But were any small bottles found in the houses of Leonard and Wilson? Wouldn't they have been found if these pills had been bought? The jury might feel that any complications in the case had been introduced by the defence in an attempt to blur their vision.

'This,' said Veale, 'is a case of deliberate poisoning. What is the alternative? Suicide does not seem to be suggested. Accident? An overdose of something? Of what? One hundred and fifty aphrodisiac pills in two cases? The answer is all too plain. It is no accident, but deliberate poisoning.'

On the facts, it was obvious that the judge would sum up against Mrs Wilson. In his summing-up he paid very great attention to the medical and scientific evidence, and restated the symptoms of phosphorus poisoning as listed by the experts.

'Who,' asked Mr Justice Hinchcliffe, 'is the only living person today who can tell what the symptoms from which Leonard and Wilson suffered were? Why is it that she has not been called to give evidence on oath on these important matters? The prosecution's case is that it is established beyond doubt that Leonard and Wilson died from phosphorus poisoning. If you accept that these men died from phosphorus poisoning, you will ask yourselves how did these two old men come to take and ingest phosphorus? Has Mrs Wilson' – it was a rhetorical question – 'helped you all she could? She has chosen not to give evidence on oath, so you are without her explanation on many important matters.' These included the details and lengths of her husbands' illnesses; the reason why a doctor was not called in for each case; her odd behaviour with Mrs Liddell on the day of Wilson's death; her trying to sell a gold watch that day; her alleged queer and untrue statement to a public house landlord that her husband was ill in hospital, when he was in fact lying dead at home. These lies and actions had all to be considered.

Pills containing phosphorus had been produced and the suggestion had been made that two men in their middle seventies had taken them as sexual stimulants. The jury should, said the judge, give that suggestion as much weight as it deserved. 'You have had no evidence called before you that either Leonard or Wilson ever possessed one of these bottles of pills.' Dr F. E. Camps, the pathologist, had expressed the view in evidence that bran found in the intestines of both men was the same sort as in brown bread. 'But there is no evidence that brown bread was eaten in either the Leonard or Wilson household. Dr Camps is not prepared to say what the cause of death was. He agrees that phosphorus was found, and Dr Barclay agrees with Dr Price in confirming that there was no other poison in the bodies.'

Because he had had to give evidence in a case at Lewes Assizes, Dr Camps had arrived a day late at Leeds, and, perhaps, created the unfortunate, and completely unfair, impression that 'the man from the South' was slighting a northern court. Camps was the first to admit that his evidence, while positively for the defence, was full of suppositions and theories. He made no other claim. Even so, he was finally somewhat humiliated by the judge, who apparently ignoring Camps' superior status as a consultant, specifically instructed the jury that they must give his evidence only the same weight as that of any of the other and several medico-legal witnesses.

The defence had asked the jury to take the view that the post-mortem examinations conducted by Dr Stewart left much to be desired, should have been carried out with greater caution, and that more microscopic sections of various parts of the bodies ought to have been taken. Said the judge, 'You will pay such attention to these criticisms as they deserve. Dr Stewart, a doctor of medicine, a distinguished pathologist, a professional man, gave independent evidence, with a view to assisting the court to come to the right conclusion.'

On 29 March, the jury, after an absence of an hour and twenty-five minutes, found Mrs Wilson guilty of both murders.

She was the first person to be convicted and sentenced for more than one murder under the new Homicide Act 1957, and the first woman to be sentenced to death under the Act.

She heard the death sentence unmoved.

The date for her rendezvous with the hangman was fixed,

provisionally, for 6 April 1958. However, her appeal was scheduled to come up in May. It did so, and was dismissed. A new date was appointed for her execution – Monday 4 June – in Durham Prison.

As it turned out, the hanging never took place. She was reprieved. No official reason was ever given. It is possible that her age – sixty-six – weighed in the balance. Equally possible is the circumstance that Lord Butler could not bring himself to order her execution, complete with the ritual donning of rubber knickers.

It is reported that five days after she arrived at Holloway to start a life sentence, inquests were held on John Knowles and John George Russell – the merry widow's husband and lover, respectively. Dr Stewart, who twice again obliged with knife, tube, and scope, came up with another phosphorus double. Detective Chief Inspector Mitchell, however, finding himself unable to produce any court-worthy evidence as to how the life-destroying phosphorus came to be in the bodies, had to stand frustratedly by as open verdicts were formally recorded.

For the much marrying Widow of Windy Nook, harbinger of epithalamial death to so many grooms, Death himself was her last bridegroom. He came to claim her in her cell in Holloway on 9 January 1963, behind the bars of the prison she had, by her actions, freely made for herself. The constant bride was aged seventy-one when she succumbed to the final groom's embrace.